The State of the American Mind

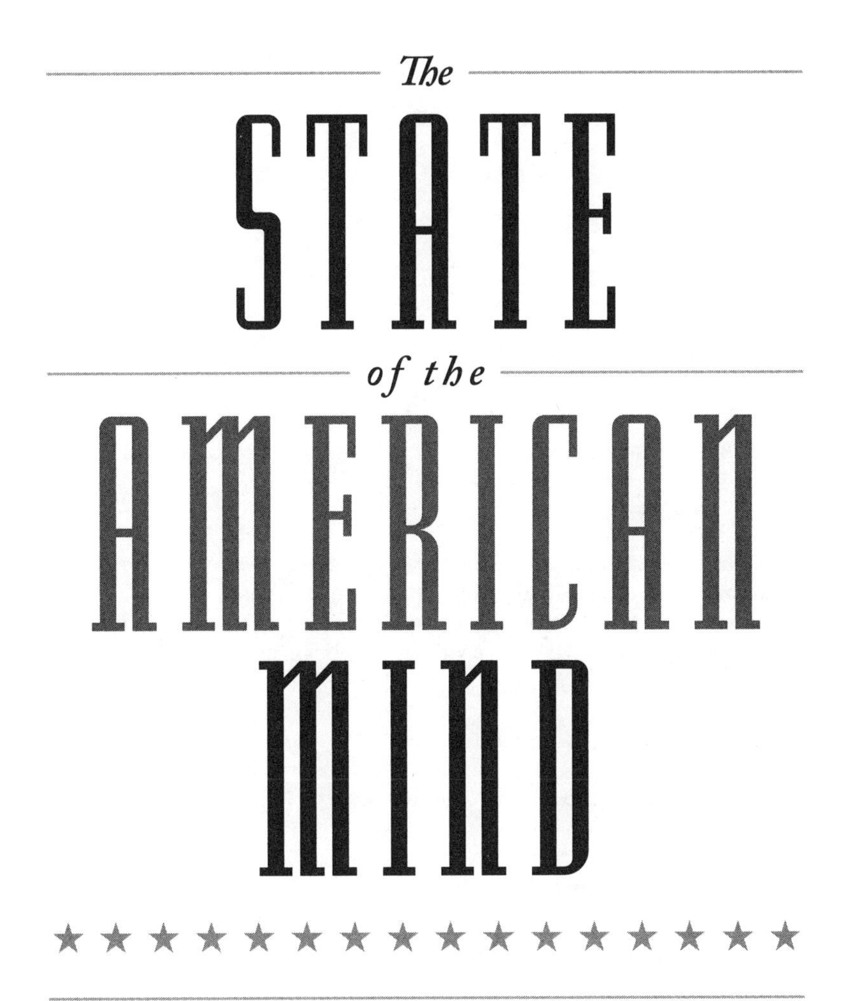

The STATE of the AMERICAN MIND

EDITED BY

MARK BAUERLEIN AND ADAM BELLOW

TEMPLETON PRESS

Templeton Press
300 Conshohocken State Road, Suite 500
West Conshohocken, PA 19428
www.templetonpress.org

Designed and typeset by Gopa and Ted2, Inc.

Library of Congress Cataloging-in-Publication Data
on file.

Printed in the United States of America

15 16 17 18 19 10 9 8 7 6 5 4 3 2 1

Contents

Foreword

AMERICA: HAVE WE LOST OUR MIND?

Mark Bauerlein and Adam Bellow

WHEN *The Closing of the American Mind* was published in 1987, even as it soared to phenomenal success, Allan Bloom may have suspected that the national object named in the title was doubly endangered. Not only was the American Mind slipping into darkness. The thing itself was already a dubious notion, at least in elite cultural and education zones. The book chronicled the deterioration of learning and mores in the institution responsible for them, the college campus, and the assumption of an "American Mind" didn't fit the times. It sounded too intellectual, too comprehensive and singular, and its patriotic undertone crossed the post-Vietnam cynicism of the professorate.

And so the book struck liberals as an out-of-touch denunciation of contemporary life. In truth, by charting a version of the American mentality it joined a long and illustrious lineage of commentary on the topic. Tocqueville's chapter "The Philosophical Method of the Americans," Emerson's "The American Scholar," and Whitman's 1855 "Preface" to *Leaves of Grass*; V. L. Parrington's *Main Currents of American Thought* (1927); and the Cold War–era symposia "Our Country and Our Culture" (*Partisan Review*) and "The National Purpose" (*Life Magazine*), to name a few famous cases—each outlined a characteristic American intelligence. They singled out an "American psychology," "Man thinking," a Cartesian "disposition of mind," and "the genius of the United States," each one a representative outlook of the American Experiment. During the Reagan era, such sweeping conceptions still retained some authority in public life.

"The American is a new man, who acts upon new principles; he must therefore entertain new ideas, and form new opinions." So said J. Hector St. John Crèvecoeur in *Letters of an American Farmer* (1782), announcing the first condition of the American Mind, the need to think anew. The Old World order of birth, court, and established church didn't apply across the ocean, not in a nation that from the start marked itself an exception in the flow of human history. Tocqueville condensed the American way into a personal standpoint: "to accept tradition only as a means of information, and existing facts only as a lesson to be used in doing otherwise and doing better; to see the reason of things for oneself, and in oneself alone." Emerson called it "self-reliance" and instructed his countrymen, "Nothing at last is sacred but the integrity of your own mind." If the American attends a church or joins a party, it's because he has deemed it worthy, not because someone told him so. Conformity disgusts him, and so does dependency. Ben Franklin set the model of success. He starts out a runaway, broke and forlorn in Philadelphia, but a strong work ethic, diligent reading, and canny business moves bring him wealth and renown. When in the opening of the *Autobiography* he offered his life as a design "fit to be imitated," he became for later generations the "self-made man" prototype. The American cherishes equality, to be sure, but only as a level playing field (the free *pursuit* of happiness), not a leveling of outcomes, which can only happen when a higher American ideal, liberty, is curtailed. Yes, America failed that ideal with slavery and Jim Crow, but the two most influential civil rights figures in our history, Booker T. Washington and Martin Luther King Jr., didn't critique the ideal of liberty. They demanded that African Americans share in it.

These traits form the American posture—independent thought and action, thrift and industriousness, delayed gratification and equal opportunity. The American Mind possesses specific knowledge, too, not just an attitude. You must remember the Declaration of Independence, the Bill of Rights, and the Bible (as our contributor Daniel Dreisbach proves), along with stories of the first colonists, the Founding, and the pioneer experience. Religious liberty, grounded in the case of the Pilgrims, must be recognized as central to civic affairs, and economic liberty as well, the freedom to make contracts and act entrepreneurially. Another root concept is popular sovereignty, which deserves all the solemnity imparted in the assertion "government of the people, by the people, for the people shall not perish from the earth." The American appreciates the divided structure of government and insists on local control, fearing the consequences of overcentralization and distant masters. However much he despises journalists, he protects a free press and relies on it to monitor elections and politicians. And while the American Mind prizes individualism, it also hails selfless civic virtue, best embodied by our Cincinnatus, George Washington, who stood for the common good and transcended politics.

These are the ingredients of the American Mind and character, but as Bloom detailed all too well, the dismantling of it was nearly complete by the mid-1980s. The characteristic knowledge and dispositions had collapsed. In Bloom's Enlightenment-leaning version, the American Mind exercised critical intellectual habits; it was cosmopolitan and broad-ranging, steeped in the past and committed to learning for its own sake. The purpose of the university was to draw youths into that formation through systematic immersion in a syllabus of great books, art, and ideas, but in the 1980s, barbarism had seized the day. Multiculturalism was busy eliminating requirements in Western civilization and inserting third-rate exertions in identity politics. Student-centered pedagogies turned the learning process upside down, disrupting the transmission of wisdom from one generation to the next. Undergraduates had more freedom than ever, and they wasted it in cheap delights.

People responded to Bloom's argument because it seemed to apply to the entire country, not just higher education. The breakdown of the curriculum reflected the breakdown of our civics and culture, they believed, and they were right, as far as a coherent and recognized American identity was concerned. In fact, the premise that the ideal American Mind had collapsed may have been the one point on which left-wing and right-wing readers of *Closing* agreed. They differed in that one group praised the development, the other mourned it.

That may have been the secret of its success. Bloom's study entered American society in the final gasp of American identity. By 1985, people had pretty much stopped talking in terms of a common, unitary American anything. It wasn't only that the American Mind had slipped into ignorance and hedonism. It was that recourse to any essential and proper feature of American individuals now came off as empty, and in some settings suspect. The cause was simple. If you assume an umbrella American condition, the argument went, you reduce the varieties of American identity and experience to one preferred form. Once you envision the American Mind, the "national character," the American Dream, or any other overarching national entity or norm, you marginalize the many peoples who don't fall under it. It comes off as selective and exclusionary, and culpable, too. When our first contributor in this volume, E. D. Hirsch, in the same year of 1987 famously compiled a "core knowledge" that every American must know, he was denounced as Eurocentric and monocultural, committed to white, male, bourgeois dominance. Hirsch believed that mastering the "cultural literacy" list was necessary to social mobility, and he offered scientific studies as proof. Indeed, he argued, keeping cultural literacy from disadvantaged groups only perpetuated their disadvantage. But his progressive aims didn't matter. Most intellectuals and academics looked at the content of his inventory and quickly judged it insufficiently diverse.

This emphasis on group differences framed standard American traits and destinies as a political ploy, a way of favoring one group under the spurious banner of an ideal, historically sanctioned role model. The logical remedy was to draw other populations into the ongoing affirmation and revision of the American Mind, American exceptionalism, and other defining national conditions. But reformers took a shorter course. Instead of ensuring that certain groups previously shut out of American identity be received within it, they discredited the ideal itself. Difference had to be respected, and the only way to do so was to deny any synthesis and displace the traditional inheritance. Why should a black sophomore study the Mayflower Compact and *Walden* in high school, instead of something out of her own culture? For decades, U.S. politicians, artists, and thinkers had read them as cardinal expressions of the American outlook, accepting them as part of an American formation. But it was high time to acknowledge her, too, not just white New England men from long ago. That was the positive intent, and to realize it in practice, the educators had to negate the seminal American heritage. We cherished the *pluribus* and abandoned the *unum*. The American Mind was one of the casualties.

★ ★ ★

This minioutline of a core American identity crumbling into group difference is, no doubt, familiar to readers, and we don't mean to rehearse the causes or judge its rightness once more. That's not what this volume is about. We accept the fact that we have lost the capacity and confidence to conceive and articulate America in essential, universal terms. Or rather, we know that essentialist definitions of American identity have no traction in educational and intellectual spheres. There, the old myths of the American Adam, Manifest Destiny, Melting Pot, and American Dream are worse than stale. They are pernicious. The sweeping mandates of diversity, multiculturalism, and cultural relativism disallow them.

We may ask, however, now that we are four decades into the diversity movement, about the condition of the dispositions and knowledge that made up the American Mind for most of our history. Certain myths may have been denounced, but not First Amendment freedoms, the Franklin work ethic, Washingtonian civic virtue, general historical knowledge, and vigorous civic engagement. The process of social differentiation wasn't supposed to reject those virtues and principles, only open them up to others, drawing more Americans into the body politic. Even as it raised the bar of equality, diversity meant no disrespect to individual liberties, so people said. Excluded and marginalized groups would become proud and patriotic, not clamorous and adversarial. Knowledge of U.S. history, literature, and the arts was to increase among them, civic participation to widen and deepen. A syllabus in English class containing more women and minority authors would inspire students to higher achievement. More women and minorities in positions of power in business and politics would assure those groups that the American Dream was theirs to pursue. Diversity itself would make workplaces more vibrant and less insular.

That was the promise of breaking up the old consensus. But when we survey the thoughts and habits of the American people today, we find the antithesis of the traditional American Mind and national character emerging again and again. One of us works in book publishing and literary culture, one in magazine publishing and higher education, and we've watched closely and sometimes participated in cultural controversies from the Canon Wars to *The Bell Curve* to liberal bias in media and on campus. Here is what we have observed:

Instead of acquiring a richer and fuller knowledge of U.S. history and civics, American students and grown-ups display astounding ignorance of them, and their blindness is matched by their indifference to the problem.

Civic virtue is a fading trait, our political sphere now typically understood as merely a contest of group interests. Patriotism and the common good are quaint notions.

Individualism has evolved from "rugged" versions of the past into present modes of self-absorption.

Not only has self-reliance become a spurious boast ("You didn't build that"), but dependency itself has become a tactical claim.

Instead of upholding basic liberties, more and more Americans accept restrictions on speech, freedom of association, rights to privacy, and religious conscience.

We aren't the only ones who have noticed an American Mind in decline. Many intellectuals and social thinkers from across the ideological spectrum express a conviction that something has gone awry in the intellectual powers of American citizens. They don't identify the same exact failing, but they agree in connecting diverse failings in our society to the way people's minds work—or don't work. Books and essays detail mental behaviors, biases of assorted kinds, "blinks" and "nudges," rational and irrational choices, narcissism and cluelessness, explaining how and where they go wrong. As we write these words, a political uproar is under way over comments by one of the architects of the Affordable Care Act, MIT professor Jonathan Gruber, who tied the act's design and passage to the "stupidity" of the American people. As commentaries flash daily in the media and politicians take sides, we wonder if the outrage lies not in the insult but in the suspicion of its truth. Perhaps the leading opinion maker on television in the last ten years, Jon Stewart, gears laugh lines to episodes of ignorance and myopia. He implies, repeatedly, it's the mental problem that matters most, not the politics.

When Barack Obama describes a large portion of the U.S. population as "bitter, [clinging] to guns or religion or antipathy to people who aren't like them or anti-immigrant sentiment or anti-trade sentiment as a way to explain their frustrations," as he did in Pennsylvania while campaigning in 2008, it sounds as if they need therapy, not better political leadership. Susan Jacoby's *The Age of American Unreason*, which warned that anti-intellectualism in America had become "a morbid disease affecting the entire body politic" (10), was the biggest nonfiction best seller of 2008. Another 2008 publication, Nicholas Carr's widely circulated *Atlantic Monthly* essay, "Is Google Making Us Stupid?" maintained that the Internet has steered our brains into speedy and shallow consciousness. One of the most prominent ideas in psychology today is Jonathan Haidt's theory that "groupish righteousness" in America is hardening biases of all kinds. One of the surest signs of this mentality emphasis is the frequent translation of earnest expression into phobic conditions, as in homophobia, Islamophobia, technophobia. . . .

★ ★ ★

These judgments, along with our own observations, have led us to conceive this volume of essays. It is an empirical approach to the problem. Except for the final entries, which are frankly general and prognostic, we downplay culture wars sallies and skirt Grand Theses. The editors' motivation may be a large speculative one—that is, to ponder the consequences of the fracturing of the American Mind—but the entries, for the most part, stick to narrow spheres and limited conclusions. We wanted it that way.

The contributors are leading voices in professional and public spheres with long experience studying American culture and society. Each one has selected an area of concern and collected numerical data, personal observations, and other concrete evidence of predominant attitudes and behaviors into a summary description. The areas range from the cognitive workings of an individual mind to rates of disability claims under Social Security, from composition exercises to personality tests, Madison on religious liberty to Freud on civil society. Following E. D. Hirsch's introduction, which maps out why widespread cultural knowledge is so important to a thriving republic, we have organized the areas into three sections:

- "States of Mind: Indicators of Intellectual and Cognitive Decline"—These essays broach specific mental deficiencies among the population, including lagging cultural IQ, low biblical literacy, poor writing skills, a low-performing higher-ed system, and overmedication.
- "Personal and Cognitive Habits/Interests"—These essays turn to specific mental behaviors and interests, including avoiding the news, impatient perception, narcissism, and conspiracy obsessions.
- "National Consequences"—These essays examine broader trends affecting populations and institutions, including rates of entitlement claims, voting habits, the culture of criticism, and higher education.

The methods vary. Some essays rest on historical facts, such as Daniel Dreisbach's review of the status of biblical literacy in America during the years of the Founding (on which he bases the civic impact of biblical illiteracy today). Others pursue statistical paths, such as Nicholas Eberstadt's compilation of data on entitlements and federal spending, which shows how vast conditions fostering the entitlement mentality have become. Still others rely on personal acquaintance—for instance, Steve Wasserman's critique of book reviewing in America, which draws upon his tenure as books editor at the *Los Angeles Times*. The settings they choose in which to display the twenty-first-century American Mind in operation include college campuses, art museums, voting booths, Facebook pages, pediatricians' offices, and blog pages.

Taken together, the essays offer a profile of the American Mind in disarray. The profile is not a partial one. The contributors provide enough population data and expert testimony for us to draw this unfortunate inference with confidence. There is no gainsaying the evidence in Greg Lukianoff's summary of "disinvitation season" that proves a chill has settled upon higher education, and that a presumption of freedom-from-offense enforces it. When readers encounter data on medical prescriptions compiled by Robert Whitaker, which show that one in five Americans took a psychiatric drug in 2010, they have no cause to quibble. Instead, they will take a crowded subway home and reflect upon the startling probability that more than a dozen passengers nearby have been diagnosed with a psychiatric disorder. And we imagine that David Mindich's portrait of the tuned-out twenty-year-old won't convince high school and college teachers of anything. No, it will corroborate what they see every day.

We assume, too, that the trends detailed in the essays will please no one. With college tuition rates at current levels, the lack of learning that usually takes place from freshman year to graduation is deplorable (see Richard Arum). And for those who know the history of voting rights in America, the fact that barely one-third of eligible citizens showed up for the 2014 midterm election, the lowest rate since World War II, is a sign of profound disengagement (see Ilya Somin).

Needless to say, such trends are antithetical to the American Mind and character in its traditional expression. The narcissistic youths in Jean Twenge's descriptions could hardly lie farther from representative figures of the past such as Frederick Douglass risking death and standing up to sadistic Mr. Covey, Thoreau heading off to the woods on the Fourth of July to build a hut and plant beans, Henry Fleming in *The Red Badge of Courage* running scared in one battle but standing firm in the next, and Alexandra in *O Pioneers!* forging a successful farm out of the bleak Nebraska hills. We have become so accustomed to emotive displays in public life and popular media that when Dennis Prager identifies our moment as the Age of Feelings, we receive it as the obvious truth. But it wasn't so many years ago that what we take as customary would have struck ordinary Americans (whose role models might have included strong, silent types such as the marshal in *High Noon* and composed ladies such as Jackie Onassis) as bizarre and outrageous. If the local newspaper and public library are fundamental institutions of a free republic, as Franklin believed, then Americans who never read one or visit the other shirk the responsibilities laid upon them by the Founders. What would John Winthrop, Nathaniel Hawthorne, and W. E. B. Du Bois think of the entitlement mentality fostered once we lost the distinction between the deserving poor and the undeserving poor?

Raising such comparisons makes many people uneasy, of course. To some it smacks of blaming the victim, and it certainly crosses the nonjudgmentalism that R. R. Reno singles out as the first premise of contemporary affairs. But we do ourselves and our nation no favors when we ignore evidence of debility and withhold criticism. When people fall short of the ideals of their country, they have to be told. The American Mind was an extraordinary creation, and it has to be remembered. Its expressions still ring with magic: "Walt Whitman, an American, one of the roughs, a kosmos"; "So we beat on, boats against the current, borne back ceaselessly into the past"; "I have a dream. . . ."

The current expressions of the American Mind, compiled and expounded in the following pages, don't ring at all. They aren't extreme or provocative; they are banal and uninspiring. Two hundred and thirty years ago, Crevecoeur could look out over the most homely American setting and testify to a historic flourishing of human beings: "Every thing has tended to regenerate them; new laws, a new mode of living, a new social system; here they are become men: in Europe they were as so many useless plants." We survey the American scene in 2015 and record unprecedented wealth, an overflow of goods that but two generations ago would have struck people as fantastical luxuries. The digital revolution continues apace, and more youths than ever before go to college and aspire to graduate school. Media have never been so profuse and diverse, while government has never provided so many people and organizations assistance and safety.

All the ingredients are in place, one would think, for the American Mind to prosper. Let us see how and where and why it does not.

Introduction

The Knowledge Requirement

WHAT *EVERY* AMERICAN NEEDS TO KNOW

E. D. Hirsch Jr.

GIVEN ALL THE discussion and fret about student achievement in the United States today, it is easy to forget that the last thirty years of public secondary education are a record not of decline but of flat performance. Overall, test scores for high school students in math, reading, and other subjects haven't much changed. Scores have fallen, yes, but it happened in the preceding two decades, from 1962 to 1979, when verbal results on the SAT slid precipitously, as shown in the figure below. I include data in the same years for combined results on the Iowa Test of Educational Development that nearly all high school juniors and seniors in the state of Iowa had to take.

The Iowa scores are important because they dispel a common

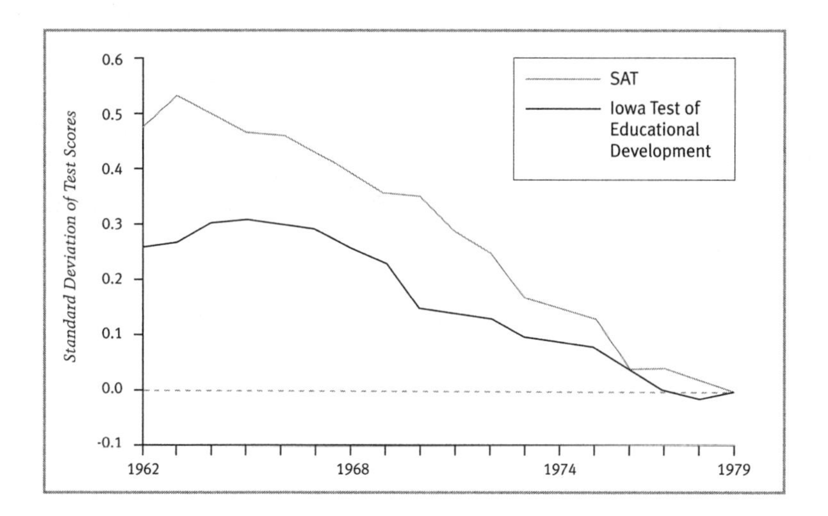

explanation for the SAT trend—that is, the belief that scores went down because more students took the exam, not because student learning had declined. Because virtually every student in Iowa sat for the test, the data undermine the excuse that democratization of the SAT caused the drop; Iowa didn't suddenly become significantly more diverse during these decades.

Other circumstances, too, provide evidence against the blame-demographics-not-the-schools theme, most importantly, the fact that the greatest expansion of SAT test takers—from 5 percent to 50 percent of seniors—occurred between 1952 and 1963, before the great decline set in. If demographics actually did create the sliding scores, then the 1952–1963 period should have produced the steepest fall in the national average. In fact, as the SAT pool contained more youths of different class, race, and ethnicity, the scores did not fall. In the following years, from 1962 to 1979 when scores did plummet, the diversity of test takers remained fairly stable.

The shortcomings of the demographic explanation led me long ago to search for other explanations for educational decline. My conclusion was a historical one: that certain ideas began to dominate teacher-training institutions in the 1930s, most prominently the idea that general knowledge was not central to an individual's education. Instead of acquiring broad awareness of the basics of science, history, civics, religion, literature, and the arts, the education schools maintained, students should "learn how to learn," to develop abstract thinking skills that they could apply fruitfully to various facts, events, and conditions as they came up in people's lives. They didn't need to study the details of the Civil War; they needed to develop critical-thinking and problem-solving habits that they could wield when the Civil War and anything else came along. After World War II, as older teachers who emphasized content knowledge retired and young ones indoctrinated in the skills-oriented approach began teaching, these ideas drifted steadily into classrooms and textbooks. Even though the ideas were not proved scientifically, they took charge of the curriculum and still shape it today. The fate of my counteridea that background knowledge ("mere facts") is essential to educational performance, that abstract skills falter without a foundation of content supporting them, is a lesson in what needs to be done to produce more competent Americans.

★ ★ ★

When my book *Cultural Literacy: What Every American Needs to Know* came out more than twenty-five years ago and stayed on the best seller list for six months, the initial enthusiasm from the general public was followed by a torrent of abuse from the academy. The public said, "We need this. At last, somebody has outlined the shared knowledge that educated people in the United States possess, and that the schools should teach." Readers understood that an engaged citizenry needed to be an informed one, too, if the people were to exercise their rights and privileges responsibly and wisely. They recognized as well that rising on the income ladder usually requires academic success, and the more general knowledge a student brings to class, the better the prospects.

Given the stunning popularity of *Cultural Literacy*, one would have expected at least some portions of our education system to have followed with a coherent curriculum designed to impart that knowledge, just as Thomas Jefferson envisioned common schools doing for everyone two hundred years ago. It didn't happen. From the academy, people in education departments judged *Cultural Literacy* as a retrograde return to the regurgitation of mere facts, while humanities professors felt indignant that anyone should try to perpetuate the existing culture at a time when the most important business of education was to change and improve American culture.

The year of publication, 1987, was at the height of the effort to make the dominant culture less male, white, and culturally middle-class. *Ms.* was to replace *Miss* and *Mrs.*, and the pronoun *anyone* was to be followed by *her* as well as by *his*. Such matters of style were part of a political effort to raise the power and status of women, minorities, and other out-groups. The great Swedish education researcher Torsten Husén observed that the push for equality in all aspects of education and cultural life after World War II was not just an American but a Western, international phenomenon. Getting caught up in all of it was dizzying and exhilarating.

But it was also depressing, because although my political sentiments fell on the left with the levelers, my research made it evident that those who attacked *Cultural Literacy* in the name of greater equality deeply missed the point. In the name of destroying cultural hegemony, the academy was preventing K–12 education from delivering the knowledge that Americans need to fulfill their democratic citizenship and that disadvantaged students need to close the achievement gap and climb the class ladder. Academic critics were so angry at the very idea of cultural literacy—that is, of a body of knowledge common to informed individuals, made use of continually in their criticisms—that they did not even try to follow the scientific evidence showing how essential that knowledge is to basic and advanced literacy. They overlooked, too, the truth that culture has an inherent resistance to change, no matter how principled and dedicated the reformers. The evidence showed that general knowledge of traditional topics in history, science, civics, literature, and the arts was necessary to success, whether the situation was an SAT reading test, a white-collar job interview, or simply a newspaper over morning coffee. Hence arose the list of "What Literate Americans Know" that my colleagues and I compiled and appended to the book, a set of terms taken for granted in public and professional spheres (e.g., abolitionism, abstract art, Alexander the Great, antibiotic, etc.). Because of the traditional, mainstream nature of the list, however, people engaged in various efforts of cultural diversification objected. To them, cultural literacy per se stood as a roadblock to their aim of carrying out effective social activism and achieving greater equality. It looked too monocultural, Eurocentric, and status quo.

Perhaps so, I answered, but it was still the reservoir of knowledge assumed by the *New York Times* and presidential campaigns, college freshman courses and professional workplaces, and not to teach it to youths was to consign them to lesser futures. To get ahead in the United States, I argued, you had to master the intellectual tools of communication and power, whether you approved of those tools or not. One could accept the admonition of liberal academics to follow the pronoun *anyone* with *her* but still not put money in her purse. These critics entirely ignored the paradox that when they deprived disadvantaged students of the dominant conventions of middle-class culture, they were also excluding those students from middle-class life—a misfortune that continues to be enacted. Upper-middle-class households have always imparted much of the knowledge that makes up that culture at home, where newspapers, books, NPR and talk radio, museum visits, and professional ambitions were commonplace. Students from lower-income households have had to rely on schools to provide the knowledge implicit in those media and experiences; but captive to bad ideas, particularly to an adversarial attitude toward that knowledge, schools all too often demurred.

A deeper point was overlooked in the debates and denunciations. The purpose of *Cultural Literacy*'s analysis was not to perpetuate a dominant group but rather to perpetuate democracy. Closing the knowledge gap not only means more economic opportunities for more people; it bolsters our republic. Citizenship requires broad, shared knowledge, including democratic values and the large vocabulary needed to communicate widely across all groups. In sum, the book proposed both a social-justice aim and a patriotic aim.

The critics of *Cultural Literacy* lost the logical and scientific argument, but sadly they won the political one. The ideas of the book have proved to be correct but have had little impact on education in the subsequent decades. As far as I could tell, the book was excluded from all syllabi in education schools, mentioned only as something evil to be avoided. When I briefly taught in an education school, the brave students who took my courses revealed to me that their professors had urged them to stay away. Metaphorically speaking, the book was burned. Although the notoriety of *Cultural Literacy* was wide in the outside world, its influence on educational policy was nugatory. Entrenched ideas are hard to change—all the more so when they are shielded by high-sounding slogans about "cultural relevance" and "social change."

For this reason, I welcome the opportunity to affirm once more the intellectual contents and traits that an individual must possess to be an active, responsible, critical, and effective citizen in the United States. In order to participate fully in the sweep of social, cultural, and political activities ranging from visiting a large city to voting to impressing others at a business luncheon, one must have a sufficient measure of general knowledge. That's the individual premise, and it holds now just as firmly as it did twenty-eight years ago. And in order for an advanced, heterogeneous, industrialized society to constitute and function as a nation, it must have a civic core, a common culture made up of shared values, beliefs, and knowledge—in the United States what Lincoln called a "political religion." That's the national premise. It is not enough that people obey the law and practice a live-and-let-live philosophy. They need to feel that they are inheritors of a meaningful past, and in a nation characterized from the start by migration, class mobility, and diversity, they must know the contents of that past—the cultural heritage of words, persons, events, ideas, discoveries, and so on, and the daily literate discourse of current events, scientific developments, ideological controversies, public policies, advents in the arts, and so forth. Cultural literacy isn't just an academic achievement or social status. It's a condition of our national success.

These individual and national arguments for cultural literacy—or to use its current name, "core knowledge"—have even greater urgency today than they did in the 1980s. Notwithstanding all the school reforms of the last thirty years, high school students have not improved their academic achievement and in some areas have slipped—a sign of persistent failure on the part of the anti-core knowledge curriculum favored by the educational establishment. Schools that have adopted the knowledge-rich curriculum developed by the organization I founded in 1986, the Core Knowledge Foundation, have performed well, but they remain scattered and largely unnoticed by school officials crafting readings, assignments, and tests in states and districts across the country.

Overall, no evidence exists that high school graduates are more knowledgeable and skilled than they were when the infamous report *A Nation at Risk: The Imperative for Education Reform* appeared in 1983. Meanwhile, our "political religion" has frayed, with partisan rancor rising, group identities and interests in increasing tension, and faith in political institutions (and in the politicians leading them) declining. Partisanship itself is no sin, and our nation has never been without it—competing interests were liberally assumed by the Founders, not suppressed, and skepticism about centralized power is part of the American character—but it seems as if today's versions lack an element that steers debate and judgment into constructive channels: points of agreement on basic and broadly understood ideals and practices. The anger, mistrust, and cynicism we see every day puts an even greater burden upon a widespread cultural literacy to keep the nation unified, or at least able to communicate effectively. That commonality of core knowledge is what every American needs to know if we are to maintain national cohesion and loyalty to one another.

★ ★ ★

The core knowledge position is, in fact, two distinct contentions. The first, more basic one is that the schools need to teach a specific, cumulative, knowledge-building curriculum in the early grades—that being the only way schools can induce equality of opportunity. The second addresses the practical task of making an index of the specific knowledge that such a curriculum should contain.

That second activity, identifying taken-for-granted knowledge, accounted for the commercial success of *Cultural Literacy* and its policy failure. The appendix of some five thousand items became the subject of cocktail-party talk and was the reason most people bought the book. Most readers didn't pay close attention to the logical arguments or the summary of scientific research. Moreover, in those days of the culture wars (recall, "Hey-hey, ho-ho, Western Civ has gotta go!"), any list that looked reactionary or "phallocentric" or "Eurocentric" was doomed from the start among academic opinion makers. Unfortunately, the ideological response to the list overwhelmed the more important, technical (and unanswered) argument in favor of teaching *some* definite, cumulative, knowledge-building curriculum in the early grades.

That bias against specific contents—the works, events, people, and ideas to be studied—for English, history, foreign languages, the arts, and the softer social sciences still holds, though math, engineering, natural sciences, and American civics do have a generally agreed-upon curriculum. Everyone concurs that students should study the Bill of Rights. Nobody quibbles over the teaching of algebra, but once you start to select episodes from U.S. history for everyone to learn, arguments begin over "Whose history?" and whether military events count more than the ordinary social experience of marginalized groups. To people outside the thought world of American education, a systematic and cumulative knowledge-based curriculum is obviously more effective than an unsystematic, noncumulative one that imparts little knowledge. Within that world, other premises reign. A fragmented elementary curriculum, emphasizing skills, was the kind we had when my book appeared, and it is the kind we still have. This approach is the fundamental cause of our poor performance in international comparisons, as well as the fundamental reason that we do less well than many other nations in narrowing the learning gap between rich and poor.

The simple solution is that every school needs to teach from pre-K through fifth grade and beyond a more or less common curriculum grade by grade, one that builds knowledge and vocabulary central to cultural literacy. This idea might seem self-evident, but in fact it impresses educators as restrictive, monolithic, and insensitive, and they dismiss it not only with the old charges of cultural imperialism but also with a thorough expulsion of all required content in the liberal arts fields, stressing instead general skills like critical thinking over specific knowledge.

Long before the days of the Internet and Wikipedia, the progressive-education tradition disparaged "rote learning of mere facts," saying, "You can always look it up." On this theory, the important educational aim was to learn how to analyze, reflect, and criticize *after* you have done the research. This conception underlies slogans such as "Don't give children a fish; teach them how to fish." Thus, in recent decades, in the teaching of reading, schools have focused less on knowledge building than on how-to strategies of reading comprehension. Instead of having students read books important to cultural literacy, schools develop abstract strategies that can be applied to any book—for instance, "Find the main idea in the text" and "Identify the author's purpose." The effort has failed. The mistaken idea that you can significantly advance reading comprehension skills by strategy sessions has induced in the early grades a culture of indifference to subject-matter coherence. The teaching of formal skills like critical thinking and comprehension strategies does cause an initial improvement in performance, but after about six lessons the improvements reach a plateau. Spending more weeks and years on such empty strategies, as our schools now do, in desperate preparation for tests, does not induce further advances. The reading performance of people leaving school has remained low and flat for thirty years. Teaching strategies instead of knowledge has only yielded an enormous waste of school time.

The relative *nongenerality* of human skills—that is, the fact that critical thinking and problem-solving skills are not easily transferable from one situation to another (because one always needs background knowledge about the situation)—is a finding that is not widely known outside of cognitive psychology. If only I had given greater emphasis in *Cultural Literacy* to that scientific point about the fruitlessness of extensive skill drills, the practical impact of the book might have been greater.

The idea of teaching general critical-thinking skills, if it could be accomplished, should naturally appeal to everybody. It appealed to me. If general critical-thinking skills could be taught, and if they could be applied fruitfully to any text whether the critical thinker was familiar with the subject matter or not, then focused critical-thinking instruction regardless of subject matter could meet the challenge of low academic achievement. I certainly believed that back in the 1970s, when I was immersed in problems of literary theory and interpretation, such as "How do you understand poetic language as opposed to ordinary language?" During those years, my colleagues and I worried less about students acquiring broad literary-historical knowledge of Shakespeare, Romanticism, and the American novel than we did about forming them into agile, astute interpreters of texts, any texts. But as I saw more and more students entering college and struggling to interpret those texts, I began to sense that the problem wasn't bad mental habits but insufficient general knowledge about the contexts of those texts. Fortunately, with advice from psychologist Robin Dawes, I found scientific support for my suspicion, and I became acquainted with the chess experiments of Adriaan de Groot, which in turn led me to the work of Karl Duncker and H. A. Simon.

That line of research emphasized the knowledge-drenched character of problem-solving skills. De Groot studied chess masters in the 1940s, testing their memory by showing them for up to fifteen seconds an actual game in which only twenty-five pieces were left. Grand masters were able to reconstruct the positions from memory with perfect accuracy, masters with 90 percent mastery, while novices could only place five or six pieces. Next, de Groot placed twenty-five pieces on the board randomly, with no relation to chess rules. Here, surprisingly, all of the subjects performed like novices. The memory advantage of the masters ended when chess knowledge (as embedded in actual game re-creations) was removed from the task. The result demonstrated that the masters' astounding memory for chess games was not an abstract mental aptitude for remembering but rather a measure of their familiarity with game situations. In a real game, certain schemata take shape; the pieces have ended up in the positions they occupy because of the strategies of the players. Masters can identify those schemata quickly, for instance, noting three pawns and a knight in a particular cluster in the middle of the board and connecting it with past games they have reviewed. That is, they don't have to remember all twenty-five pieces, only a few schemata that they recognize because, as masters, they know up to fifty thousand positional patterns. In other words, what look like the same abstract memory processes in masters and novices are, in fact, quite different mental actions.

These and other findings such as the famous "radiation problem" that Duncker identified show that people cannot easily transfer old solutions to new domains. The belief that we can readily direct general skills from one particular problem to another, unrelated one—the assumption behind present-day American schooling—turns out to be false. To apply a formal skill in that way (say, to find the main idea in a paragraph) is an uncertain and time-consuming way of thinking critically, the slow and error-ridden method of novices. By contrast, people who are well informed about the subject matter of a problem or text use shortcuts that quickly identify a way through the problem or the significance of the words. The conclusion of cognitive research concerning skills is this: Broad knowledge of many domains is the only foundation for wide-ranging problem-solving and critical-thinking skills. More broadly, the only way in which citizens in our nation can be discerning, critical, and engaged is by possessing general awareness of the principles, events, figures, ideas, and trends underlying current matters and situations. Hence broad knowledge is what the schools, media, and policies should try to impart. The "teach the child *how to* fish" educational theory, on which our present public school system is based, is mistaken. Ideas have consequences, and mistaken ones about skills have led to the disappointing results of early schooling, a perpetuation of achievement gaps, and the oft-documented ignorance of the citizenry.

★ ★ ★

The dismal record in civics knowledge compiled by the National Assessment of Educational Progress (NAEP, or the "Nation's Report Card") is startling. This result reflects the general de-emphasis of facts in favor of supposedly general skills that don't exist. But another factor has been at work. After World War II, with the United States by far the most powerful and influential nation in the world, complacency about the United States reigned. Few emphasized the tradition that assigned to schools the task of teaching to youths basic American ideals, events, documents, and history in order to help unify and sustain this artificially patched-together nation. Moreover, many people became disillusioned with government policies—with militarism, Watergate, the Vietnam War. All over the country, particularly in humanities departments and education schools, an emphasis developed on national shortcomings.

The emergence of this adversarial mind-set as establishment thinking in the education sphere eventually prompted a fine response from my late friend, the distinguished philosopher Richard Rorty, who wrote the following in an op-ed in the *New York Times*:

> Most of us . . . still identify with our country. We take pride in being citizens of a self-invented, self-reforming, enduring constitutional democracy. We think of the United States as having glorious—if tarnished—national traditions. Many of the exceptions to this rule are found in colleges and universities, in the academic departments that have become sanctuaries for left-wing political views. I am glad there are such sanctuaries, even though I wish we had a left more broadly based, less self-involved and less jargon-ridden than our present one. . . . [Their] focus on marginalized groups will, in the long run, help to make our country much more decent, more tolerant and more civilized. But there is a problem with this left: it is unpatriotic. In the name of "the politics of difference," it refuses to rejoice in the country it inhabits. It repudiates the idea of a national identity, and the emotion of national pride.

When the chairman of the National Endowment of the Humanities proposed some town meetings to "explore the meaning of American identity," Rorty continues, some prominent academics denounced him as nationalistic and pronounced the idea of a shared national identity as "evil." But, Rorty insisted,

> A nation cannot reform itself unless it takes pride in itself—unless it has an identity, rejoices in it, reflects upon it and tries to live up to it. Such pride sometimes takes the form of arrogant, bellicose nationalism. But it often takes the form of a yearning to live up to the nation's professed ideals. . . . If we fail in such identification, we fail in national hope. If we fail in national hope, we shall no longer even try to change our ways. If in the interests of ideological purity, or out of the need to stay as angry as possible, the academic left insists on a "politics of difference," it will become increasingly isolated and ineffective. An unpatriotic left has never achieved anything. A left that refuses to take pride in its country will have no impact on that country's politics, and will eventually become an object of contempt.

The founders of American education—Rush, Webster, Jefferson, Mann—believed rightly that the new nation was an experiment that could only be sustained by schools that taught students the particularity and promise of a nation based not on place or descent but on a set of ideas. These founding thinkers understood that continual nation making, the passing along of those ideas and reverence for them, was needed to sustain this new type of post-Enlightenment nation. Lincoln put it well in his Lyceum Address of 1838.

> Let reverence for the laws be breathed by every American mother, to the lisping babe, that prattles on her lap—let it be taught in schools, in seminaries, and in colleges; let it be written in Primers, spelling books, and in Almanacs—let it be preached from the pulpit, proclaimed in legislative halls, and enforced in courts of justice. And, in short, let it become the political religion of the nation; and let the old and the young, the rich and the poor, the grave and the gay, of all sexes and tongues, and colors and conditions, sacrifice unceasingly upon its altars. (32)

Note the key phrase "all sexes and tongues, and colors and conditions." All were to be Americanized, not just the descendants of Great Britain and the prosperous landowners. That ideal was the central theme of the early common-school movement, as seen clearly in the 1848 account of the history of the common school in New York State—one of the most thrilling books I've ever read—which I quote at length in my book *The Making of Americans*. The making of American patriots continued to be a self-conscious aim of schools and schoolbooks well into the 1930s, to our good fortune. The common-school idea helped create the United States and sustain it as a national community. It made the fragile experiment largely a success.

Rorty's worry proved well-founded. In foundations of education courses, teachers are required to read books by Paolo Freire and others that attack the nation-building idea in favor of the politics of difference. But Rorty's observations and his implied prescription are sound. In the United States, there's a difference between nationalism and patriotism that is particularly American. Before the American experiment, nations still had a connection with the word "nation," which comes from *nation*, meaning "birth." American patriotism is not based on birth but on a set of Enlightenment ideas of equality, freedom, and toleration. Nationalism defines one group over against others. It sees differences as inherent and essential. The transnational patriotism of the United States, symbolized by the flag, can accommodate all tribes within a larger conceptual loyalty learned in childhood. A vigorous and successful United States could not have evolved if our schools had not deliberately sustained those ideals through reiterations of founding documents, national myths about courageous heroes who fought for those principles, and historical episodes that put American values to severe tests—in a word, the knowledge that Americans must know.

★ ★ ★

These are the keys to improving the quality and equity of American education, society, and politics. First, students should be taught systematically and cumulatively the most enabling knowledge across the whole spectrum of subject matters. Second, they should be taught the universal principles that formed the United States and the history of its triumphs and failures in living up to those principles. For the past half century we have retreated from those two simple curricular ideas, and we have paid a heavy spiritual and material price. We have lost our collective nerve, and we have increased economic inequality.

One minimal, tough-minded (and incomplete) way of defining "the most enabling knowledge" is simply to ask this question: What do people who earn over one hundred thousand dollars per year know in common, but which remains unknown to people who earn twenty-five thousand dollars or less? The answer is guaranteed *not* to be some general "how to think" skill. That idea has been tried; it has failed, and according to cognitive science it must fail. The answer must be specific knowledge and vocabulary over a wide spectrum. One attempt to answer that question was the research that led to the list in *Cultural Literacy*, the items summarized as "provisional," an effort to "illustrate the character and range of the knowledge literate Americans tend to share." No doubt an amended list would be needed today.

Such a knowledge inventory would determine what people need to learn both inside and outside school. Teachers would present it in an age-appropriate way from pre-K through twelfth grade, while adults would learn it through discerning choices for themselves and their children in leisure hours (books, newspapers, knowledge-rich media). Such demands are not merely theoretical. An attempt to formulate such a curricular sequence has been used and refined in Core Knowledge schools for over twenty years, with demonstrable positive effects on achievement and equity. It's available online for free. If a more effective sequence can be formulated, so much the better.

Action item: The next time people downplay the importance of knowledge in the areas of history, politics, literature, economics, natural science, social science, technology, and the arts for individuals and for societies—if you hear them repeat the convenient and popular falsehood that knowing how to think is much more important than facts; if they say that twenty-first-century skills of critical thinking and problem solving and collaboration are more important than old-fashioned traits such as being well read, bookish, up-to-date on current events, and willing to investigate the truth claims by advertisers, politicians, and other influential voices; if they de-emphasize curiosity about what happened in our nation fifty years ago and other knowledge-aimed impulses—ask them, "How do you know what you believe is correct?" Then ask them how they make those assertions jibe with the work of a whole army of cognitive scientists who have established the knowledge-based character of human skills and intelligence. To Ben Franklin's answer to the lady who asked him outside the Constitutional Convention what he and the others had created, a republic or a monarchy, "A republic, if you can keep it," we must say. "And we shall keep our Republic by making all of our citizens knowledgeable, inquisitive, informed." As James Madison famously put it, "A popular Government without popular information, or the means of acquiring it, is but a Prologue to a Farce or a Tragedy; or, perhaps both. Knowledge will forever govern ignorance. And a people who mean to be their own Governors, must arm themselves with the power which knowledge gives" (103).

References

Lincoln, Abraham. "Address to the Young Men's Lyceum of Springfield, Illinois, January 27, 1838." In *Lincoln: Speeches and Writings, 1832–1858*. New York: Library of America, 1989.

Madison, James. Letter to W. T. Barry, August 4, 1822. In Vol. 9 of *Writings of James Madison*, ed. Gaillard Hunt, 9 vols. New York: G. P. Putnam's Sons, 1900–1910.

Rorty, Richard. "The Unpatriotic Academy." *New York Times*. February 13, 1994.

Part One

* * * * * * * * * * * * * * * *

States of Mind

Indicators of Intellectual and Cognitive Decline

* * * * * * * * * * * * * * * *

1

The Troubling Trend of Cultural IQ

Mark Bauerlein

ANY BROAD DISCUSSION of the American Mind has to take into account an extraordinary finding first noticed in the middle of the twentieth century and confirmed and publicized widely in the 1980s and beyond. From World War I to World War II, cognitive psychologists discovered, the average score of U.S. soldiers on mental tests rose significantly, and in the decades after that, scores on IQ tests continued the trend. It came to be known as the "Flynn Effect," named for New Zealand social scientist James R. Flynn, whose studies brought to widespread attention the intelligence gains by adults and children in the United States and elsewhere.

IQ tests always set the mean at 100, adjusting the scale accordingly over time so that it appears that test takers from year to year achieve the same cumulative score (a 100 places one at the fiftieth percentile). But if we were to maintain the same scale over the decades, without recalibrating it to keep the mean the same, we would find it rising, as follows for the Weschler Intelligence Scale for Children (WISC):

100.00 (1947–48) 107.63 (1972) 113.00 (1989) 117.63 (2002)

And here are the scores for the Weschler Adult Intelligence Scale (WAIS):

100.00 (1953–54) 107.50 (1978) 111.70 (1995) 115.07 (2006)

An average child in 2002, that is, would have scored seventeen points above average in the late 1940s, while an average adult in 2006 would beat the average in the early 1950s by fifteen points. In other words, an average person in 2002 (the fiftieth percentile) would fall into the eighty-fifth percentile in the 1947–48 group. This advance is remarkable, one that few scientists would have thought possible. As Flynn's studies circulated in the 1980s and after, psychologists analyzed the data and pondered their causes and implications at length. What made American intelligence climb so rapidly, and will the gains continue? Do the numbers indicate that Americans are, in fact, getting smarter—more knowledgeable, critical, ingenious, and reflective?

Explanations for the rising scores have varied, with researchers advancing several factors in different proportions, including improvements in early childhood nutrition and education, more people going to college, reduced exposure to toxins (particularly lead), a more demanding cognitive environment in the workplace and in leisure activities (created by technology and media), and the expansion of practices of hypothesizing and abstract reasoning. Flynn favors the latter cause, noting that IQ test questions mostly ask people to detach facts from concrete situations and apply logic to them, identifying patterns, similarities, and analogies, not invoking real-world knowledge. They require subjects to perform certain mental operations—for instance, examining numbers in sequence and predicting the next one to come, or observing objects in two pictures and determining relationships between them, then looking at a third picture and selecting a fourth picture (out of five provided) that forms the same relationship to it. Knowledge helps, but mainly knowledge that supports abstract inferences (such as familiarity with classification schemes and mathematical processes), not factual knowledge such as what happened on December 7, 1941. The actual objects in the pictures themselves don't matter, only the abstract relations one can draw. Consider the question, "What do dogs and rabbits have in common?" A concrete answer might be, "Well, dogs help you hunt rabbits," while an abstract one would go,

"Both are mammals." As Flynn notes in discussing this example in *Are We Getting Smarter? Rising IQ in the Twenty-First Century* (2012), IQ exams such as Raven's Progressive Matrices test for the abstract choice. He terms it a "habit of mind," a readiness to treat objects in a conditional, scientific way. "If you are unaccustomed to using logic for anything but to deal with the concrete world," he writes, "and indeed distrust reasoning that is not grounded in the concrete, you are not amenable to the change of gears that Raven's requires" (13). If a test question began, "Suppose two friends start from Point A and reach Point B five minutes apart . . . ," a hyperconcrete mind might think, "Why don't they drive the same speed?" while an abstract-habit mind would comfortably accept the opening as a working premise. Rising IQ scores, then, measure a particular kind of cognitive disposition that, in fact, primary and secondary education in the twentieth century had increasingly stressed. The gains are real, and they mean we are getting smarter—*if, that is, we define intelligence as this capacity for abstraction.*

Indeed, if we take the numbers at face value, we have to believe that American adults and children are much smarter than they were a half century ago, as if evolution accelerated so fast that it concentrated thousands of years of development into several dozen. The average child in 2010 would have been exceptional in 1950, the ordinary twenty-first-century adult able to run circles around a mid-twentieth-century adult whenever an abstract intellectual problem arose. That's what fifteen points represent—clear and distinct superiority, a marked gap in mental talent easy to demonstrate (hand both of them a Sudoku puzzle). A score of 117 puts someone in the top 15 percent of the population.

And yet, given this dramatic advance, those of us in the worlds of education and employment are stuck with a discordant fact. Why, we wonder, do so many high school students, college students, and younger workers seem so terribly deficient in basic knowledge and skills? Their reasoning abilities may have jumped forward, their ability to learn may make the 1950s mind appear lethargic, but their reading comprehension hasn't improved at all. One source of long-term data on reading comes from the National Assessment of Educational Progress (NAEP—the "Nation's Report Card"), which shows scores for seventeen-year-olds flat since the test began in the early 1970s (National Center for Education Statistics). We have average scores on the SAT verbal exam going back even farther, and they underwent a shocking decline of fifty-four points from 1962 to 1980. The score has wavered up and down by a few points ever since (Adams). More youths are going to college, yes, but the numbers of them requiring remedial coursework in math and writing keep climbing, the rate of those in need standing at 10 percent for selective schools, 30 percent at less selective colleges, and 60 percent at two-year institutions, according to the National Center for Public Policy and Higher Education. Employers, too, constantly grumble about the lack of readiness of college graduates for their workplaces. A fall 2013 report by Chegg queried one thousand hiring managers on the skills of recent college graduates, and the rate of those who judged them "Very/Completely Prepared" for the following tasks came up as follows:

- "Working on tasks independently": 58 percent
- "Writing to sum up results": 51 percent
- "Solving problems through experimentation": 49 percent
- "Making a persuasive argument": 43 percent

At the same time, Chegg asked college students the same question, and they judged themselves "Very/Completely Prepared" at much higher rates, for instance, 70 percent on "Writing to sum up results" (Korn). More substandard results come from a 2013 ACT report on the entire adult population, not just recent graduates, that identifies three "cognitive assessments" ("Reading for Information," "Applied Mathematics," and "Locating Information") that tally more closely the mental aptitudes tested by IQ questions. "Less than half (45%) of the examinees with a high level of education met the Locating Information skill requirements for 4 of the 5 occupations with a large number of openings and for 3 of the 5 highest-paying occupations requiring a high level of education," the ACT concluded. "Only 19%

of the examinees with a low level of education met or exceeded the Locating Information skill requirement." Overall, "Significant foundational skills gaps exist between the skills of examinees with either a low or high level of education and the skills needed for jobs requiring a low or high level of education." Clearly, the gains reported on IQ tests haven't spread to school and work.

If we drill down into the IQ data, however, the mismatch starts to make sense. The WISC (child) and WAIS (adult) IQ tests have several parts, each one testing a different mental function. The Digit Span subtest has subjects repeat a list of numbers that have been presented orally (testing memory and attention). The Block Design on the children's test asks subjects to organize blocks according to a given model (testing spatial reasoning and motor skills), while the Vocabulary exam for adults tests how many words they know and how well they can deploy them. Other subtests include Visual Puzzles, Similarities, Arithmetic, Coding, Matrix Reasoning, Symbol Search, and Information (a straightforward measure of general knowledge derived from culture). If we look at child scores, we see that the rates of improvement over the decades have varied for each subtest, sometimes sharply, the difference masked when we combine them into an average score. At the high end, we find Similarities climbing 23.85 points from 1950 to 2004, while Coding jumped 18 points and Block Design 15.9 points. At the low end, the Information subtest showed an improvement of only 2.15 points, while Arithmetic inched up only 2.3 points and Vocabulary results added 4.4 points. The lesser subtest outcomes explain why academics have stalled for U.S. schoolchildren. Flynn sets NAEP reading scores alongside Information and Vocabulary data for the years 1972 to 2002, when general-information knowledge was flat and vocabulary moved minimally. On the NAEP reading exams, elementary and middle-school students showed some improvements, but twelfth-graders none at all, leading Flynn to conclude, "Today's children may learn to master basic reading skills at a younger age, but are no better prepared for reading more demanding adult literature" (18). The small vocabulary IQ gain is reflected in better NAEP reading scores by nine-year-olds, but it doesn't help seventeen-year-olds whose reading tests contain passages with diction exceeding that gain.

The Information subtest factors into reading scores as well, a connection that laypersons, educators, and even professors of education often fail to appreciate. The significance of general information begins with the fact that texts always have unstated meanings—content that is implicit in the sentences and taken for granted as known by readers. The 2009 NAEP reading assessment for twelfth-graders, for instance, chose as one passage a rental agreement and asked test takers to respond to prompts such as, "The name of the tenant must be filled in on the rental agreement in two places. Identify the two places and explain why the name of the tenant needs to appear in each of them." The passage didn't explain what a rental agreement is, define key terms ("tenant," "disclosure"), or introduce the diction and style of legal language. Successful test takers had to know something about property rights and contracts in order to read quickly and answer the questions confidently. Those who didn't stumbled as they read, laboring to discern meanings that others apprehended automatically. Examine any newspaper story, press release, scientific report, contemporary novel, or other commonplace text and you find the same thing: buried knowledge that sets readers on a comprehension continuum, those at the high end having the knowledge that lets them proceed fluently, and those at the low end not having it and faltering. If you don't know anything about rental situations and have never seen a legal contract, critical thinking skills won't much help. Those abstract mental abilities measured by other subtests, at best, help readers to make imperfect inferences from whatever aspects of the text are familiar. But that's a time-consuming and chancy process. Relevant prior knowledge, in contrast, allows readers to recognize implicit references and situations in a snap. The contrast has become clear in eye-tracking studies. Readers with some knowledge about the topic of the text move their eyes swiftly and linearly through the text, whereas low-knowledge readers' eyes move haltingly, doubling back and slowing down. Their ensuing scores reflect their ease or difficulty.

The more background knowledge one has, then, the more agile and capacious a reader can be, which is why the Information and Vocabulary IQ trends are so important to the state of the American Mind. Other IQ subtest scores give ample reason for optimism, but the disappointing stagnation of general knowledge and vocabulary among the young in the last sixty years means that the benefits of the Flynn Effect may be limited to bounded spheres in which general knowledge and word breadth don't count so much, such as undemanding entertainments and unskilled labor, but not in the civic sphere, traditional cultural settings such as performance halls, or any place related to a marketplace of ideas, not to mention professional and managerial workplaces. Better spatial reasoning may help people read a map and navigate a video game, but it won't help them choose better schools for their children, catch biblical references in President Obama's speeches, decide which mayoral candidate to vote for, or evaluate the trustworthiness of various news programs.

Adults have produced steady IQ gains on knowledge-driven subtests, rising 17.8 points in Vocabulary and a not-so-impressive 8.4 points in Information since 1950, the latter likely a result of many more people going to college and picking up general knowledge by enrolling in basic courses in U.S. history, economics, psychology, English, and other core subjects. (The virtually flat Information scores for youths indicate that the boost must happen after age seventeen.) Given the explosion of college attendance in the second half of the twentieth century, not to mention the proliferation of information about the world through the advent of television, we have to judge the adult improvement in Information a disappointment. Set alongside Vocabulary, Coding (16.15 points—a typical coding task is to copy a series of numbers and symbols in sequence within a time limit), and Similarities (19.55 points), Information looks like less of a positive development than it does a result casting doubt upon the capacity of abstract cognitive skills to incorporate concrete facts about history, politics, arts, and culture and make people curious about them. In contrast to Arithmetic, though, where adults gained only 3.5 points, Information looks gigantic (Flynn judges the minimal adult gain on Arithmetic "unexpected and shocking" [22]). Still, if adults and children raised their abstract, fluid intelligence so much, why couldn't they have raised their general knowledge at parallel rates? What would have happened in college if students had entered with a significant knowledge gain already under way?

We can sharpen the question by focusing on Vocabulary and identifying an empirical puzzle. As adults have raised their general knowledge IQ by 8 points, presumably they have retained the knowledge long after they left college, got married, and had children. Greater knowledge certainly affects interests and conversation in the home, and we would expect a more knowledge-rich environment to have influenced the children, producing a parallel rise. But that hasn't happened, as the 6-point difference between the two groups indicates. As for Vocabulary, it should have shown an even firmer correlation between adult and child IQ, because vocabulary learning for small children transpires mainly through the environment that adults provide, including their conversation and reading material. Here, however, we find the most conspicuous gap of all between older and younger Americans. As noted above, from 1950 to 2004, WISC scores for Vocabulary rose 4.4 points, while WAIS results soared 17.8 points, a 13.4-point difference. Adults have grown smarter with words, but children haven't absorbed it and become smarter with words themselves. Why?

Flynn interprets this discrepancy as an effect of "cultural segregation," but he doesn't elaborate on what it is and how it works except to refer to a teenage subculture that commenced in the 1950s and crafted a "teenage-speak" that insulated them from "adult-speak." Other social scientists and intellectuals have often noted and lamented the phenomenon, however, but no amount of criticism and regret has slowed the process. Over the course of the twentieth century, observers say, adolescence emerged as a distinct stage of life, a time after childhood and before adulthood in which teenagers stayed in school, congregated with one another, and adopted their own manners, idioms, fashions, music, movies, and gathering places. The great education researcher James Coleman termed it "the adolescent society" in his study of values in high schools in the late 1950s, a new historical phenomenon that allowed adolescents unprecedented independence, peer-to-peer contact, and spending money. Before 1910, most American youths left school before reaching ninth grade, learning to read and write and do arithmetic, then going to work on the farm, in the kitchens, and as delivery boys, seamstresses, and factory workers. In 1909, only 8.8 percent of Americans graduated from high school, the rest of them spending their teen years around adults, not with one another. No fifteen-year-old at the time could refer to "my social life," because the adolescent society didn't exist. Once they outgrew childhood, the adult world pressed in and oriented youths toward work and money and sustenance, and the life of the teenager in 1965 would have been unimaginable.

As the twentieth century progressed and average years of schooling lengthened—by 1960, 70 percent of youths earned a high school diploma—teenagers passed more and more hours with one another, 185 days a year in close quarters in school buildings and much of the rest of their time hanging out together. They shuffled from room to room all day in groups of twenty-five, ate together in the lunchroom, played sports and joined clubs after school, and had the leisure to linger in each other's company before heading home. Naturally, all the hours together had an effect. A youth subculture developed and was soon noticed by sociologists and journalists, while films such as *Rebel without a Cause* (1955) and *The Blackboard Jungle* (1955) appeared and dramatic profiles of teens were published such as *Life* magazine's "The 'Hot-Rod' Problem: Teenagers Organize to Experiment with Mechanized Suicide" (November 1949) and the *New Yorker*'s "A Caste, A Culture, A Market II" (November 1958), Dwight Macdonald's examination of the sociopathologies of this new age group ("Like other tribes, the teenagers have their folkways"). As adolescents became more conscious of themselves as distinct, claiming their own social space and defining it against adult matters—as the rock and roll band The Who put it, "Don't try to dig what we all say"—age segregation set in, and the adult voice that carried authority in 1920 waned. The more youth-to-youth contact happened, the more peer pressure intensified and the less adult pressure was exerted. Elvis filled their thoughts more than Eisenhower or Eliot, and the shenanigans of the school cafeteria impressed them more than family dinner table talk or popular poems.

The problem, of course, is that youth speech isn't as sophisticated as adult speech, nor is it as stocked with the material that helps them understand the world (not to mention IQ Vocabulary questions and reading-test passages). The lingo of youth banishes big words; topics center on social doings, while museums, bookstores, and historic sites have the status of foreign lands. Adolescent subculture is just that—adolescent—and youths immersed in it emerge with dawdling vocabulary and information knowledge, what we may call Cultural IQ, as Weschler subtest scores prove. In 1950 and today, if adult conversation and interests don't counteract youth content, intellectual development slows. However much novels such as *The Catcher in the Rye* (1951), declarations such as the Port Huron Statement (1962), commentaries like Charles Reich's *The Greening of America* (1970), and films such as *The Breakfast Club* (1985) cast American teens as estranged from grown-ups, tired of adult conformism and hypocrisy, and even poised at the vanguard of a social upheaval, those youths still needed nearby adults to pass on language and facts not found among themselves. If they shunned the elders, they narrowed the pipeline of eloquence and knowledge. The famed Generation Gap of the 1960s wasn't just a cultural difference between old and young, swing music versus rock and roll, *Time* magazine versus *MAD Magazine*, suits and hats versus T-shirts and jeans. It was an intelligence breakdown, too, the rising cultural autonomy of kids meaning a falling transfer of verbal and informational awareness. As the "Don't trust anyone over thirty" message circulated (even as mere posturing), as more music and movies catered to adolescent audiences and more kids not only stayed in high school but proceeded to college and extended peer immersion into their early twenties, a fundamental human tradition deteriorated. The parent-to-child and employer-to-young-worker acculturation process gave way to peer-to-peer interaction, which didn't raise vocabulary and information IQ but only intensified youth consciousness.

The fact that Americans realize large vocabulary gains and some informational gains in college is only a partial consolation. Colleges can't efficiently assume a duty handled by parents and mentors of various kinds (bosses, coaches, priests . . .) whose instruction happens at more impressionable ages and often for hours at a time. Not all kids go to college. Just two-thirds of high school students head to postsecondary institutions after they graduate, and the increase in the rate of youths admitted to college and staying there to earn a degree is apparently slowing down. According to the U.S. Census Bureau's American Community Survey, the percentage of Americans ages forty-five to sixty-four who have earned a bachelor's degree is 28.6, and the percentage of Americans ages twenty-five to thirty-four who have done so is 31.5, a meager increase given the tenacious emphasis on higher education in our culture in the last fifty years (National Center for Higher Education Management Systems). Universal college attendance has been a policy position of the G. W. Bush and Obama administrations, for instance, and the Common Core State Standards initiative developed out of the aim of preparing low-income as well as middle-class students for college, but the universalization mandate runs squarely against materials in the challenging parts of the college curriculum (for instance, math and science) that only those with above-average intellectual talent can digest.

Charles Murray outlines that conflict in *Real Education: Four Simple Truths for Bringing America's Schools Back to Reality* (2008), in which he cites data from the College Board that set college readiness at a score of 1180 on the SAT (verbal and math), which only one out of ten seventeen-year-olds in the United States attain. This scant percentage shouldn't surprise us, Murray notes, recalling that "for many years, the consensus intellectual benchmark for dealing with college-level material was an IQ of around 115, which demarcates the top 16 percent of the distribution. That was in fact the mean IQ of college graduates during the 1950s" (69). The portion of people who have graduated from college has soared since the 1950s, of course, but as the cohort figures cited above show, not so much in the last few decades, indicating that this intelligence deficiency may form a barrier that keeps graduation rates in the low thirties. Indeed, the very fact that American youths haven't raised their Word and Information IQs may become even more dynamic as more of them enroll in postsecondary courses and try and fail to stick it out to the end, a trend indicated by the large numbers of first-year students who are placed into remedial courses and drop out before the semester is over. Given that the main reason students struggle to handle coursework is their inability to comprehend "complex texts" such as legal opinions and modern poetry whose vocabulary and syntax are too dense and unfamiliar, Vocabulary IQ stands out as crucial to success (ACT, *Reading between the Lines*). Unless college-educated parents and mentors pass along their word and information knowledge more successfully, or rather, unless adolescents pay more attention to adults and less to one another, matriculation and graduation rates will flatten. When that happens, not only will youth Vocabulary and Information IQs remain sluggish, but so will adult scores. If adult Vocabulary and Information climbed because of the historic rise of college enrollments that started in the early 1960s, when the rate of increase levels off, those IQ scores will, too.

The solution is easy to conceive but impossible to implement. Parents and mentors need to spend more time conversing with youths, reading the newspaper together, going on cultural outings, taking walks, and otherwise cutting into the ample after-school hours of social life and adding grown-up affairs to the menu of adolescence. But how can we change habits and preferences that have the force of history behind them? How can a parent in a single-parent home find the time and energy to do so, especially with sulky teens who relate only to one another? How can mentors curtail youth culture when the goods and styles of it form a mega-industry that showers kids with marketing and plays upon status and consumer competition? The parents and mentors inclined to heed our exhortations probably already recognize the problem and strive to restrain it—they don't need our advice—while the others haven't the space to listen or the disposition to act. The cultural liberation of youth was a genuine revolution in human society, and few things in this world have stronger momentum than cultural mores and values that settle into people's heads as the way reality operates. I know of no way to slow this hazardous social experiment except to broadcast as widely as possible the intellectual damage it has done and will continue to do.

References

ACT. *The Condition of Work Readiness in the United States*, 2013, http://www.act.org/workreadiness/.

———. *Reading between the Lines: What the ACT Reveals about College Readiness in Reading*, 2006, http://www.act.org/research/policymakers/pdf/reading_report.pdf.

Adams, Marilyn Jager. "Advancing Our Students' Language and Literacy: The Challenge of Complex Texts." *American Educator* (Winter 2010–11): 3–11, 53.

Coleman, James S., with John W. C. Johnstone and Kurt Jonassohn. *The Adolescent Society: The Social Life of the Teenager and Its Impact on Education*. New York: Free Press, 1961.

Flynn, James R. *Are We Getting Smarter? Rising IQ in the Twenty-First Century*. Cambridge: Cambridge University Press, 2012.

Korn, Melissa. "College Kids Give Themselves an 'A' for Job Readiness." *Wall Street Journal*, October 29, 2013.

Life. "The 'Hot-Rod' Problem: Teenagers Organize to Experiment with Mechanized Suicide." November 7, 1949, 122–28.

Macdonald, Dwight. "A Caste, A Culture, A Market II." *New Yorker*, November 29, 1958, 57–107.

Murray, Charles. *Real Education: Four Simple Truths for Bringing America's Schools Back to Reality*. New York: Random House, 2008.

National Center for Education Statistics. *NAEP 2012: Trends in Academic Progress*, http://nces.ed.gov/nationsreportcard/subject/publications/main2012/pdf/2013456.pdf.

National Center for Higher Education Management Systems. "Education Levels of the Population," http://www.higheredinfo.org/dbrowser/?level=nation &mode=map&state=0&submeasure=245.

National Center for Public Policy and Higher Education and the Southern Regional Education Board. *Beyond the Rhetoric: Improving College Readiness through Coherent State Policy*, June 2010, http://www.highereducation.org/reports/college_readiness/CollegeReadiness.pdf.

2

Biblical Literacy Matters

Daniel L. Dreisbach

At the first presidential inauguration of the millennium, George W. Bush delivered an address rich with biblical language and allusions, including references to at least four books of the Bible. Pledging a national commitment to serve those in poverty, for example, Bush mentioned the biblical parable of the Good Samaritan (Luke 10:30–36). Media pundits wondered about the source of this strangely archaic language. A veteran CBS political commentator confessed, "There were a few phrases in the speech I just didn't get. One was, 'When we see that wounded traveler on the road to Jericho, we will not pass to the other side'" (Meyer).

A stream of opinion surveys and widely reported anecdotes document an alarming decline in biblical literacy among Americans; that is, there is ignorance of key biblical texts, stories, characters, doctrines, themes, rituals, and symbols (Pew Research; Bible Literacy Project). For example, when asked in January 2004 to name his favorite book of the New Testament, Democratic presidential candidate Howard Dean, eager to show that his party was as religion friendly as Republicans, answered, "Job" (Teather). At a November 2, 2011, briefing, White House press secretary Jay Carney elaborated on the president's invocation of God in chastising the House of Representatives for not acting more quickly on a jobs bill. "I believe the phrase from the Bible is," Carney said, "'The Lord helps those who help themselves'" (Carney). The White House later issued a correction, noting, "This common phrase does not appear in the Bible." On April 1, 2013, the *New York Times* issued the following correction of an article on Pope Francis's first Easter message: "An earlier version of this article mischaracterized the Christian holiday of Easter. It is the celebration of Jesus' resurrection from the dead, not his resurrection into heaven" (*New York Times*).

It was not always so. There was a time when politicians and polemicists such as John Winthrop, Patrick Henry, Tom Paine, Abraham Lincoln, and William Jennings Bryan could pack a missive or stirring oration with biblical language, themes, and allusions and expect their biblically literate audiences to recognize their sources and meanings. George Washington routinely incorporated biblical language and allusions into his working vocabulary. Consider, for example, a line from a 1785 letter brimming with a half dozen biblical phrases:

> I wish to see the sons and daughters of the world in Peace and busily employed in the more agreeable amusement of fulfilling the first and great commandment, *Increase and Multiply*: as an encouragement to which we have opened the fertile plains of the Ohio to the poor, the needy and the oppressed of the Earth; any one therefore who is heavy laden, or who wants land to cultivate, may repair thither and abound, as in the Land of promise, with milk and honey: the ways are preparing, and the roads will be made easy, thro' the channels of Potomac and James river. (Washington 28:206–7)

Patrick Henry's oratorical style is said to have been modeled on that of itinerant evangelists of the Great Awakening, and his most celebrated address—the "give me liberty or give me death" declamation delivered before the Virginia Convention on March 23, 1775—sounded like a revivalist lay sermon. The former slave Frederick Douglass was among the assembled throngs in Washington, DC, to witness Lincoln's second inauguration in March 1865. After hearing the president's brief speech in which he mentioned God fourteen times, quoted the Bible four times, and referenced prayer three times, Douglass famously quipped that Lincoln's "address sounded more like a sermon than a state paper" (441).

Americans, apparently, have long been more biblically literate than their European contemporaries. In 1781 Benjamin Franklin, then serving as the U.S. minister to France, wrote a letter to his old friend the Reverend Doctor Samuel Cooper, pastor of Boston's influential Brattle Street Church. Some months before, the Congregationalist clergyman had sent Franklin a copy of the sermon he had delivered on the commencement of the Massachusetts government under a new constitution. The sermon, Franklin responded, gave him an "abundance of Pleasure," and he said he intended to translate and print the sermon for a European audience. He explained, however, that he would need to insert biblical references for European readers even though such citations were unnecessary for Cooper's biblically literate American audience:

> It was not necessary in New England where every body reads the Bible, and is acquainted with Scripture Phrases, that you should note the Texts from which you took them; but I have observed in England as well as in France, that Verses and Expressions taken from the sacred Writings, and not known to be such, appear very strange and awkward to some Readers; and I shall therefore in my Edition take the Liberty of marking the quoted Texts in the Margin. (Franklin, 35:70)

That Americans from the colonial era to the twentieth century were biblically literate is no surprise because they lived in an overwhelmingly Protestant culture. Protestant theology reveres the Bible as the revealed word of God and emphasizes its role as authority in all matters of faith and practice (as encapsulated in the popular phrase of the Reformation, *sola scriptura* [scripture alone]). One would expect the Bible to occupy a place of prominence in such a culture.

The Pilgrims followed by the Puritans who settled in New England were children of the Protestant Reformation. They set sail for the New World on a mission to build Bible commonwealths based on Reformed theology and biblical law as they understood it. They were a people whose beliefs, values, and culture were shaped by the Book; as one scholar put it, "In a manner that finds no exact parallel in any other nation, the Bible has become America's book" (Gunn, 1); another stated, "The Bible is not merely the fertile soil that brought Americanism forth. It is the energy source that makes it live and thrive" (Gelernter, 42). If there was one book that seventeenth-, eighteenth-, and nineteenth-century Americans read and consulted frequently, it was the Bible. According to Lawrence A. Cremin, the Bible is "the single most important cultural influence in the lives of Anglo-Americans" (40). It promoted high literacy rates among the populations and created a common mentality among immigrants from different countries; people of diverse sects; across distant regions north, south, and west; and farmers and merchants.

In addition to its profound influence on language, letters, law, and politics, the Bible informed how Americans thought of themselves and their place in the world. Even before the Puritans arrived in the New World to establish Bible commonwealths, their leader, John Winthrop, described a sacred mission to remake society and to be, in the words of Matthew's Gospel, a "city set upon a hill" that would serve as an example to all the world. This mission in various iterations would inspire intrepid settlers to tame the continent in pursuit of manifest destiny and lead the nation into wars in foreign lands in order to make the world "safe for democracy." These missions were believed to be "sacred," shaped by beliefs and ethics derived from biblical precepts.

After three and a half centuries of common standing in America, however, biblical literacy has undergone a precipitous decline, according to social science data and anecdotal evidence. Often-cited surveys recently conducted by Gallup, the Barna Group, and the Pew Research Center, for example, report that only half of American adults can name one of the four Gospels, and an even smaller percentage can identify the first book of the Bible.

Because of the Bible's role in shaping people's thoughts and speech during the forming of our nation, it matters deeply that Americans today know so little about the Bible and its influence on their culture. It matters because the Bible has informed diverse aspects of the culture, and the Bible continues to influence culture in innumerable ways. To understand themselves and where they come from, Americans must know something about the Bible. Moreover, biblical literacy is essential to understanding not only the Christian tradition and Christianity's continuing influence in the world today but also core cultural components of Western civilization and the intellectual roots of the American political experiment. Biblical literacy, in short, mattered to America's Founders, and it still matters to those engaged now in cultural and civic life.

Why Biblical Literacy Mattered

Since the first settlements in the New World, the Bible has been woven into the fabric of American social, legal, and political culture. For many colonial families, the Bible was a cherished household possession passed down from one generation to the next. Sociologist Robert N. Bellah observed, "The Bible was the one book that literate Americans in the 17th, 18th, and 19th centuries could be expected to know well" (12). The Bible was important to Americans both for religious reasons and for the development of key components of their culture, including language and literature, education, law, and politics, providing the shared background knowledge within which daily affairs transpired.

The first laws crafted in British North America, such as the "Articles, Lawes, and Orders, Divine, Politique, and Martiall for the Colony in Virginea" (1610–11) and the Massachusetts Body of Liberties (1641), drew extensively not only on English common law but also on Mosaic law. Many early colonial codes were apparently framed with a copy of the Pentateuch at hand. And lest there be any doubt, these codes often included references to specific biblical authority for legal provisions contained in them.

For centuries, the Bible was a central text and mental framework in American education. No text was more widely used, influential, or illustrative of the Bible's influence in education than *The New-England Primer*. This slender manual, ubiquitous in colonial homes and schools, was replete with biblical passages, allusions, and doctrines, so much so that we can say that schoolchildren learned reading, writing, arithmetic, geography, and civics through the lens of the biblical text. First published in Massachusetts in the late 1600s and reprinted in numerous editions over the course of two centuries, the *Primer* was "the most widely read school book in America for 100 years," according to R. Freeman Butts and Lawrence A. Cremin, historians of American education (69). It imparted biblical principles in multiple ways, including through alphabet lessons drawn from scriptural texts, biblical passages (such as the Ten Commandments and the Lord's Prayer), Christian creeds (such as the Apostles' Creed) and catechisms (such as the Westminster Assembly's "Shorter Catechism"), and miscellaneous prayers, hymns, poems, and other devotional material. Its biblical content was so pervasive that it has been called "The Little Bible of New England" (Ford, 1). A famous rhyming couplet illustrating the letter *A* in one of the *Primer*'s alphabet lessons is, "In ADAM's Fall/We sinned all." Significantly, this lesson commenced with the fall and the doctrine of original sin, concepts essential to understanding the founding generation's view of human nature and the necessity for imposing restraints on civil magistrates through a variety of checks and balances and the separation of powers. Other popular children's books of the seventeenth, eighteenth, and nineteenth centuries similarly drew on scripture.

From the colonial era to the founding era, Americans looked to the Bible to propose models, appeal to precedents, and set normative standards for the ordering of public life. The founding generation thought that the Bible, among other sources ancient and modern, provided models for, inter alia, republicanism, separation of powers, and due process of law. There were late eighteenth-century Americans, for example, who thought that the Hebrew Commonwealth, which encompassed approximately a half millennium of Jewish history from the exodus until Saul was anointed king, was a model of and divine precedent for a form of republican government worthy of emulation in their own commonwealths (see, generally, Dreisbach, "A Peculiar People"). They were well aware that ideas like republicanism and federalism found expression in traditions apart from the Hebrew example. The political models they found in the Hebrew scriptures, however, reassured pious Americans that these models enjoyed a divine imprimatur.

In cultures shaped by the Protestant Reformation, including North America, a chain of links connects Reformation theology to the vernacular Bible, the vernacular Bible to literacy education, literacy education to a broader pursuit of education, and education to republican self-government. The Protestant notion of the "priesthood of all believers" renounced the church and its priests as *the* mediator between God and man and empowered each individual to read and reason about matters of faith. This challenged control by elites and opened doors to lay leadership in religious concerns and, eventually, in the broader society. A diminished role for the church and its priests as essential interpreters in issues of faith meant that ordinary believers needed access to the Bible in a reliable, vernacular translation so that they could gain firsthand knowledge of God's communications with humankind. Accordingly, many early reformers such as Martin Luther and William Tyndale devoted years at great personal costs, to translating the Bible into a vernacular tongue. The advent of new printing technology and a demand for accessible, inexpensive Bibles sparked an explosion in printed material, starting with Bibles and Bible commentaries and quickly expanding to newspapers and other literature on a wide range of topics.

Notwithstanding accessible, inexpensive vernacular Bibles, the persistence of illiteracy meant that individuals still had to rely on others for knowledge of God's Word. Therefore, Protestants promoted literacy, and Reformed communities enjoyed the highest literacy rates in recorded history. This was especially true in British North America where, according to Harry Stout, a Bible could be found in "virtually every household, and the regional literacy rates were perhaps the highest in the world" (30). "A Native of America, especially of New England, who cannot read and wright is as rare a Phenomenon as a Comet," John Adams reported in 1765 ("[Fragmentary Draft]," 1:257). In his 1800 assessment of education in America, Pierre Samuel Du Pont de Nemours observed, "Most young Americans . . . can read, write and cipher. Not more than four in a thousand are unable to write legibly—even neatly." He attributed America's high literacy rate to frequent Bible reading, which, he also said, "tend[s] to increase and formulate ideas of responsibility" (3–4). The vernacular Bible, together with an ability to read, proved powerfully liberating. It empowered ordinary people—men and women, rich and poor, priest and parishioner—to search and study scripture and to think for themselves about matters most vital to their consciences. More generally, expanding literacy unleashed an energizing spirit of inquiry. Thus, from its inception, the Reformation fostered literacy and, in turn, promoted education more generally.

The children of the Reformation, including many American Founders, came to believe that a literate, well-educated populace, guided by biblical morality, was essential for self-government. If their bold experiment in republican self-government was to succeed, many founders believed that the populace must be educated and virtuous. Indeed, the political literature of the founding era is replete with the assertion that education and religion are the indispensable twin pillars on which their system of self-government rested. The populace, first, must be sufficiently educated that citizens could make well-informed decisions about how best to govern themselves. Second, the people must be sufficiently virtuous that their personal responsibility and discipline would facilitate the social order and political stability necessary for a regime of self-government. In sustaining this second pillar—civic virtue—the founders believed that religion must play a vital role in the polity, either for genuinely spiritual or utilitarian reasons. They believed the moral instruction found in the Bible could provide the internal moral monitors that citizens required to maintain the social discipline necessary to govern themselves. Even those founders who rejected the Bible as divine revelation valued the Bible—especially the moral teachings of Jesus—as an instrument for promoting personal discipline and social control.

A moral people respected social order, legitimate authority, oaths and contracts, private property, and the like; the Bible and the Christian religion, it was believed, nurtured such civic virtue. Thus, the Bible was thought indispensable to a regime of republican self-government. For example, believing that "without national morality a republican government cannot be maintained" and that "the Bible contains the most profound philosophy, the most perfect morality, and the most refined policy, that ever was conceived upon earth," John Adams described the Bible as "the most republican book in the world" (Letter to Benjamin Rush, 75–76). Adams was not alone among his contemporaries in expressing this idea. John Dickinson, often called the "penman of the Revolution," similarly remarked, "The Bible is the most republican Book that ever was written" (Notes).

Starting with the first colonial settlements, Americans looked to the Bible for instruction in numerous aspects of life, including education, law, and politics. The Bible, as a handbook for teaching civic virtue and instilling a civic temperament, was thought particularly important to maintaining a regime of republican self-government.

Why Biblical Literacy Still Matters

Biblical literacy still matters because the Bible not only offers insights on and enriches an understanding of American history and culture but also provides a shared cultural vocabulary that facilitates broad social engagement and conversations on a wide array of religious and civic concerns. The Bible has played a foundational role in shaping American national identity, crafting a sacred national mission and defining the nation's place in the world. Scripture has also been an invaluable source for shaping Americans' beliefs and values. In short, from the first western settlements to the present day, the Bible has informed how Americans see themselves and their place in the world.

In particular, the Old Testament accounts of bondage, exodus and liberation, a promised land, and finally nationhood have acted as powerful formative metaphors of American self-identity. Americans have embraced specific narratives, rooted in biblical culture, as a chosen people and a covenanted people who, like Israel of old, were led miraculously out of bondage into a promised land flowing with milk and honey and, most important, liberty. So pronounced was this theme in the founding era that one patriot preacher declared, "It has been often remarked that the people of the United States come nearer to a parallel with Ancient Israel, than any other nation upon the globe. Hence, 'OUR AMERICAN ISRAEL,' is a term frequently used; and common consent allows it apt and proper" (Abbot, 6).

From the Pilgrim Fathers to the Founding Fathers, and even to the present day, Americans have seen themselves reliving the exodus story. The contours of the analogy have differed depending on who made it and when, but the comparisons have often been elaborate, and sometimes tortured. The political repression and religious persecution the settlers had endured in England and from which they fled was their Egyptian bondage. The Stuart monarchs (and, later in the revolutionary year, George III) were their intransigent Pharaoh; the treacherous waters of the Atlantic Ocean, which they traversed in search of the promised land, was their Red Sea. In the new Canaan, like the ancient Israelites, they had to contend with a forbidding terrain and hostile inhabitants. The Native Americans they encountered were their Moabites and Philistines. In the founding era, George Washington was frequently referred to as their Moses.

Significantly, even Americans most influenced by the Enlightenment and skeptical of the miraculous aspects of the exodus story have embraced this vision of America, the American people, and their collective identity and mission in providential history. On July 4, 1776, the Continental Congress appointed John Adams, Thomas Jefferson, and Benjamin Franklin to a committee to design "a seal for the United States of America." Franklin proposed an image of Moses extending his hand in anticipation of God's supernatural parting of the Red Sea, allowing the children of Israel to escape Pharaoh's army (Exodus 14). Jefferson similarly recommended a portrayal of the "Children of Israel in the Wilderness, led by a cloud by Day, and a Pillar of Fire by night" (Exodus 13:21–22; Dreisbach and Hall, 229). Remarkably, both men, sons of the Enlightenment, drew on familiar Old Testament images of Israel miraculously delivered from Pharaoh's bondage just as Americans had been providentially delivered from the tyranny of George III, as fitting allegorical portrayals of the new nation's plight.

Their choices were unsurprising; biblical citations echoed throughout the former colonies, including the political literature. After reviewing political writings published from 1760 to 1805, Donald S. Lutz counted more citations of the Bible than of any European thinker or school of thought (Lutz, "The Relative Influence"). Lutz found that Deuteronomy, the fifth book of the Pentateuch, "is the most frequently cited book, followed by Montesquieu's *The Spirit of the Laws*" (Lutz, *A Preface*, 136). He further noted, "Saint Paul is cited about as frequently as Montesquieu and Blackstone, the two most frequently cited secular authors, and Deuteronomy is cited almost twice as often as all of Locke's writings put together" (Lutz, *The Origins of American Constitutionalism*, 140). It should be added here that Lutz focused on political writings and that his method defined a citation as "any footnote, direct quote, attributed citation, or use of a name in exemplifying a concept or position" ("The Relative Influence," 191). The study did not capture unattributed direct quotations, paraphrases, or allusions to the Bible, which students of the era know are found abundantly in this literature.

This national narrative embodied in the Bible has imbued Americans with a sacred purpose. The inescapable implication of being God's new "chosen people" in a new "promised land" was that there was something extraordinary—exceptional, if you will—about America's place and role in God's unfolding plan for humanity. America's role as God's "new Israel" has carried with it both blessings and burdens, among them a responsibility to be a model polity for the world, a shining city on a hill. This vision has inspired generations of Americans to expand ever westward on a mission of manifest destiny, to embark on global Christian missionary outreach, and to fight wars on distant continents in order to make the world "safe for democracy." The themes of bondage, exodus, and liberation figured prominently in the abolitionist campaigns of the mid-nineteenth century and found similar expression in the civil rights movement a century later.

Conclusion

Biblical literacy is essential to understanding those Americans and people around the world for whom the Bible still matters and still informs their worldview. Many movements, developments, and conflicts at home and abroad, although not exclusively or even primarily about Christianity, are difficult to comprehend without an awareness of biblical Christianity. This includes controversies involving just war, civil rights, abortion, definitions of marriage, homosexuality, origins of life, and blasphemy. Without the biblical framework underlying those issues as they have unfolded in American history, people will not fully understand each other. In America, the biblical presence has run so deep that the deterioration of biblical literacy amounts to a deterioration in civic discussion, a cognitive failure on all parties to communicate.

Given the impact of Christianity and the Bible on Western civilization, we may say that every educated mind in the United States—Jews, Christians, other religious believers, and even atheists—must be acquainted with the basic stories, themes, claims, and symbols of Christianity and its sacred text, the Bible. In advice to his son, John Quincy Adams affirmed, "To a man of liberal education, the study of history is not only useful, and important, but altogether indispensable, and with regard to the history contained in the Bible, . . . 'it is not so much praiseworthy to be acquainted with it as it is shameful to be ignorant of it'" (J. Q. Adams, 34—a statement quoting Cicero on the importance of knowing one's country). The vernacular Bible has informed the language, letters, arts, architecture, law, politics, social structures, and other essential components of Western culture, extending from the most deeply felt spiritual beliefs to the most mundane secular practices. The calendar in common use is shaped by Christianity as revealed in the Bible, and numerous "holy days" in the public calendar celebrate explicitly Christian events. Familiar idioms, figures of speech, symbols, and proper names in Western cultures have biblical origins. Without knowledge of the Bible, it is difficult to appreciate the works of the greatest artists, writers, and composers in western history. Absent the King James Bible in particular, the English-speaking world would have never known Milton's *Paradise Lost*, Bunyan's *Pilgrim's Progress*, Handel's *Messiah*, the Negro spirituals, Lincoln's Gettysburg Address, Johnson's *God's Trombones*, and Seeger's "Turn! Turn! Turn!" Furthermore, those who lack biblical literacy find it difficult to appreciate the thoughts expressed in works such as these that draw so richly on the Bible.

In an increasingly fragmented society in which citizens lack a common language to engage in social discourse, there is an apparent need for shared points of reference and a common cultural vocabulary that will facilitate meaningful communications across various social divides, especially on volatile issues of religion and politics. Religious and cultural literacy lifts barriers to communication in a pluralistic and democratic society and helps citizens to join in conversations about how best to order public life and govern themselves. Given the Bible's pervasive cultural influence, the continuing influence of Christianity in the modern world, and the often contentious nature of religious controversies, biblical literacy is vital for effective and efficient communications and valuable social engagement in a pluralistic society.

Declining biblical literacy rates in twentieth- and twenty-first-century America have accompanied the increasing secularization of culture and a general decline in educational standards. Furthermore, a U.S. Supreme Court ruling on state-sponsored prayer and Bible reading in public schools was widely misunderstood by educators and the general public as expelling religion from the classroom, prompting schools to avoid studying religion altogether (U.S. Supreme Court). A few educators, public intellectuals, and organizations have sounded the alarm that unless parents, churches, and schools make a deliberate effort to teach children about the Bible and its influence, this illiteracy will only increase. Biblical literacy matters because the Bible reveals much about America's past, continues to inform basic components of culture today, and contributes to a common cultural vocabulary that enables Americans across social divides to engage in meaningful conversations about the issues that matter most to them.

References

Abbot, Abiel. "Traits of Resemblance in the People of the United States of America to Ancient Israel. In a Sermon, delivered at Haverhill, on the Twenty-eighth of November, 1799, the Day of Anniversary Thanksgiving." Haverhill, MA: Moore and Stebbins, 1799.

Adams, John. "[Fragmentary Draft of a Dissertation on Canon and Feudal Law, February 1765]." In *Diary and Autobiography of John Adams*, ed. L. H. Butterfield, 4 vols. Cambridge, MA: Belknap Press of Harvard University Press, 1961.

———. "Letter to Benjamin Rush, 2 February 1807." In *The Spur of Fame: Dialogues of John Adams and Benjamin Rush, 1805–1813*, ed. John A. Schutz and Douglass Adair, 75–76. San Marino, CA: Huntington Library, 1966.

Adams, John Quincy. *Letters of John Quincy Adams, to His Son, on the Bible and Its Teachings.* Auburn, NY: Derby, Miller, and Co., 1848.

Bellah, Robert N. *The Broken Covenant: American Civil Religion in Time of Trial.* New York: Seabury Press, 1975.

Bible Literacy Project. "Bible Literacy Report: What Do American Teens Know and What Do They Need To Know?" 2005, http://www.bibleliteracy.org/secure/documents/bibleliteracyreport2005.pdf.

Butts, R. Freeman, and Lawrence A. Cremin. *A History of Education in American Culture.* New York: Holt, Rinehart, and Winston, 1953.

Carney, Jay. "White House Press Briefing," November 2, 2011, http://www.whitehouse.gov/the-press-office/2011/11/02/press-briefing-press-secretary-jay-carney.

Cooper, Samuel. *A Sermon Preached before His Excellency John Hancock, Esq; Governour, the Honourable the Senate, and House of Representatives of the Commonwealth of Massachusetts, October 25, 1780. Being the Day of the Commencement of the Constitution, and Inauguration of the New Government.* Boston: T. and J. Fleet, and J. Gill, 1780.

Cremin, Lawrence A. *American Education: The Colonial Experience, 1607–1783.* New York: Harper and Row, 1970.

Dickinson, John. "Notes," n.d. R. R. Logan Collection, Historical Society of Pennsylvania. Copy provided courtesy of the John Dickinson Writings Project, University of Kentucky.

Douglass, Frederick. *Life and Times of Frederick Douglass.* Hartford, CT: Park Publishing, 1882.

Dreisbach, Daniel L. "A Peculiar People in 'God's American Israel': Religion and American National Identity." In *American Exceptionalism*, ed. Charles W. Dunn. Lanham, MD: Rowman and Littlefield, 2013: 55–76.

Dreisbach, Daniel L., and Mark David Hall, eds. *The Sacred Rights of Conscience: Selected Readings on Religious Liberty and Church-State Relations in the American Founding.* Indianapolis, IN: Liberty Fund, 2009.

Du Pont de Nemours, Pierre Samuel. *National Education in the United States of America.* Trans. B. G. Du Pont. Newark: University of Delaware Press, 1923.

Ford, Paul Leicester, ed. *The New-England Primer.* New York: Dodd, Mead and Co., 1899.

Franklin, Benjamin. "Letter to Samuel Cooper, 15 May 1781." In *The Papers of Benjamin Franklin*, eds. Barbara B. Oberg et al., 35:70. New Haven, CT: Yale University Press, 1999.

Gelernter, David. "Americanism—and Its Enemies." *Commentary* 119 (January 2005): 41–48.

Gunn, Giles. "Introduction." In *The Bible and American Arts and Letters*, ed. Giles Gunn. Philadelphia: Fortress Press, 1983: 1–9.

Lutz, Donald S. *The Origins of American Constitutionalism.* Baton Rouge: Louisiana State University Press, 1988.

———. *A Preface to American Political Theory.* Lawrence: University Press of Kansas, 1992.

———. "The Relative Influence of European Writers on Late-Eighteenth-Century American Political Thought." *American Political Science Review* 78 (1984): 189–97.

Meyer, Dick. "Clinton Rains on Dubya's Parade." CBSNews.com, January 20, 2001, http://www.cbsnews.com/news/Clinton-rains-on-dubyas-parade/.

New York Times. "Correction: April 1, 2013." To Elisabetta Povoledo, "Pope Calls for 'Peace in All the World' in First Easter Message," March 31, 2013, http://www.nytimes.com/2013/04/01/world/Europe/pope-francis-calls-for-peace-in-all-the-world-in-first-easter-message.html.

Pew Research Center, the Pew Forum on Religion and Public Life. "U.S. Religious Knowledge Survey," September 28, 2010, http://www.pewforum.org/2010/09/28/new-pew-forum-on-religion-public-life-survey-explores-religious-knowledge-in-the-us/.

Stout, Harry S. "Word and Order in Colonial New England." In *The Bible in America: Essays in Cultural History*, eds. Nathan O. Hatch and Mark A. Noll. New York: Oxford University Press, 1982: 19–38.

Teather, David. "Democrat Hopeful Walks with God in 'Bible Belt.'" *The Guardian*, January 4, 2004, http://www.theguardian.com/world/2004/jan/05/usa.uselections2004.

U.S. Supreme Court. *School District of Abington Township v. Schempp* and *Murray v. Curlett*, 374 U.S. 203 (1963).

Washington, George. "Letter to Marquis de Lafayette, 25 July 1785." In *The Writings of George Washington*, 37 vols., ed. John C. Fitzpatrick, 28:206–7. Washington, DC: Government Printing Office, 1931–1940.

3

Why Johnny and Joanie Can't Write, Revisited

Gerald Graff

Complaints that American high school and college graduates can't write have been pervasive for so long that they almost go without saying. Last year, when the Society for Human Resource Management asked managers about the skills of recent college graduates, 49 percent of them rated those graduates deficient in "the knowledge and basic skill of writing in English" (Goodbaum). A few years earlier, in 2006, a survey sponsored by the Conference Board posed the same questions to human resource professionals, and 81 percent of them judged high school graduates deficient in written communications, 47 percent of them said the same of two-year college graduates, and 28 percent of four-year college graduates. A 2012 survey of employers by the *Chronicle of Higher Education* concluded, "When it comes to the skills most needed by employers, job candidates are lacking most in written and oral communication skills."

More bad news comes from the standardized test universe—for instance, the SAT exam, which added a writing component in 2006. Since then, the national average has dropped every year except 2008 and 2013, when it was flat. (The 2012 SAT reading result marked the lowest figure since 1972.) In the 2013 administration of the ACT exam, only 64 percent of the 1.8 million test takers achieved a "college-ready" score in English. On the 2011 National Assessment of Educational Progress exam in writing (the "Nation's Report Card"), only 24 percent of twelfth-graders reached "Proficient."

The findings of these surveys and tests are often framed as a national crisis. Bad writing means lower productivity in the workplace, and it also spells deteriorating discourse in the civic sphere. Since the quality of our writing reflects the quality of our thinking, slovenly writing breeds weak citizens—people who are slow to see through propaganda and nonsense, unable to detect contradictions, and poor at grasping the implications of consequential policy choices. Show me a student writer who by page five of an essay has forgotten the claim he made on page one (and won't bother to go back and check), and I'll show you someone who will probably bring that mental laziness into the workplace and the civic arena. Today's student who can't see that she is not saying anything when she writes, "In Flaubert's *Madame Bovary* there are many characters introduced and involved in the story," or "In *1984* many themes and situations arise right from the beginning of the story"—two opening sentences I have received in essays—is on her way to becoming tomorrow's uncritical thinker and apathetic nonvoter. What may appear at first glance an academic problem is, in fact, a far-reaching political and economic consequence. If students don't learn to write well, they are unable to think clearly and argue responsibly, to the detriment of our prosperity and civic health.

Still, blaming student writers for these problems would be a mistake. To understand why so many American students write badly, we need to look at the confusing ways that writing is taught, all the way from kindergarten to graduate school. Since no consensus has ever existed among educators about how to teach people to write, writing instruction across the grades and education levels is a mishmash of inconsistent and often contradictory advice that is bound to confuse any student who pays attention to it. But writing instruction tends to be poor or ineffective even when it is taught in a consistent way, as it often is in K–12 and college writing programs where all teachers follow a common approach. As a result, students graduate from high school unprepared for the twenty-first-century workplace and are ill equipped for the rigors of democratic society in an age of information and ubiquitous media. It isn't that students fail to absorb writing instruction properly; rather, we teach writing in confusing and unhelpful ways.

The weaknesses of writing instruction belie the view we often hear from prominent educational commentators these days that "we now know," if we did not previously, the key elements of a good education. Here, for example, is Diane Ravitch in her recent book *Reign of Error: The Hoax of the Privatization Movement and the Danger to America's Public Schools*:

> We know what works. What works are the very opportunities that advantaged families provide for their children. In homes with adequate resources, children get advantages that enable them to arrive in school healthy and ready to learn. Discerning, affluent parents demand schools with full curricula, experienced staffs, rich programs in the arts, libraries, well-maintained campuses, and small classes. (6)

But if "we know what works," as Ravitch assures us, why are American students not doing better? Because, according to Ravitch, they are being held back by the destructive impact of "concentrated poverty and segregation" and the underfunding of schools. But such a diagnosis fails to explain the bad or mediocre academic performance of students who aren't poor or segregated and come from families and schools with all the advantages in her list. If upper middle-class households are part of an environment that "works," then why do so many youths from those households perform so inadequately on reading and writing exams? Why do they go to college and write C papers for their freshman composition instructors or end up in remedial writing classes? I can speak with some authority on these questions, having taught many such students in my college courses. Since some get by with Cs, Bs, or even As, and many graduate, they might seem to offer evidence that the educational system functions reasonably well and that we do indeed "know what works," as Ravitch says. But my experience and research based on closer examination of the quality of academic work these students produce suggest that, in the title of the best-known recent book on college students' prowess, these students and the institutions they attend are "academically adrift." (Arum and Roksa)

Still, other commentators and many politicians would agree with

Ravitch that "we know what works," but they argue that poor teaching is the factor that most prevents schools from effectively putting what is known into practice. Train more good teachers, according to this view, and student performance will significantly improve. Though such a diagnosis better explains the weak academic performance of many affluent students than do poverty and segregation, it, too, is limited, not just by the inherent nebulousness of "good teaching," but by the failure to consider that even when teachers are good (by whatever measure we use), their students come away confused if the different teachers' courses convey mixed messages about how to do academic work.

My own view is that "we" *don't* in fact know what works—at least not if the object is to educate the great majority of students and not just only the highly achieving few. We certainly don't know what works in the teaching of writing. Many writing instructors who otherwise meet the qualifications for good teachers—being well informed on their subject, up to date on the research in their fields, and sensitive to their students' needs—don't have a clue how to help weak student writers write better.

Indeed, the wild inconsistency I mentioned at the outset in the content of writing instruction in both K–12 schools and colleges is a symptom of this cluelessness among professionals. We would not likely see such inconsistency, after all, if any one or two approaches to teaching writing had had any discernible success. To mention just a few examples of this inconsistency, some K–12 teachers (but not all) virtually equate good writing with correct grammar, but when and if those students get to college they are often told that grammar is overrated, if not completely unimportant. In some cases, students encounter these confusingly conflicting attitudes toward grammar side by side *both* in K–12 and college. In a similarly confusing way, "writing" in K–12 often means creative writing or personal narrative, but in college the term shifts without warning to mean rigorous exposition, analysis, and argument. This shift often comes as a surprise or shock to students—if they become aware of it at all—because neither K–12 schools nor colleges take responsibility for informing students about it, much less explaining and justifying it.

These mixed messages often come to a head in the indications students receive from different teachers about whether an academic paper is supposed to have an argument or not. Some college teachers view argument as central to academic writing while others either don't mention it at all or soft-pedal it, warning students not to be too argumentative, perhaps because argument is allegedly "binary," male, or a reflection of hegemonic Western rationality. A correspondent at another university reports that some of his department colleagues assume that argumentative writing is the natural academic genre and thus focus on it exclusively for the entire term. But a few other colleagues are so convinced that argument is complicit with an oppressive hegemonic epistemology that they refuse to teach the argumentative essay altogether. Interestingly, most members of the department are unaware that this conflict exists at all, and the question of what the department's students may make of the conflict doesn't arise.

To take another mixed message students receive, one teacher may grade students down for summarizing the assigned text—writing in the margin of the paper, "Hey, I've *read* the book. I want to know what *you* think." The next teacher, however, may grade the same student down for *not* summarizing, saying, "I don't care what *you* think. I want to know how well you've read the assigned text." Undergraduates can give you many more examples of such contradictions, though they often view them (as do many college teachers and administrators themselves) as normal or even as a healthy manifestation of intellectual diversity and therefore don't notice the damage being done to their chances of learning to write. Of course, exposure to a diversity of views can be beneficial to learning, but this benefit is negated when the diversity takes the form of continually having the rug pulled out from under you as you go from course to course, teacher to teacher, and level to level of education.

Such radical inconsistencies in writing instruction, then, are one factor that undermines its chances for success. But again, even when writing instruction is consistent, as it is in programs that adopt a particular approach and get instructors to follow it, instruction generally fails to produce adept writers. Sometimes, the advice that informs the instruction is mistaken or confused; other times, when the advice is sound and well taught, students still can't internalize it effectively because studying abstract principles and reading exemplary models don't enable students to apply the principles or imitate the models. Learning to write is a bit like learning to hit a golf ball or a tennis backhand: learning *about* the correct way to do it or seeing it done by an expert won't necessarily enable a novice to do it better.

Since it's not possible within the scope of this essay to survey the range of writing instruction at the various educational levels, I limit myself to examining one representative approach to writing used in many K–12 school districts across the country, one that reflects the questionable thinking that is typical of much other current writing instruction. The "Six Traits of Writing" model of instruction and assessment (or "Six Traits Writing Process"—see Long and Gardiner) operates on the sensible enough premise, as explained on the website from which I quote hereafter, that "a complex activity like writing" must be broken down into its components "to make it more manageable." The Six Traits approach tries to provide such a helpful breakdown by isolating the following aspects of writing and focusing "on only one trait at a time":

- Idea development
- Organization
- Voice
- Word choice
- Sentence fluency
- Conventions

Breaking writing down into discrete components in this way, according to the Six Traits site, enables writers, with practice, to "become more critical of their own work and . . . make improvements in their writing." Equally important, according to the site,

"The six traits give teachers and students a common vocabulary for talking and thinking about writing."

These premises are seemingly reasonable, and whether they work in a classroom depends to a large extent on variables such as how they are translated into practice and what other materials are used to supplement them, including readings, models of good writing, and so forth. Still, despite these variables, we can assess such a program's potential to improve student writers. In order to do so, I offer a look at a seven-page handout titled the "Six Traits Writing Rubrics," which teachers and students in many fifth-grade classes use in Chicago-area elementary schools. In my judgment, at least, things are not encouraging.

To begin with, though the document is only seven pages long, my first reaction on reading it was "too much information." The number of categories and concepts represented on just the first two pages—for example, covering "idea development" and "organization"—is too large to be assimilated by fifth-graders—or even high school or college students. Furthermore, the terms presented here are often confusing in themselves and lacking any coherent connection between them.

Since presenting students with as few as six "traits" of any academic practice is likely to overwhelm even college undergraduates who are not already familiar with the practice, I can only imagine the effect of doing so on fifth-graders. And the number of concepts that students need to process here is far more than six. Expecting inexperienced students at any educational level to take away very much from such visual and conceptual overkill seems wildly unrealistic and a prescription for losing all but the small minority of high achievers in the class. In teaching a complex and confusing subject like writing, you are doing well if you can get one key point across, and the more you pile on related or subordinate points, the more you risk inducing cognitive overload.

Strike one, then, against the Six Traits of Writing is that, despite its claims to simplify the process of writing, it actually drowns students in far more advice than most will be able to handle (in this

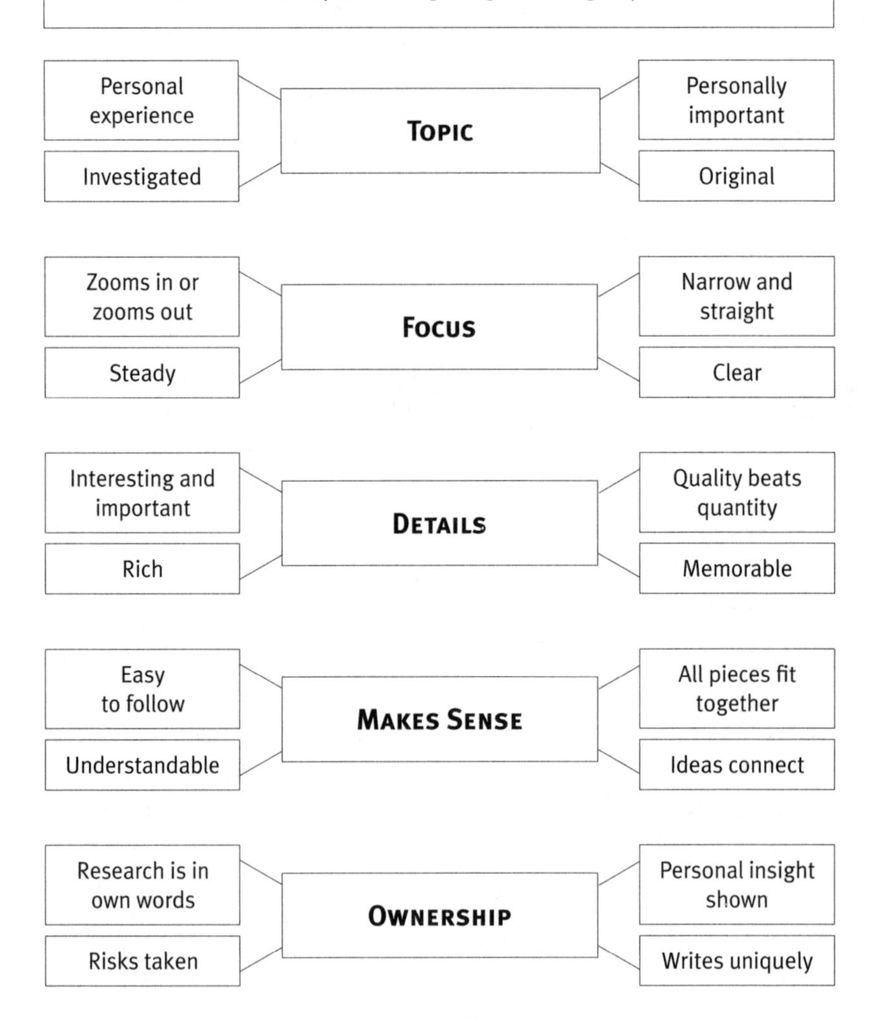
IDEA DEVELOPMENT
Like the foundation of a house, Idea Development serves as the solid base on which a good piece of writing rests. If you start with a solid idea, your writing can grow as big as you want.
Personal experience
Investigated
TOPIC
Personally important
Original
Zooms in or zooms out
Steady
FOCUS
Narrow and straight
Clear
Interesting and important
Rich
DETAILS
Quality beats quantity
Memorable
Easy to follow
Understandable
MAKES SENSE
All pieces fit together
Ideas connect
Research is in own words
Risks taken
OWNERSHIP
Personal insight shown
Writes uniquely

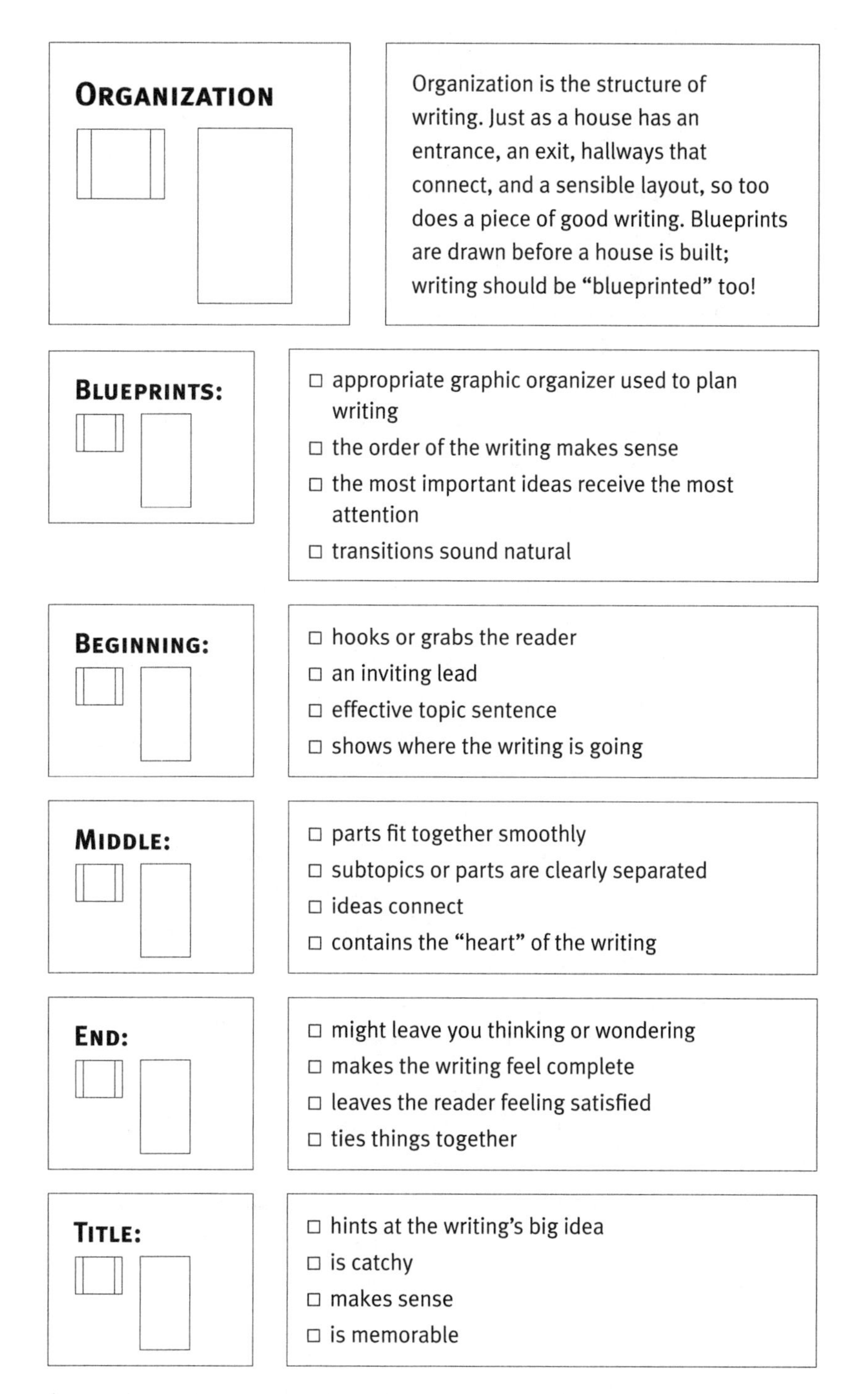

ORGANIZATION

Organization is the structure of writing. Just as a house has an entrance, an exit, hallways that connect, and a sensible layout, so too does a piece of good writing. Blueprints are drawn before a house is built; writing should be "blueprinted" too!

BLUEPRINTS:

- ☐ appropriate graphic organizer used to plan writing
- ☐ the order of the writing makes sense
- ☐ the most important ideas receive the most attention
- ☐ transitions sound natural

BEGINNING:

- ☐ hooks or grabs the reader
- ☐ an inviting lead
- ☐ effective topic sentence
- ☐ shows where the writing is going

MIDDLE:

- ☐ parts fit together smoothly
- ☐ subtopics or parts are clearly separated
- ☐ ideas connect
- ☐ contains the "heart" of the writing

END:

- ☐ might leave you thinking or wondering
- ☐ makes the writing feel complete
- ☐ leaves the reader feeling satisfied
- ☐ ties things together

TITLE:

- ☐ hints at the writing's big idea
- ☐ is catchy
- ☐ makes sense
- ☐ is memorable

respect mirroring the school and college curricula themselves). But even if we reduce the number of traits and boxes, as any sensible teacher is likely to do, little here will help students to write better. I think it unlikely that student writers who have trouble staying focused on an issue or an argument throughout the length of a paper or a paragraph will find very useful the "Idea Development" page's urging to be "steady," "clear," and "narrow and straight," whatever these phrases may mean. Nor can I imagine such student writers getting much help in developing ideas from reading, "Like the foundation of a house, IDEA DEVELOPMENT serves as the solid base on which a good piece of writing rests. If you want to start with a solid idea, your writing can grow as big as you want."

Still, you might object, studying such rubrics and reading about the similarities between a house and an essay at worst won't do any harm and at best might spark some useful reflection on writing. After all, some students may actually get something out of these prompts, unlikely though it may seem to a jaded observer. But if I'm right that the American school and college curricula induce cognitive overload, then even seemingly harmless advice figures to deepen students' confusion by crowding out more helpful advice and lessening its chances of being noticed. The more stuff we throw at students, the less the likelihood that the part of it they need the most will stick. And the more stuff teachers try to teach, the less the chance that faculties will be able to get on the same page in the messages about writing they send to students and thus the more likely their students will be confused.

But what, then, about the claim that the Six Traits of Writing provides "teachers and students a common vocabulary for talking and thinking about writing"? Given the mixed messages about how to write that most students receive, such a common vocabulary is indeed a necessary condition for improving writing. Unfortunately, the common vocabulary offered by the Six Traits is not a good one, though buried within its diffuseness and terminological overkill are doubtless some things worth salvaging.

All right, you may say, carping and griping are easy. What do *you* have to offer that figures to be any better than the kind of thing you complain about? For starters, I would answer, we should do what the Six Traits of Writing promise but do not deliver: break writing down into its components "to make it more manageable." To do that effectively, however, so that student writers can actually put the lessons into practice, six components are five too many. For students to be able to assimilate it and put it into practice, writing instruction needs to highlight one big thing and rigorously subordinate everything else to it. Briefly put, my candidate for this one big thing is *argument*, or what Cathy Birkenstein and I, in a college textbook, call "They say/I say" argument.

Why select this two-sided form of argument, which highlights the need for writers to respond to others? Because this is the way communication works in the real world, not to mention in a democratic society, where we don't make assertions out of the blue, but are motivated to speak or write by something said or thought by others—in academic courses, usually something said in an assigned text. Indeed, a text is likely to seem unintelligible or pointless to readers unless it is framed as a response to something "they say," something others have said or might say or think. Consider a statement such as, "The characters in *The Sopranos* are very complex." The statement is admirably clear, but if it were simply asserted in isolation, it would leave us wondering why the speaker or writing is making it—what is the point? The answer becomes clear once the statement is reframed as a response to others—"Some argue that *The Sopranos* caricatures Italian Americans, but actually the characters in the series are very complex." In other words, unless we frame our arguments as responses, what we are saying may be clear, but why we are saying it at all will not be.

To speak and write with the kind of point and purpose expected in real-world communication, then, students need to learn to summarize somebody else's argument and use that summary to motivate their own. I call this kind of communication "Arguespeak," which is the dominant language not only of higher education but also of the civic and public sphere outside academia and of the professional workplace. The "they say/I say" framework helps student writers find a genuine stake, a purpose for writing, for proving one point right and another wrong, and in the process it simplifies the task of writing and motivates students to do it well. To teach writing more effectively, schools and colleges need to drum home this message over and over with enough repetition and redundancy so that it has a chance to stick, settling into their minds as an intellectual habit, which is to say that it can't come across as one teacher's message among so many others that it is lost on students or forgotten.

In other words, students need to be taught that effective writing follows the "they say/I say" format, and that's *all* they should be taught, at least until they grasp that principle, internalize it as a way of understanding things, and can put it into practice. Anything else that competes with that lesson or can't be subordinated to it will get in the way, overload the beginner, and prevent student writers from making progress. This proviso is less draconian as it sounds, however, for "they say/I say" writing is open to infinite variations and permutations that students can and should explore once they master the central framework.

But simply telling students *about* writing in the "they say/I say" form won't enable them to practice it, any more than reading about the fundamentals of the golf swing will enable a 30-handicapper to break par. For students to write better, they need to *see* what the moves of good writing look like and not just be told about them or be expected to spot them by reading exemplary models. Though a few students will learn to write better by reading model essays such as George Orwell's "Politics and the English Language" (or whatever that work's fifth-grade equivalent may be), most will not, notwithstanding those who think that student writing would improve if teachers assigned more challenging or higher-quality reading. Though reading complex, challenging texts is a necessary part of the process, such reading will not enable most students to imitate their rhetorical moves.

For such imitation to become possible, the central moves of Arguespeak need to be isolated and represented to students in a schematic form that they can recognize in their reading and try out in their own writing:

> Writer ______ argues that ____________________. Though I agree with his premise that ____________, I can't go along with his conclusion that ____________ ____________________. For one thing, ____________ ____________________. My point here, however, is not __________, but ______________.

This is an example of the "argument templates" (as we call them) that Birkenstein and I present in our textbook. A fifth-grade equivalent might look like this:

> My mom and dad say kids should not be allowed to ______________, because ____________. My own view, though, is ____________________. An example of what I'm talking about is something that recently happened in our house, when I did ____________________ and was punished for it. I can see why my parents punished me, but ______________________.

★ ★ ★

> In ________, the book our class read last week, the point is that bullying is bad, mainly because ______________. I agree with this, but it's not that simple if you're a boy. For example, ______________.

Working with these kinds of templates in writing assignments is more likely to give fifth-graders a sense of what it feels like to write their way into a discussion about ideas and problems—or to develop their distinctive voice, for that matter—than following abstract prompts on "idea development," "voice," and so forth. In the process they will thus realize how writing actually works in the real world, where writers never "develop ideas" in isolation, but do so only in response to provocations by others. Lastly, such templates can be rigged to induce student writers to put themselves in the shoes of others, their parents, or a writer they are reading, and therefore hasten their growth out of egotistical ways of thinking.

I'm aware that my arguments here go directly against the grain of much current educational thinking, particularly the mantra that no one-size-fits-all model can possibly do justice to the diversity of academic subjects and of student "learning styles." That kind of thinking, however, though it is easy to accept because it avoids conflict and leaves teachers free to do whatever they please, has resulted in massive confusion on the part of teachers and students, and not just about writing but about how academic work is done. The "they say/I say" model offers a means of cutting through this confusion by giving student writers access to the domain of Arguespeak, showing them how to perform the indispensable tasks of summarizing others' arguments (what "they say") and responding with their own ("I say").

As I noted at the outset, the implications extend far beyond the classroom. Students who learn to write Arguespeak in the "they say/I say" mode will be better prepared not only for academic work but for the demands of today's workplaces as well as the civic sphere, where we need to engage with coworkers and fellow citizens and weigh the opinions of others before advancing our own. Models that emphasize students' "personal voice" and abstractions such as "idea development" prepare them for neither work nor citizenship. In the civic sphere, where we often justifiably lament the low quality of public debate and the pervasiveness of knee-jerk polarization and groupthink, much of the problem stems from our refusal to take the first step of "they say," that of summarizing the other side clearly and fairly. Teaching students to begin with an opinion they may or may not agree with, forcing them to examine a position far from their own experience, trains them for democratic civics in which ideas, values, and policies are weighed in open forums.

The Six Trait writing approach I have described in this essay (and other similar ones) projects a claustrophobically isolated picture of the writer and his or her words and thoughts, omitting precisely the basic democratic relationship of writer-to-writer, "opinionator-to-opinionator," which gives focus and purpose to the task. Young people who learn "they say/I say" and thus get in the habit of summarizing the views of others will recognize that their opinions properly exist in a marketplace of opinions, and they will in turn be apt to look upon fellow citizens as interlocutors rather than as foes, seeing others as rivals for power and influence, perhaps, but not as enemies. In this sense, "they say/I say" is the writing practice best suited to the civic practices of democracy (all the more in the age of the blogosphere and of talk-back radio and TV), practices requiring that citizens become articulate users of Arguespeak, enter the marketplace of ideas, listen to all sides, and make their arguments in the ways that are proper to an open society.

References

Arum, Richard and Josipa Roksa. *Academically Adrift: Limited Learning on College Campuses*. Chicago and London: University of Chicago Press, 2011.

Birkenstein, Cathy, and Gerald Graff. *They Say/I Say: The Moves That Matter in Academic Writing*. New York: Norton, 2007.

The Chronicle of Higher Education. "The Role of Higher Education in Career Development: Employer Perceptions," December 2012, https://chronicle.com/items/biz/pdf/Employers%20Survey.pdf.

The Conference Board. *Are They Really Ready to Work? Employers' Perspectives on the Basic Knowledge and Applied Skills of New Entrants to the 21st-Century U.S. Workforce*, 2006, http://www.p21.org/storage/documents/FINAL_REPORT_PDF09-29-06.pdf.

Goodbaum, Beth. "Survey Reveals the Skills That College Grads Lack the Most." *Industry Market Trends*, July 19, 2013, http://news.thomasnet.com/IMT/2013/06/19/study-reveals-the-skills-that-college-grads-lack-the-most/.

Long, Vince, and Steve Gardiner. "The Interactive Six Trait Writing Process." The Literate Learner, http://www.literatelearner.com/6traits/page_template6t.php?f=main.

National Center for Education Statistics. *The Nation's Report Card: Writing 2011*, "Executive Summary," http://nces.ed.gov/nationsreportcard/pubs/main2011/2012470.asp.

Ravitch, Diane. *Reign of Error: The Hoax of the Privatization Movement and the Danger to America's Public Schools*. New York: Knopf, 2013.

4

College Graduates

SATISFIED, BUT ADRIFT

Richard Arum

COLLEGES AND UNIVERSITIES have worked hard to attract seventeen-year-olds to their campuses and keep them engaged and satisfied for the next four years while they embark on what for many of them will be prolonged periods of emerging adulthood. After all, competitive colleges focused on the *U.S. News & World Report* rankings recognize that the nature of the applicant pool figures highly, and a boost in the number of applicants and in their average SAT/ACT scores can move an institution a few steps up the list. Less competitive colleges worry about filling seats. Given the institutional imperative of catering to teenagers' preferences, the dramatic growth in institutional investments in student support services and social amenities—including student counseling, athletic facilities, student centers, and dormitories—is not surprising, nor is a corresponding disinvestment in academic programs and full-time faculty. While colleges have raised tuition at twice the rate of inflation annually over the past several decades, funds are by definition limited, and resource allocation decisions in most colleges and universities have come to follow a clear institutional logic. If an institution is forced to compete for a typical seventeen-year-old, investments in social amenities rather than academics are rational as students, acting as consumers choosing from a range of "brands," prefer these services (Jacob et al.).

The extent to which many colleges and universities focus more on promoting student social engagement than academic rigor likely has consequences for human capital formation in the United States. For many Americans, college is the final academic threshold when they acquire general education and specific knowledge in a major, not to mention advanced literacy and numeracy. A decline in an institution's focus on academics has an effect on the students; a slackening of standards can undermine incentives for learning, leaving graduates ill equipped for graduate programs and professional and technical workplaces. If one is to consider the implication of changes in collegiate academic rigor for human capital formation, however, it is imperative to situate this examination in a broader context that considers changes in educational attainment and cognitive performance in the United States and abroad.

Changes in IQ and Educational Attainment

If one analyzes exclusively the current condition of undergraduate education in the United States, one would have good reason to be dismayed. Undergraduate education, however, is only one part of a larger system of education and human development. Over the past hundred years, individuals have demonstrated significant increases in IQ or general cognitive capacity measured at early ages (Flynn). The causes of these increases are imperfectly understood, but potentially are related to improved nutrition, sanitation, prenatal care, and early environmental exposures.

In addition to the gains in IQ, the population as a whole has also been attending school for longer and longer periods of time. For example, from 1940 to 2012, the percentage of young adults with high school diplomas (or equivalent GEDs) increased from 38 percent to 90 percent, and the percentage of college graduates increased from 6 percent to 34 percent. From 1995 to 2012 the percentage of young adults with master's degrees or greater increased from 4.5 percent to 7.2 percent (young adults defined as ages 25 to 29; see National Center for Education Statistics, Digest, table 9). Although this expansion has been impressive and the United States historically has led the world in mass education, recent decades have seen many countries surpass the United States in college degree completion. For example, 48 percent of young adults now complete college in Norway; 43 percent in Finland; 41 percent in Iceland; and 40 percent in Korea, Switzerland, and the United Kingdom (Organisation of Economic Co-operation and Development, *Education at a Glance*, table A1.3a; individuals ages 23–34).

Two other confounding factors are worth noting. First, recent decades have seen greater academic rigor and stable or slightly improved performance in K–12 education. For example, high school students have increased hours spent studying over recent decades, and student scores on standardized National Assessment of Educational Progress (NAEP) math and English tests have improved since the early 1970s for individuals ages nine and thirteen, while remaining stable for seventeen-year-olds (National Center for Education Statistics, *Nation's Report Card*—increases in high school hours derived from the author's analysis of data sets in National Center for Education Statistics data sets.) In addition, while the academic quality of undergraduate education might be suspect, doctoral and professional program quality is another matter. Colleges and universities are typically deeply committed to the promotion of research, academic scholarship, and scientific discovery in an effort to gain both prestige and external funding—institutional efforts that are well aligned with high-quality doctoral training.

Given this overall context, problems with undergraduate education might be less consequential than otherwise would be the case for human capital formation in this country. Nevertheless, it is worth focusing specifically on the character of college, not only because of its exorbitant cost to individuals and the public, but since what happens or fails to happen in college likely has implications for the cognitive development of individuals attending these institutions as well as for shaping attitudes and dispositions of young adults. As eighteen- to twenty-three-year-olds have come increasingly to experience prolonged periods of "extended adolescence" or "emerging adulthood," this age span likely has a more significant formative impact and lasting consequence for individual life courses.

Declining Academic Rigor

Many college students today experience college life as being less about academics than about engagement in social activities and the development of sociability, sensitivity to others, and social networks. This interpersonal emphasis, too, is considered rational by students as the economic returns to college are often perceived as not a product of increased individual knowledge and productivity, but simply a reflection of earning a credential (i.e., signaling) or social network formation. That is, if students assume that the widely known adage "It's not what you know, it's who you know" is operative in society, why would they waste time in college investing valuable hours in gaining useless book knowledge and refining technical and cognitive skills? This would especially be the case if grade inflation and declining academic standards had undermined the need to do so.

Indeed, Josipa Roksa and I found in our research that 36 percent of students at four-year colleges reported studying alone five or fewer hours per week—that is, less than one hour per day. When we examined these students' transcripts, we found that in spite of their modest effort these individuals had managed to earn a 3.2 grade point average. Apparently, it does not take a great deal of effort to demonstrate satisfactory academic performance in today's colleges and universities. Forty-five percent of students reported that in the prior semester they did not have a single course that required more than twenty pages of writing over the entire semester; 32 percent did not have even one class that assigned more than forty pages of reading per week (Arum and Roksa, *Academically Adrift*). With such meager academic demands, why would a student study alone more than an hour per day? Unsurprisingly, many college students today decide instead to invest time in other activities in college. In the University of California system, for example, researchers have documented that students spend more than three times as much time socializing and entertaining themselves than they do studying (Brint and Cantwell).

Students in the University of California system devote twelve hours per week studying compared to forty-three hours in the following pursuits: twelve hours socializing with friends, eleven hours using computers for fun, six hours watching television, six hours exercising, five hours on hobbies, and three hours on other forms of entertainment. Given the investment of colleges in social amenities, such as state-of-the-art athletic facilities and student centers, as well as the institutional promotion of increased social engagement on campus, indulging in social as opposed to academic pursuits becomes increasingly compelling.

Is there anything unusual or different about the limited investment of contemporary students in academic activities in college? A set of empirical comparisons clearly suggests an affirmative response. Labor economists Philip Babcock and Mindy Marks, for example, have demonstrated that full-time college students' hours studying have dropped in half from twenty-five hours per week to approximately twelve or thirteen hours per week over the past few decades. This decline held regardless of whether the analysis was disaggregated by parental education, race, institutional type, or major. When one compares full-time college students' academic engagement (i.e., hours in class and studying) to their peers in Europe, only full-time college students in the Slovak Republic spend less time on academics than do students in the United States (Orr et al.).

The lack of academic rigor in colleges and universities certainly has consequences for the extent to which students develop competencies and skills—a topic I address shortly. It is also worth considering how the erosion of academic standards is potentially associated with the development of attitudes, behaviors, and dispositions aligned with adult success. Interactions between youth and adult authorities in schools are experienced as direct manifestations of the norms and expectations of the larger society, shaping what values students ultimately internalize. When college administrators and educators are overly permissive and unduly tolerant of shoddy work and egregious misbehavior, students internalize those values and apply them as expectations of the larger society, failing to develop an appreciation for the relationship between individual accomplishment and grit, perseverance, and effort. Recent research suggests that not only are students working fewer hours, but they are considerably more likely to report plagiarizing and cheating on exams than in prior decades. For example, in a longitudinal comparison of students in nine colleges, 26 percent of students in 1963 reported copying from other students on tests at these schools, compared to 52 percent in 1993 (McCabe et al.). In addition, research from the Wabash Center of Inquiry in the Liberal Arts demonstrates that, as students progress through college, rather than becoming more academically motivated, they become less so (Salisbury et al.).

College Graduate Competencies

One could adopt various approaches to determine the level of competencies that college graduates possess when they leave college. For example, one could directly ask students and various other higher education stakeholders to make these judgments. When one conducts such an exercise, a stark divergence of opinion emerges, one that reflects a troubling lowering of academic standards on campus, this time not among students alone. College administrators and students are quite satisfied with the performances of colleges in producing learning outcomes. For example, in a recent Gallup poll, 96 percent of provosts state that the colleges at which they are employed do a good job of preparing students for the workforce (56 percent report their institutions are "very effective" and 40 percent report "somewhat effective"; see Gallup). In another survey conducted by UCLA's Higher Education Research Institute, students, too, are quite content: 85 percent of graduating seniors report that they are satisfied with their colleges, and the vast majority of them report that they learned a great deal while enrolled (Spinosa et al.). In the Gallup findings, though, when researchers asked people off-campus for their opinions, a remarkable contrast emerged: only 43 percent of the public and 33 percent of employers believe that colleges are preparing students with the skills and competencies necessary to succeed in the workforce.

Given these divergent judgments, it is worth foregrounding what objective assessments of student performance have indicated in recent years. While higher education is designed to develop student capacities in a number of areas, including general competencies and subject-specific skills, assessments of performance on generic as opposed to subject-specific assessments are more widely available at this time for comparative purposes. One can use generic assessments of higher education to focus on two distinct questions: How much do students learn while in college, and what levels of competency do they have when they graduate?

To ascertain student learning reliably requires a pre-post test design. In the United States, two large-scale projects have tracked students longitudinally as they progress through a diverse set of colleges and universities to identify their improvement on generic assessments. Josipa Roksa and I have reported results of student gains on the Collegiate Learning Assessment (CLA)—a measure of performance in critical thinking, complex reasoning and writing. The CLA performance task provides students with a set of documents to evaluate critically, and then to synthesize and utilize the information in a logical written argument that an employer might ask a college graduate to undertake. For example, students must write a memo with recommendations on whether their company should purchase a particular airplane model after they have considered journalistic and federal reports of an accident, correspondence between their supervisor and a vendor of the plane, and a technical manual. Student improvement on responses to these tasks is, to say the least, disappointing. Over four years of college, students gain 0.47 standard deviations on the measure. If we translate the results into a different scale, still using the CLA performance task, we find that if the assessment were scored on a range from zero to one hundred points, 36 percent of students would not have moved up even one point during four years of college (Arum and Roksa, *Aspiring Adults Adrift*).

These paltry results are repeated by an alternative multiple-choice assessment of critical thinking and complex reasoning, the ACT's College Assessment of Academic Proficiency (CAAP), taken by several thousand students at a different set of colleges and universities. In the CAAP exam, students are given passages to consider that include information in multiple formats and then asked sets of multiple-choice questions requiring them to clarify, analyze, evaluate, and extend arguments. When Charles Blaich and his colleagues at the Wabash Center of Inquiry in the Liberal Arts examined the scores, they identified gains of 0.44 standard deviations. These improvements are roughly half of what was found when researchers several decades ago estimated similar assessments of student growth (Pascarella and Terenzini).

College graduate student performance can also be identified cross-nationally. Such comparisons are perhaps particularly apt, given that in a globalized economy multinationals often have the opportunity to utilize human capital from across national borders. The Organisation of Economic Cooperation and Development's *Programme for the International Assessment of Adult Competencies* provides a reliable estimate of cross-national variation in generic competencies in twenty-three developed countries. The assessments measure an individual's ability to understand and use information from written tests; to use, apply, interpret, and communicate mathematical information and ideas; and to use technology to solve problems and accomplish complex tasks. The results for U.S. college graduates on these assessments are not impressive: on most measures assessed, they score below the average of college graduates in other countries (*OECD Skills Outlook 2013*, figures 3.9, 3.10, 5.5). In addition, the results for the U.S. population as a whole are even more discouraging when compared to results on prior OECD assessments of adult competencies. In spite of a larger percentage of adults in the United States having gone to college and at increased costs over recent decades, the OECD notes, "There are few signs of improvement. Today, adults in the U.S. have similar or weaker literacy skills to their counterparts in the mid-90s, and the average basic skills of young adults are not very different from older adults" (*Time for the U.S. to Reskill?*, 13).

Conclusion

The evidence above, considered as a whole, suggests that U.S. colleges and universities underperform with respect to developing human capital for recent cohorts of college graduates. Individuals who have undergone four or more years of instruction and managed to graduate enter the workforce with gains on generic competencies from college inferior to those of graduates from prior decades, and they face growing competition from graduates from other developed nations. The crucial years of intellectual maturation from ages eighteen to twenty-three are not yielding the gains in knowledge, discernment, and analytical capacity that they should, and that are necessary to a productive workforce and responsible citizenry. These shortcomings, however, have been partly mitigated by countervailing forces at play in the education system and society as a whole that contribute independently to human capital formation. Nevertheless, colleges and universities are not doing enough to ensure that college graduates experience their rightful intellectual growth and cognitive development and make successful transitions to adulthood. This failure likely has consequences for the long-term global competitiveness of our economy and the capacity of future citizens to engage and participate actively in a democratic society. In fact, Josipa Roksa and I uncovered in our studies not only a deterioration of academic progress but a civic dimension, too: a large percentage of recent college graduates not only failed to make significant gains in critical thinking and complex reasoning during their four years of college, but they also failed to develop dispositions associated with civic engagement. Two years after graduating college, 32 percent of individuals reported to us that they read a newspaper in print or online never or monthly (not weekly or daily), and 39 percent reported that they discussed politics or public affairs with friends, family, or coworkers in person, on the phone, or online monthly or never (*Aspiring Adults Adrift*).

The problem of inadequate academic rigor and limited undergraduate learning is not surprising when one considers the existing incentive structures present in higher education. Students often define their college enrollment in instrumental terms and are frequently satisfied with earning a credential that demands only minimum academic effort. Faculty are typically rewarded for their scholarship, not their teaching, and when the latter is assessed, course evaluations are employed that ask whether students *liked* the class that was taught. Administrators are asked to focus on producing improved instructional metrics on multiple indicators—applications, yield, entering student characteristics, graduation rates, external research awards, fund-raising—that is, everything but student learning.

It doesn't have to be this way. College and universities do not require more money to improve academic rigor and attention to undergraduate learning. The United States spends on college approximately twice as much per student as what is spent in European countries for at best roughly comparable student learning outcomes (for cross-national data on expenditures per student, see OECD, *Education at a Glance*). If colleges and universities had more money, there is no reason to believe that, absent fundamental changes in the system, improved student learning outcomes would be an institutional objective or outcome. At this point in time, change requires political will, not increased resources.

To improve academic rigor and student learning, colleges and universities need to recommit themselves organizationally to those core elements of their institutional missions. As new technological tools become increasingly available to provide, assess, and improve instruction, there are fewer and fewer reasons not to act. The ideal path forward will be for institutions themselves to take responsibility for addressing these problems by promoting cultures that value teaching, learning, and assessment. Change and accountability work best when organized at the institutional level. Further delays in colleges and universities internally addressing these issues, however, will only bring closer the specter of externally imposed accountability systems. While centralized oversight would likely be counterproductive, in the face of institutional inertia around improved student learning, teaching, and assessment, one cannot expect public funding and student indebtedness to increase indefinitely without more being required from U.S. colleges and universities.

References

Arum, Richard, and Josipa Roksa. *Academically Adrift: Limited Learning on College Campuses.* Chicago: University of Chicago Press, 2011.

———. *Aspiring Adults Adrift: Tentative Transitions of College Graduates.* Chicago: University of Chicago Press, 2014.

Babcock, Philip S., and Mindy Marks. "The Falling Time Cost of College: Evidence from Half a Century of Time Use Data." *Review of Economics and Statistics* 93 (2011): 468–78.

Brint, Steven, and Allison M. Cantwell. "Undergraduate Time Use and Academic Outcomes: Results from UCUES 2006." University of California–Berkeley, Center for Studies in Higher Education, Research and Occasional Paper Series, 2008, http://cshe.berkeley.edu/sites/default/files/shared/publications/docs/ROPS-Brint-TimeUse-9-24-08.pdf.

Flynn, James R. "Massive IQ Gains in 14 Nations: What IQ Tests Really Measure." *Psychological Bulletin* 101 (1987): 171–91.

Gallup, Inc. "What America Needs to Know about Higher Education Redesign," 2014, http://www.gallup.com/strategicconsulting/167552/america-needs-know-higher-education-redesign.aspx.

Jacob, Brian, Brian McCall, and Kevin M. Stange. "College as a Country Club: Do Colleges Cater to Students' Preferences for Consumption?" NBER Working Paper no. 18745. Cambridge, MA: National Bureau of Economic Research, 2013.

McCabe, Donald L., Linda Klebe Treviño, and Kenneth D. Butterfield. "Dishonesty in Academic Environments: The Influence of Peer Reporting Requirements." *Journal of Higher Education* 72 (2001): 29–45.

National Center for Education Statistics. "Digest of Education Statistics: 2012," http://nces.ed.gov/programs/digest/d12/.

———. "High School and Beyond: National Educational Longitudinal Study," http://nces.ed.gov/surveys/hsb/index.asp.

———. "The Nation's Report Card, Trends in Academic Progress, 2012," http://nces.ed.gov/pubsearch/pubsinfo.asp?pubid=2013456.

Organisation of Economic Co-operation and Development. "Education at a Glance 2013: OECD Indicators," OECD Publishing, http://dx.doi.org/10.1787/eag-2013-en.

———. "OECD Skills Outlook 2013: First Results from the Survey of Adult Skills," OECD Publishing, http://skills.oecd.org/skillsoutlook.html.

———. "Time for the U.S. to Reskill? What the Survey of Adult Skills Says," OECD Publishing, 2013, http://skills.oecd.org/Survey_of_Adult_Skills_US.pdf.

Orr, Dominic, Christoph Gwosc, and Nicolai Netz. *Social and Economic Conditions of Student Life in Europe: Synopsis of Indicators, Final Report, Eurostudent IV, 2008–2011*. Hannover, Germany: Eurostudent, 2011.

Pascarella, Ernest T., and Patrick Terenzini. *How College Affects Students: A Third Decade of Research*. San Francisco: Jossey-Bass, 2005.

Salisbury, M., C. Blaich, and C. Loes. "Increasing Students' Intrinsic Motivation to Learn: Evidence from a National Study (June 2012)," presentation at the 2012 forum of the Association for Institutional Research, New Orleans, LA.

Spinosa, Hanna, Jessica Sharkness, John H. Pryor, and Amy Liu. "Findings from the 2007 Administration of the College Senior Survey (CSS): National Aggregates." University of California, Los Angeles: Higher Education Research Institute, 2008.

5

Anatomy of an Epidemic

Robert Whitaker

WHEN WE THINK of events and trends in the past three decades that have shaped the American Mind in a profound way, one statistic should not be overlooked: the dramatic rise in the number of people, children and adults, who are taking prescribed psychotropic medications. These drugs, which are prescribed to ameliorate symptoms of schizophrenia, depression, hyperactivity, and other psychiatric disorders, alter the chemistry of the brain, and notably so. Indeed, an individual who takes a psychiatric medication for a longer period of time ultimately ends up with a different brain—and thus a different mind—than before exposure to the drug. A psychotropic drug's impact on mood, behavior, and cognition is profound, so when a significant percentage of people in a society are taking psychotropic medications, the society as a whole is changed. The widespread use of the drugs has a potent collective impact.

Given that these are *prescribed* drugs, we might assume that this is a story of a great medical advance, with people getting effective treatment for psychiatric disorders of all types. But the discovery and increased use of these drugs didn't arise from a scientific breakthrough that produced a cure for an established disease or from an improved understanding of the biology of psychiatric disorders. Such scientific discovery is the usual foundation for a medical advance. Psychiatric drugs, however, do not fix any known biological abnormality, and as I documented in my 2010 book, *Anatomy of an Epidemic*, the dramatic increase in their use over the past twenty-five years has been accompanied by an astounding *rise* in the number of disabled mentally ill in American society. The burden of mental illness in our society has increased in the past three decades, rather than decreased.

The remarkable growth in the use of psychiatric drugs in our society can be traced to the publication in 1980 of a then-obscure diagnostic manual by the American Psychiatric Association (APA). The APA's third edition of its *Diagnostic Statistical Manual* (DSM III) marked a turning point in American life, for it changed what we expect of our children, our sense of self-governance, and even our understanding of free will.

To understand why DSM III was so transformative, it is necessary to review the history that led up to it. The modern era of psychiatry began in 1954, when Thorazine arrived in asylum medicine. That drug is remembered today as the first antipsychotic, and it is said to have kicked off a "psychopharmacological revolution." That name, *antipsychotic*, told of a drug that was a specific antidote to psychosis and conjured up comparisons to antibiotics, which had revolutionized internal medicine only a decade earlier. In the late 1950s and early 1960s, psychiatry introduced new antidepressant and antianxiety drugs, too, the field apparently having discovered antidotes to these common problems.

Although psychiatry provided the medications with names that told of wonder drugs, Americans—for the next two decades—viewed them with a fair amount of unease. Thorazine and other antipsychotics were often depicted in popular culture as "chemical straightjackets" that turned patients in mental hospitals into "zombies." The public understood Valium to be a tranquilizer, and during the 1970s the media was filled with stories about how it could be addictive. In general, the public didn't think of depression and anxiety as biological ailments, and in that regard, their sentiments were in line with the second edition of the APA's *Diagnostic and Statistic Manual.* DSM II, published in 1968, reflected Freudian conceptions of neurosis and the human mind, with most psychiatric problems seen as rooted in psychological conflicts that weren't likely to be "cured" by a pill.

For various reasons, the 1970s turned into a difficult time for psychiatry, with the leaders of the APA often speaking about how their field was in a fight for "survival." Psychiatry's fall from public grace had begun in the 1960s, when Thomas Szasz and a handful of other academics launched an antipsychiatry movement that challenged psychiatry's legitimacy, arguing that it served more as an instrument of social control than as a medical profession. Then, in the early 1970s, ex-patients formed "Liberation Fronts," protesting that electroshock and antipsychotic drugs, when administered against their will, were more like torture than medical therapies. These criticisms ultimately portrayed psychiatrists as "not real doctors," a charge that naturally stung the profession, and to cap it all off, the field also faced criticism from within the scientific community. Researchers reported in medical journals that psychiatric diagnoses were unreliable, and the effectiveness of its talk therapies unproven.

Faced with these many challenges, the APA decided in 1973 to revise its diagnostic manual. Columbia University psychiatrist Robert Spitzer was named to head the project, and he appointed a task force that included a number of biologically oriented psychiatrists. The revised manual, Spitzer said, would serve as a "defense of the medical model as applied to psychiatric problems" (Wilson, 405). Psychiatry, as it sought to restore its image, would wrap itself in the white coat of the medical profession. The manual, explained APA president Jack Weinberg in 1977, would "clarify to anyone who may be in doubt that we regard psychiatry as a specialty of medicine" (Kirk, 114).

In DSM III, Spitzer and his colleagues adopted a disease model for categorizing psychiatric disorders. Freudian concepts present in DSM II were scrapped, and psychiatric problems were instead conceptualized as discrete ailments. A diagnosis would be made based on whether the symptoms characteristic of that particular disorder were present; treatment would focus on ameliorating those symptoms. "The development of DSM-III," said Gerald Klerman, a former director of the National Institute of Mental Health, "represents a fateful point in the history of the American psychiatric profession . . . [and] its use represents a reaffirmation on the part of American psychiatry to its medical identity and its commitment to scientific medicine" (Klerman, 539).

The future of psychiatry was foretold at that moment. The APA had adopted a model that was certain to spur the increased use of drug treatments, given that medications, in the eyes of the FDA, were treatments that lessened the symptoms of a disease. The 494-page DSM III also identified a long list of possible diagnoses, 265 in all, 83 of which were newly created, without any obvious precedent in DSM II. As Spitzer later confessed, among other advantages, "The pharmaceuticals companies were delighted with DSM [III]" (Ronson, pp. 44–45).

In 1981 the APA established a "division of publications and marketing" to "deepen the medical identification of psychiatrists" and promote its new model. Soon the public was hearing that researchers were making great progress in identifying the biology of mental disorders. In 1984 Nancy Andreasen, the future editor in chief of the *American Journal of Psychiatry*, wrote a best-selling book titled *The Broken Brain*, which told of how psychiatry was undergoing a "revolution," with the field coming to understand that psychiatric disorders were diseases (of the brain), "just as diabetes, heart disease, and cancer are" (29–30).

In 1988 Eli Lilly brought Prozac to market, and it seemed that the revolution in care that had been promised was now here. This new drug didn't just reliably lift depression, it made people feel "better than well." The reason that it was so effective, *60 Minutes* and other media reported, was that it fixed a "chemical imbalance" in the brain (Angier; for the *60 Minutes* reference, see Duncan and Miller). The publicity told of a drug that was, in fact, like insulin for diabetes, an antidote to a known pathology, and soon pharmaceutical companies were bringing other such wonder drugs to market. They introduced a number of SSRI antidepressants, and in the mid-1990s the public was introduced to a new class of "atypical antipsychotics," which were also said to be "breakthrough medications" that worked by fixing a chemical imbalance in the brain. With this general understanding of psychiatric drugs taking hold in the public mind, our use of such medications exploded, such that in 2010, more than one in five Americans took a psychiatric drug (Medco).

Such is the narrative of progress that drives our societal understanding of mental illness today and our use of psychiatric drugs. The major psychiatric disorders are brain diseases, and researchers have developed safe and effective drug treatments for them. But, as a review of the scientific literature reveals, this narrative has a false story at its core.

Investigating the Chemical Imbalance Theory

The origins of the chemical imbalance theory of mental disorders goes back farther than the DSM III to the 1960s, when researchers were first discovering how brain neurons communicate. The transmission of signals along a neuronal pathway relies on chemical messengers, which are known as *neurotransmitters*. A *presynaptic neuron* releases a neurotransmitter into the tiny gap between neurons, which is called the *synaptic cleft*, and the neurotransmitter then binds with receptors on the second neuron (called the *postsynaptic neuron*). The neurotransmitter is then quickly removed from the synaptic cleft by one of two methods. Either it is taken back up by the presynaptic neuron, or an enzyme metabolizes the neurotransmitter and the metabolites are carted off as waste.

The chemical imbalance theory arose when researchers discovered how antidepressants and antipsychotics interrupted this messaging process. The first generation of antidepressants, tricyclics and monoamine oxidase inhibitors, were discovered to retard the removal of two neurotransmitters, serotonin and norepinephrine, from the synaptic cleft. This increased the levels of these two chemical messengers, and thus, if the drugs lifted depression, researchers hypothesized that depression was due to abnormally low levels of these molecules. In a similar vein, antipsychotics were found to block dopamine receptors, thereby decreasing dopamine activity in the brain, and thus researchers hypothesized that perhaps schizophrenia was due to too much dopamine activity.

Once these hypotheses were advanced, investigators sought to determine whether people diagnosed with depression actually suffered from low serotonin or low norepinephrine, or whether patients diagnosed with schizophrenia actually had overactive dopamine systems. In the case of depression, researchers eventually focused on serotonin, rather than norepinephrine, as the likely culprit, but once they developed ways to measure indirectly serotonin levels in the brain, they did not find that this neurotransmitter was abnormally low in depressed patients. Indeed, as early as 1983, National Institute of Mental Health (NIMH) investigators concluded that "elevations or decrements in the functioning of serotonergic systems per se are not likely to be associated with depression" (Maas et al., 1169). Scientists continued to investigate serotonergic function in depressed patients throughout the 1980s and 1990s, and they regularly failed to find any notable deficit. As psychiatrist Stephen Stahl wrote in his 2000 textbook *Essential Psychopharmacology*, "There is no clear and convincing evidence that monoamine deficiency accounts for depression; that is, there is no 'real' monoamine deficit" (cited in Lacasse and Leo, 1212; serotonin is a monoamine).

The history of investigations into the dopamine theory of schizophrenia is a bit more complex. First, researchers looked at whether the dopaminergic neurons in schizophrenia patients released abnormally high amounts of dopamine. In studies of patients who had never been medicated, researchers did not find that to be so. Next, researchers looked at whether the postsynaptic dopaminergic neurons in schizophrenia patients had too many receptors for this neurotransmitter, as this would also lead to an "overactive" dopamine system. By the mid-1980s, researchers concluded that this did not appear to be the case. The situation led John Kane, a well-known psychiatrist at Long Island Jewish Medical Center, to conclude in 1994 that there was "no good evidence for any perturbation of the dopamine function in schizophrenia" (Kane and Freeman, 23).

While a number of researchers have continued to investigate dopamine function in patients with psychotic disorders, no characteristic pathology has been identified (and so no antipsychotic drug to address a specific pathology can be developed). As Stephen Hyman, former director of the NIMH, wrote in 2002, "There is no compelling evidence that a lesion in the dopamine system is a primary cause of schizophrenia" (Nestler, Hyman, and Malenka, 392).

The low-serotonin theory of depression and the dopamine hyperactivity theory of schizophrenia were the two pillars of the chemical imbalance theory of mental disorders. Investigations into other psychiatric disorders—ADHD, for instance—also failed to find any characteristic chemical abnormality that was then corrected by a drug. In 2005 Kenneth Kendler, coeditor in chief of *Psychological Medicine*, summed up this long investigation in this way: "We have hunted for big simple neurochemical explanations for psychiatric disorders and have not found them" (434).

A Paradigm for Understanding Psychotropic Drugs

Although decades of investigations into the chemical imbalance theory of mental disorders failed to confirm the theory, the research did foster a nuanced understanding of how the brain *responds* to a psychiatric drug. And therein lies a story of science that is little known to the public, and underappreciated even by most researchers.

As noted above, Thorazine and other first-generation antipsychotics were found to block a particular type of dopamine receptor, known as the D_2 receptor. This thwarts the transmission of messages along dopaminergic pathways in the brain. What researchers discovered is that in response to this drug blockade, the brain accelerates such activity. The brain, researchers note, is trying to retain a "homeostatic equilibrium." Presynaptic neurons put out more dopamine than normal, at least for a period of time, while postsynaptic neurons increase the density of their D_2 receptors. Antipsychotics were found to trigger the very abnormality—an increase in dopamine receptors—that had been theorized to cause psychosis in the first place.

The same was found to be true of antidepressants. SSRI antidepressants accelerate serotonergic activity; in response, the brain tries to put the brake on this system. Presynaptic neurons put out less serotonin than normal (at least for a while), and the postsynaptic neurons decrease the density of their receptors for the neurotransmitter. Antidepressants drive the brain into a low serotonergic state. In 1996, NIMH director Stephen Hyman and Eric Nestler summarized this research in a paper subtitled "A Paradigm for Understanding Psychotropic Drug Action." These drugs, they wrote, "create perturbations in neurotransmitter functions." In response, the brain goes through a series of compensatory adaptations, which are designed to "permit cells to maintain their equilibrium in the face of alterations in the environment or changes in the internal milieu." At the end of this process, they concluded, the person's brain functions in a manner that is "qualitatively as well as quantitatively different from the normal state" (152–53, 161).

In sum, psychiatric drugs, which the public was informed are normalizing agents, are better understood, from a scientific standpoint, as agents that create abnormalities. They induce the very changes hypothesized to cause the illness in the first place.

Long-Term Outcomes

The fact that psychiatric drugs cause compensatory adaptations does not mean they necessarily fail to provide a benefit over the long term. But this understanding of the drugs' effects does provide insight into why they might have so many side effects, and why they might be problematic over time. The story of their long-term effects can, in fact, be dug out from a thorough review of the scientific literature, and the literature tells a surprisingly consistent tale.

There isn't space in this essay to review in detail the scientific record (which I wrote about in *Anatomy of an Epidemic*). But the bottom line is that antipsychotics, antidepressants, and the collection of drugs used to treat bipolar disorder worsen outcomes over the long term. Moreover, as researchers have tried to understand why antipsychotics and antidepressants would have this long-term effect, they have theorized it may be because the drugs trigger compensatory adaptions in the brain that oppose their initial intended effects.

This paradox in outcomes—that drugs that are effective over the short term could worsen outcomes over the long term—first surfaced in studies of the antipsychotics. In the 1970s, three NIMH-funded studies that assessed outcomes of schizophrenia patients for one to three years all found higher relapse rates in the patients regularly treated with antipsychotics. A retrospective study conducted by J. Sanbourne Bockoven, which compared five-year outcomes for psychotic patients hospitalized in 1947, with five-year outcomes for patients hospitalized in 1967, found that the drug-treated patients had higher relapse rates and were much more socially dependent—on welfare and unable to work—than the earlier cohort. This research prompted William Carpenter, who had led one of the three NIMH-funded studies, to pose a troubling prospect: "We raise the possibility that antipsychotic medication may make some schizophrenic patients more vulnerable to relapse than would be the case in the natural course of the illness" (Carpenter et al., 19).

A researcher from McGill University in Montreal, Guy Chouinard, put together a biological explanation to explain why the drugs might have that effect. The fact that the brain, in response to an antipsychotic, increased the density of its dopamine receptors meant that it was now "supersensitive" to dopamine. This could lead to severe relapses upon drug withdrawal, he said, and yet, if patients stayed on an antipsychotic indefinitely, a significant percentage would develop persitent psychosis. "New schizophrenia symptoms or original symptoms of greater severity will appear," Chouinard wrote (23).

This picture of antipsychotic drugs naturally startled the psychiatric field, which soon did its best to put this thought out of mind. Nevertheless, numerous studies since then have provided evidence that antipsychotics worsen long-term outcomes, at least in the aggregate. In two World Health Organization studies that compared longer-term outcomes in three developing countries to outcomes in the United States and other developed countries, patients in the developing countries fared much better, and in the poor countries, only 16 percent of patients were regularly kept on antipsychotics (Jablensky et al., table on 64). The best long-term prospective study of schizophrenia outcomes in the United States, conducted by Martin Harrow, found that recovery rates at the end of fifteen years were eight times higher for those who got off antipsychotics than for those who stayed on an antipsychotic, and that the off-medication group was also much less likely to experience psychotic symptoms at the ten-year and fifteen-year follow-ups (Harrow and Jobe, 409). The fact that the medicated patients suffered more persistent psychotic symptoms, Harrow wrote, might be due to the "buildup of excess dopamine receptors, or supersensitive psychosis" (Harrow, 964). Researchers at the University of Toronto, in animal studies, also concluded that antipsychotics "fail" over time because they trigger an increase in dopamine receptors (Samaha, 2985).

The evidence that antidepressants worsen long-term outcomes is equally compelling. Prior to the arrival of antidepressants, major depression was understood to be an episodic disorder. Hospitalized patients could be expected to recover from an episode, and studies found that about half of all patients would never again be rehospitalized. Antidepressants seemed to quicken the recovery process, but as several psychiatrists observed in the late 1960s and early 1970s, their depressed patients, once treated with an antidepressant, were now relapsing much more quickly. Were the drugs inducing a change to a more chronic long-term course? A number of studies found that depressed patients were indeed relapsing frequently, and in 1994 Giovanna Fava, editor of *Psychotherapy and Psychosomatics*, wrote that it was time for psychiatry to confront this troubling body of evidence. "Within the field of psychopharmacology, practitioners have been cautious, if not fearful, of opening a debate on whether the treatment is more damaging [than helpful]. . . . I wonder if the time has come for debating and initiating research into the likelihood that psychotropic drugs actually worsen, at least in some cases, the progression of the illness which they are supposed to treat" (125).

Naturalistic studies of depressed patients support this conclusion. In the past twenty years, study after study has found that over the long term, those who avoid antidepressants have better outcomes. They are less likely to be depressed years later, and they are more likely to be working. For instance, in an NIMH study that followed patients for six years, the medicated patients were seven times more likely to become "incapacitated" (Coryell, 1126). In 2010 Rif El-Mallakh, an expert in mood disorders at the University of Louisville, reviewed this evidence and concluded that it appears that SSRIs induce a "treatment resistant depressive state" in a significant percentage of patients" (771).

The decline in bipolar outcomes in the modern era is also well recognized. People so diagnosed today have more episodes and are more likely to become rapid cyclers. Whereas 75 percent or so in the prelithium era would remain employed, today that functional outcome has dropped to around 33 percent. Bipolar patients today, who are regularly put on a cocktail of drugs, show signs of cognitive decline, whereas that didn't used to be the case. In a 2007 paper, Nancy Huxley and Ross Baldessarini, from Harvard Medical School, aptly summarized this deterioration in outcomes: "Prognosis for bipolar disorder was once considered relatively favorable, but contemporary findings suggest that disability and poor outcomes are prevalent" (183).

Unfortunately, this story has unfolded away from the public eye. American psychiatry has not incorporated these poor long-term outcomes into its clinical practice guidelines and its textbooks, and the NIMH has similarly failed to inform the American public of the worsening long-term outcomes in the modern era.

Anatomy of a Global Epidemic

In essence, the story of science detailed above serves as a counternarrative to the conventional narrative of progress that psychiatry likes to tell. In this counternarrative, the biological causes of mental disorders remain unknown. Psychiatric drugs do not fix chemical imbalances but instead induce them, and the drugs worsen outcomes over the long term. These are dueling narratives, and if the conventional narrative is true, we should expect that the burden of mental illness in our society during the Prozac era would have declined. If the counternarrative is true, then we should expect that the burden of mental illness would have grown worse.

Here are the data.

In 1987 there were 1.25 million adults in the United States who received either a monthly Supplemental Security Income (SSI) or Social Security Disability Insurance (SSDI) payment because they were disabled by a mental disorder, a disability rate of 1 in every 184 Americans. In 2011, there were 4.8 million adults on the disability rolls due to mental illness, a disability rate of 1 in every 65 Americans. The disability rate among adults ages eighteen to sixty-five nearly tripled during that twenty-four-year period. The publication of DSM III also marked the moment when we began medicating children regularly, as it was in that manual that attention deficit disorder was first identified as a discrete illness, and here are the disability data for youth under age eighteen: The number receiving an SSI payment due to mental illness rose from 16,200 in 1987 to 728,000 in 2011, a forty-five-fold increase. (For these data, see the Social Security Administration's annual statistical reports on the SSDI and SSI programs, 1987–2011, the *Social Security Bulletin, Annual Statistical Supplement*, 1988–1992, and annual statistical reports on the SSI program, 1996–2011.)

There may have been any number of social factors that contributed to the increase in the number of disabled mentally ill in our society. There may have been a loosening of eligibility criteria, welfare reform may have led poor people to turn to the disability system for support, and many people may have stayed on disability in order to retain access to medical care. However, if widespread use of psychiatric drugs is, in fact, a driving factor of the disability epidemic, then similar increases in disability should have occurred in other countries that have adopted this paradigm of care, even though social factors in those countries may be very different. The epidemic wouldn't be specific to the United States, and that is indeed the case. In Australia, New Zealand, Iceland, the United Kingdom, Germany, Denmark, Sweden, and other countries, the number of disabled mentally ill has increased dramatically in the past twenty years, with these countries regularly reporting disability numbers that have doubled, tripled, or even quadrupled since 1990.

The cross-cultural data support this conclusion: The widespread use of psychiatric medications increases the burden of mental illness in a society. The global epidemic tells of a failed paradigm of care.

This failure is taking a great financial toll on American society. The adult on disability receives a monthly living payment, food stamps, and free medical care. The child on disability is likely to move to the adult disability rolls at age eighteen, and thus have a "career" as a mental patient receiving such financial assistance. The disability numbers also tell of millions of lives that have been diminished in profound and lasting ways. And beyond that, this paradigm of care is weakening our society as a whole.

Transforming the American Mind

We could look at this failure of modern psychiatric care as simply a story of failed medical care. Treatments that we believed to be helpful and even necessary have not proven to be so, at least not in terms of how they affect overall outcomes. While many people find the medications helpful over the short term and some do well on them over the long term, the drugs nevertheless increase the likelihood that a person will become chronically ill and disabled by the disorder. That medical story is surely of great import to our society, given that one in five Americans now takes a psychiatric drug. But the harm done by our current paradigm of care extends beyond the long-term effects of the drug treatment.

The APA, through its *Diagnostic and Statistical Manual*, sets the boundaries for determining what is to be considered "abnormal" in our society. The APA has informed the American public that the various diagnoses should be thought of as "discrete" illnesses, and the fourth and fifth editions list nearly three hundred such disorders. This profusion of diagnoses and loosened criteria for making a diagnosis casts a very wide net for psychiatry, and it certainly serves the commercial interests of both psychiatry and the pharmaceutical industry. It also leads to an understanding that mental illness is rampant in our society. But beyond that, the APA's manual provides us with an impoverished philosophy of what it means to be human.

The human mind, of course, is a messy place. We are emotional creatures, and we naturally struggle with those emotions. But in the DSM, the "normal" human mind is supposed to be quite well ordered, never too battered by unpleasant emotions or surprising behaviors. Melancholy, anxiety, extreme states of happiness . . . all can fall outside the boundaries of "normal" in the DSM. Indeed, the DSM is a manual that seems to have been authored by individuals who have never read Shakespeare and witnessed in his dramas the stories of men and women riven by jealousies, greed, rivalries, and the grip of romantic love.

The DSM, through its narrowing of what is to be deemed "normal," has also redefined childhood, and what we expect of our children. Forty years ago, few children were seen as having a mental illness. Schoolyards were populated by nerds, goof-offs, teachers' pets, bullies, and so forth, and society understood that children could be expected to gain more control over their behavior as they grew up. But then the APA, when it published DSM III, started constructing a variety of diagnostic categories for childhood behaviors and moodiness, and the transformation of American childhood was under way. Today, the child who is antsy and talks too much in school is likely to be diagnosed with attention deficit hyperactivity disorder. The moody teenager becomes a candidate for a diagnosis of bipolar disorder. The child in foster care is likely to be deemed "bipolar," or suffering from "oppositional conduct disorder," and prescribed an atypical antipsychotic. Children so diagnosed hear that there is something wrong with their brains and that they aren't normal, and this message, quite apart from the long-term effects of the drugs they may be prescribed, can damage a child's sense of self-worth and self-confidence. Indeed, when the diagnosis is combined with drug treatment, it can put a child onto a career path as a lifelong "mental patient."

Finally, the chemical-imbalance story has reshaped Americans' thinking about free will and the capacity of humans to be responsible for their emotional states and for their actions. If our moods and behaviors are understood to be governed by molecules in our brain, which are beyond our control, we are less likely to think of ourselves as resilient beings who, when confronted with distressing feelings, can choose to make changes that will help us regain our emotional health. The chemical imbalance story even encourages us to explain away our bad behavior. If we gamble too much or fail to apply ourselves at work, then this may be the fault of our brain chemistry. The chemical imbalance story encourages us to think of ourselves as victims, born with brains that can't cope well with the demands of the world.

Such are the many ways that American society has been transformed by DSM III and the Prozac era. The burden of mental illness in our society has notably increased. We have embraced an impoverished philosophy of mind; our children grow up in an environment ever ready to declare them mentally ill; and our society has been encouraged to think that our behaviors and moods are governed by brain chemicals that are beyond our control, diminishing our sense of self-responsibility. This is a loss, rather remarkable in scope, that has arisen from our societal belief in a narrative of progress that is, in so many ways, belied by science.

References

Andreasen, Nancy C. *The Broken Brain.* New York: Harper and Row, 1984.

Angier, Natalie. "New Antidepressant Is Acclaimed but Not Perfect." *New York Times*, March 29, 1990.

Carpenter, William T., Thomas H. McGlashan, and John S. Strauss. "The Treatment of Acute Schizophrenia without Drugs." *American Journal of Psychiatry* 134 (1977): 14–20.

Chouinard, Guy. "Severe Cases of Neuroleptic-Induced Supersensitivity Psychosis." *Schizophrenia Research* 5 (1991): 21–33.

Coryell, William, et al. "Characteristics and Significance of Untreated Major Depressive Disorder." *American Journal of Psychiatry* 152 (1995): 1124–29.

Duncan, Barry, and Scott Miller. "Exposing the Mythmakers: How Soft Sell Has Replaced Hard Science." *Psychotherapy Networker* (March/April 2000), http://www.psychotherapynetworker.org/populartopics/depression/494-exposing-the-mythmakers.

El-Mallakh, R., et al. "Tardive Dysphoria: The Role of Long-Term Antidepressant Use in Inducing Chronic Depression." *Medical Hypothesis* 76 (2011): 769–73.

Fava, Giovanni A. "Do Antidepressants and Antianxiety Drugs Increase Chronicity in Affective Disorders?" *Psychotherapy and Psychosomatics* 61 (1994): 125–31.

Harrow, Martin. "Does Long-Term Treatment of Schizophrenia with Antipsychotic Medications Facilitate Recovery?" *Schizophrenia Bulletin* 39 (2013): 962–65.

Harrow, Martin, and Thomas H. Jobe. "Factors Involved in Outcome and Recovery in Schizophrenia Patients Not on Antipsychotic Medications." *Journal of Nervous and Mental Disease* 195 (2007): 406–14.

Huxley, Nancy, and Ross J. Baldessarini. "Disability and Its Treatment in Bipolar Disorder Patients." *Bipolar Disorders* 9 (2007): 183–96.

Hyman, Steven E., and Eric J. Nestler. "Initiation and Adaptation: A Paradigm for Understanding Psychotropic Drug Action." *American Journal of Psychiatry* 153 (1996): 151–61.

Jablensky, Assen, et al. "Schizophrenia: Manifestations, Incidence, and Course in Different Cultures." *Psychological Medicine* 20, monograph (1992): 1–95.

Kane, John M., and Hugh L. Freeman. "Towards More Effective Antipsychotic Treatment." *British Journal of Psychiatry* 165, suppl. 25 (1994): 22–31.

Kendler, Kenneth S. "Towards a Philosophic Structure for Psychiatry." *American Journal of Psychiatry* 162 (2005): 433–40.

Kirk, Stuart A. *The Selling of DSM: The Rhetoric of Science in Psychiatry.* New York: Aldine de Gruyter, 1992.

Klerman, Gerald L. "A Debate on DSM-III." *American Journal of Psychiatry* 141 (1984): 539–42.

Lacasse, Jeffrey R., and Jonathan Leo. "Serotonin and Depression: A Disconnect between the Advertisements and the Scientific Literature." *PLOS Medicine* 2 (2005): 1211–16.

Maas, J. W., et al. "Pretreatment Neurotransmitter Metabolite Levels and Response to Tricyclic Antidepressant Drugs." *American Journal of Psychiatry* 141 (1984): 1159–71.

Medco. "America's State of Mind." 2010, http://apps.who.int/medicinedocs/documents/s19032en/s19032en.pdf.

Nestler, Eric J., Steven E. Hyman, and Robert C. Malenka. *Molecular Neuropharmacology.* New York: McGraw-Hill, 2002.

Ronson, Jon. "Bipolar Kids: Victims of the 'Madness Industry'?" *New Scientist*, June 8, 2011: 44–47.

Samaha, Anne-Noel, et al. "'Breakthrough' Dopamine Supersensitivity during Ongoing Antipsychotic Treatment Leads to Treatment Failure over Time." *Journal of Neuroscience* 27 (2007): 2979–86.

Social Security Administration. Annual Statistical Reports on the SSDI and SSI programs, 1987–2011.
———. Annual Statistical Reports on the SSI Program, 1996–2011.
———. *Social Security Bulletin*. Annual Statistical Supplement, 1988–1992.
Wilson, Mitchell I. "DSM-III and the Transformation of American Psychiatry: A History." *American Journal of Psychiatry* 150 (1993): 399–410.

Part Two

★ ★ ★ ★ ★ ★ ★ ★ ★ ★ ★ ★ ★ ★ ★ ★ ★

Personal and Cognitive Habits/Interests

★ ★ ★ ★ ★ ★ ★ ★ ★ ★ ★ ★ ★ ★ ★ ★ ★

6

A Wired Nation Tunes Out the News

David T. Z. Mindich

Which do you prefer: "Obamacare" or the Affordable Care Act? *Jimmy Kimmel Live* posed this question in a person-on-the-street video in September 2013. The Affordable Care Act beat out Obamacare, despite the fact that the two are the same thing. It made for good humor and deserved embarrassment for interviewees, but in a more profound way, the loser was American democracy, a system that relies on an informed electorate.

Other comedians have plumbed the shallows of Americans' knowledge. In his "Jay Walking" segments on the *Tonight Show*, Jay Leno spent many years showing the cluelessness of average citizens. So did Canadian comedian Rick Mercer with his "Talking to Americans" segments, in which he provoked Americans to say the darnedest things, even famous Americans like Mike Huckabee and then-Texas governor George W. Bush, who seemed pleased in 2000 when Mercer told him about the endorsement of his candidacy by Canadian "Prime Minister Jean Poutine" (Poutine is a popular Canadian dish involving fries and gravy—see Thornton; Mercer).

Just as we might do with a plate of poutine, we should take these videos with a grain of salt; comedians like to highlight the foolish. But what is the actual state of political knowledge among the American electorate? How much interest do they have in current events? Given the importance in the United States of a free press and a citizenry that follows it—after all, though they often despised journalists, the Founders wrote them into the First Amendment—we rightly regard news consumption and political knowledge as essential to the

American outlook. In history and in principle, the American Mind attends closely to political affairs, with a zealous appetite for information on the doings of their representatives. Current evidence in recent years, however, sets this fundamental civic inquisitiveness in grave decline. My own discussions with young people suggest a tale of two electorates, the tuned in and the tuned out. Tuned-in citizens are, by definition, news consumers, but they also tend to have a basket of behaviors ranging from voting to volunteering to political affiliation. Tuned-in citizens also tend to have more faith that their role in society can make a difference. This faith is coupled with an acceptance that some media outlets can be trusted to provide useful information and that at least some politicians work for the common good, at least some of the time. Tuned-out citizens often display the opposite of these characteristics and behaviors. They don't trust the usefulness of following the news or politics at all, believing that their role as individuals doesn't matter. They doubt that news can be a force for informing an electorate, and they doubt that politicians are ever noble. In a word, most of the tuned-out people I speak with display a deep cynicism about news and politics, which in turn contributes to a deep political paralysis (Mindich).

Sometimes the consequences of ignorance can harm a policy debate. During the health-care debate in 2009, a *Wall Street Journal*/NBC poll found that half of all Americans believed, erroneously, in the existence of death panels (Patterson). Sometimes the consequences of ignorance can be devastating. In 2003 and 2004, polls showed that more than two-thirds of Americans assumed a connection between Iraq and the September 11 terrorist attacks, a misperception that persisted well after the Bush administration pulled back from that claim (Milbank and Deane). In 2014, researchers asked Americans to locate Ukraine on a blank map. The farther their guesses were from Ukraine's actual location—and some guessed as far as Alaska and Australia—the more likely they were to support military intervention (Dropp et al.).

This problem is not new. In 1995 a poll found that 17 percent of Americans could name three or more Supreme Court justices; 59 percent could name three of the Three Stooges (Biskupic). But while the problem of Americans' indifference to news and politics is long-standing, it takes on greater importance when we realize that it's getting worse. In 1990 an important study called "The Age of Indifference" concluded that young Americans were far less likely to follow the news than their elders did. This was a shift from the 1940s through the 1970s. "Watergate was of equal interest to young and old," said the study's sponsor, the Times Mirror Center for the People & the Press. But in the decade following Watergate, polls began to show "diminished interest in current affairs among younger people" (Times Mirror).

In the two decades that followed the 1990 Times Mirror Center report, I and other researchers, particularly the pollsters at the Pew Research Center for the People & the Press, showed that that gap had not only persisted but grown larger.

According to Pew's latest news consumption survey, the number of Americans who read a newspaper "yesterday" declined from about half in 2000 to 23 percent in 2012. Among the under-thirty crowd, only 13 percent had read a newspaper "yesterday" in 2012, and that figure includes digital newspapers. In the first decade of the 2000s, more than half of young people said they watched TV news "yesterday"; by 2012, only one-third did (Pew Research, "In Changing News Landscape").

Only 5 percent of eighteen- to twenty-nine-year-olds say they "follow news about 'political figures and events in Washington' very closely" (Beaujon). Thus, it is no surprise that young people know far less about basic political facts and show less regard for political knowledge than their elders do. In 2011 Pew asked respondents if they could identify the Speaker of the House. Forty-three percent of Americans knew Boehner was the speaker, but only 21 percent of those under age thirty knew (Pew Research, "Well Known"). Significantly, the young were not always less informed than their elders, as "The Age of Indifference" explained.

This may be one of the big surprises of our day: that the under-thirty crowd lags behind the news practices and political involvement of its elders, both in terms of what their elders do today and what they did as youths. Why are most young Americans politically disengaged? Fired up by Obama's 2008 election and cinched together by Facebook, Twitter, and Instagram, the wired-up Millennials have every reason to be the most politically engaged generation ever. But with the exception of a politically engaged minority of young people (more about them later), they are not. Despite the fact that they have the means to stay informed, most of them don't take the time to do so. As a longtime college professor, I've seen firsthand that young people I come in contact with continue to be intelligent, idealistic, and thoughtful. But too many seem uninterested in keeping up with even the basic outline of the national and international narrative.

★ ★ ★

"Where the press is free, and every man able to read, all is safe," Thomas Jefferson famously wrote. But a free press and literacy, while clearly prerequisites of democracy, are not sufficient. One adage states that America is a system designed by geniuses so that it could be run by idiots, and the Constitution does provide checks against our greatest mistakes of the moment (see, for example, Friedman). But nothing in our Constitution protects us against the long-term ravages of neglect by the people themselves.

And make no mistake: This is a long-term problem. Despite the fact that youth is—by definition— fleeting, the habits that young people form can last a lifetime. Writing in the *New Yorker* in 1998, Robert M. Sapolsky, a neuroscientist, explored why certain habits are formed early. Sapolsky looked at three habits—listening to music, eating sushi, and body piercing—and discovered that the three each have expiration dates: the thirties for musical tastes and sushi, the twenties for one's first encounter with body piercing (Sapolsky). The news habit fits this pattern. Research has shown that the news habits of a generation don't change much. The twenty somethings of the 1990s and 2000s, now in middle age, tend to be about as tuned in or tuned out to news today as they were back then. What changes over time relates to what is called "cohort replacement": each age cohort—or generation—is replaced by another with potentially different news habits. In the last decades of the twentieth century, the median viewer age of TV news was about fifty; in 2013 the median viewer age of MSNBC and CNN was about sixty and Fox News was sixty-five (Carter).

Not that watching the news on television is in itself the answer to our problems. Media critics over the last decade have pointed out, correctly, that watching Fox News negatively correlates to political knowledge. In other words, if you watch Fox News, you are less likely to know basic political facts than if you consume nearly anything else (Patterson; Greenwald).

In 2012 Pew asked respondents four basic questions about tax policy, the unemployment rate, who controls the House of Representatives, and the nation that Angela Merkel leads (Germany). In a finding similar to other surveys, Fox News viewers fared poorly (only 16 percent answered four questions correctly). While critics of Fox News are correct in their assessment of that network's audience, one recent study suggests that viewers of other broadcast news networks, including CNN, fare no better (Pew Research, "In Changing News Landscape").

And that shouldn't surprise us. As many Americans drifted away from politics and political news, the networks chased after them with fluff. CNN has been among the worst offenders, giving over its Headline News Network, once a serious place for straight news, to a circus show of entertainment, fashion, and sensational crime news. In 2011 CNN and Headline News aired more than five hundred stories about Casey Anthony, a woman accused of killing her daughter (Anthony was found not guilty). Similarly, CNN's obsession with Lindsey Lohan could be one of the reasons that a 2010 poll found that actress to be more recognizable than any cabinet member except Hillary Clinton (Patterson). In 2013, researchers published a

"Twerkyria index," showing the ratio of tweets about twerking, a suggestive dance, and Syria. In the United States, that ratio was 10:1 (Watercutter).

At a 2005 meeting of top news executives in New York to which I was invited because of my research about young people and news, I had an opportunity to meet the then-president of CNN, Jonathan Klein. I told him and the other news executives that chasing young viewers with entertainment was a mistake and offered them a parable as an illustration. I told the news executives to imagine that I, as a professor, decided to appeal to my students by mixing up some alcohol-laced Jell-O shots and bringing them to class.

If I brought Jell-O shots to class, I told the executives, some of my students would be thrilled. But most would be horrified. First, they would correctly understand that a geeky middle-age professor would have no idea how to mix Jell-O shots. Second, the vast majority of my students, even the party animals, don't come to class to party. They come to class to be informed, challenged, and inspired. Ideally, class for most is an intellectual oasis, a refuge.

I used my fictional story to explain to Klein that his company was making a huge mistake by watering down Headline News to include *Nancy Grace*, *Showbiz Tonight*, and other fluff. Viewers aren't going to CNN for Jell-O shots. CNN should be the place they go for intelligence, information, and democracy. The off-the-record ground rules of the conference prevent me from reporting the response to my story, but as history is my witness, my words had zero impact on CNN programming. In fact, CNN has continued to dilute the seriousness of its network.

Most media and most public discourse are and forever will be the intellectual equivalent of Jell-O shots. But journalists should be in a different business. They are the folks who protect important discourse. They educate. They enlighten. They investigate. They comfort the afflicted and afflict the comfortable. And that's what this is all about. It's about democracy. "The role of the press," wrote the late James W. Carey, a Columbia journalism professor, "is simply to make sure that in the short run we don't get screwed and it does this best not by treating us as consumers of news, but by encouraging the conditions of public discourse and life" (Carey).

The health of our democracy is reason enough for CNN and other news outlets to recommit to serious news. But there is also a financial incentive. Despite the conventional wisdom, quality sells. The Project for Excellence in Journalism, in a study of 146 local TV news programs, discovered that the quality of a newscast correlated strongly with its ratings success (Rosenstiel et al.). A recent survey has shown clearly that viewers are finding many newscasts to be "too sensational, too contentious, too repetitive, and too flimsy—in other words, too much like showbiz and too little like news" (Patterson, 127). Thus, no one should be surprised that, with entertainment-infused news programming, CNN has lost nearly half of its primetime viewers, according to Pew's 2013 "State of the News Media" report. Providing quality news informs the public, and only an informed public will demand quality news. The declines in news quality and an informed citizenry are, therefore, mutually reinforcing.

Given that having an engaged citizenry is so important to our democracy, what can be done about this problem? I offer three solutions.

1. Do Quality Journalism

If the Pew Center's polls reveal ways in which Fox, CNN, and other TV newscasts are not living up to their potential, there is a flip side. Some quality outlets attract news consumers who are very informed. In order, the top outlets for informed audiences are the *Rachel Maddow Show*, the *New Yorker*, the *Wall Street Journal*, NPR, the *Daily Show*, *Hardball*, the *New York Times*, and the *Economist* (Beaujon). This list has some important implications. First, these outlets are not only successful but smart. While they don't share much ideologically—with the *Wall Street Journal* displaying a right-wing bias in its opinion pieces and the others on the list a centrist or leftwing bias—the news outlets are all intelligent. Further, none of them pander to their audience. Yes, the *Daily Show* slips in more than its share of bathroom humor, but it also cares deeply about politics, offering intelligent interviews and trenchant (albeit humorous) analysis.

By the way, the *Daily Show* is not part of the problem. Jon Stewart's jokes are designed for an intelligent, politically savvy audience, suggesting that those who watch the *Daily Show* are consumers of other quality news outlets, too, like the *New York Times* and NPR. An interesting fact: Heavy news consumers tend to be generalists; that is, they consume not only a quality newspaper but quality broadcast news as well. And people who have one or more news apps on their cell phones tend to be heavy news consumers across media (Pew Research, "In Changing News Landscape").

Unlike the *Nancy Grace* show, whose very existence suggests that CNN's management has little respect for its audience, the *Daily Show* assumes that its audience wants to hear, among other things, a sophisticated argument about the hypocrisy of supporting war while voting against a bill that compensates 9/11 first responders, an argument Stewart made repeatedly in 2010 and 2011.

These quality outlets offer a lesson for the rest of journalism. Respect your readers or viewers, treat them like serious thinkers, and you will not only inform them but they will return that respect and come back tomorrow, hungry to be informed and empowered. If I have one quarrel with Jon Stewart, it's that he sometimes dismisses what he does as nonjournalism. If I have one wish, it would be that he start an annual tradition, let's say every April Fools' Day, of conducting a serious, no-jokes newscast. One of the most famous news broadcasts in history was Edward R. Murrow's show that revealed Joseph McCarthy's hypocrisy. Murrow's mix of analysis, righteous indignation, and use of McCarthy's own words could be seen as an early template for what Jon Stewart's team does every day; it can still be an important model for news analysis today.

2. Broaden the Engaged Minority

The *Daily Show*, the *Colbert Report*, and the *New York Times* tend to attract a younger audience, Pew's research shows. This is not a contradiction to the findings presented above. An engaged minority of young people has always existed, and today is no exception. In fact, there has never been a better time to be an engaged citizen. Quality journalism—local, national, and international—exists in every town and every village, and anyone with a basic Internet connection can consume ten lifetimes worth of news.

The Internet can sate even the thirstiest news consumer and in this way is the most comprehensive news source ever created. But if the Internet can feed the news appetite, it can—and does—feed other appetites as well. For years, young people have been claiming that they have no time to follow the news, but this argument is bogus: the young and the not-so-young consume vast amounts of media (Mindich). Clay Shirky, in *Cognitive Surplus*, reminds us that Americans watch hundreds of billions of hours of television a year. And we know that the Internet has added countless hours of mindless diversion. For proof, check out what people are consuming in computer labs and Internet cafes and on their smartphones. For some, it's the *New York Times*; for far more, it's Facebook.

In a recent book about the news consumption habits of Millennials, Paula Poindexter noted the importance of caring about every generation's news consumption. Imagine, Poindexter asks rhetorically, if the Coca-Cola Company didn't work hard to get the latest generation interested in soda. It would risk losing lifetime customers. So why aren't we doing more to interest young people in news (Poindexter, 119–20)?

Over the years, some of the proposed solutions to the problem have started and ended in the newsroom. But this issue is societal. We know, for example, that college-bound high school students will study vocabulary and math and spend time volunteering in the community. Why? They study in part because of standardized tests, and they volunteer in their communities in part because the National Honor Society requires volunteerism. But if colleges and universities signal to high school kids that news knowledge and political engagement are also important, it could have a big impact. We certainly don't want colleges and universities telling young people that they need to embrace a particular political party or ideology. But if colleges and universities promoted the importance of civics classes and high school newspapers in particular and community engagement in general, the impact on news awareness would be a positive one.

3. Promote News on Social Media

"Begin with a clear conception that the subject of deepest interest to an average human being is himself," wrote Horace Greeley, the nineteenth-century newspaper editor. "Next to that, he is most concerned about his neighbors. Asia and the Tongo [*sic*] Islands stand a long way after these in his regard" (Parton, 522).

In some ways, Facebook embodies Greeley's words; sometimes it feels like a collective effort to focus on minutiae. And for too many Facebook residents, the gaze at one's navel, and the navels of one's peers, prevents a sustained examination of Asia, the Tonga Islands, and other matters of importance.

But it's not all insular news. Some people, particularly those with politically engaged Facebook friends, get a good deal of news from the social network. And unlike online chat rooms that are tailored to people who share narrow political ideologies, Facebook, recent studies have found, can be a good place to debate issues with an open mind (Manjoo). Researchers have found that getting news from Facebook friends deepens one's understanding of a subject (Pew, "State of the News Media"). This is not surprising. In my conversations with young people over the last couple of decades, I've found a strong correlation between those who discuss news and those who consume it (Mindich). The reason is that we tend to consume media that feeds our conversations. When your friends talk about sports, you will follow sports in order to participate in the conversation. The same is true for news. The mind-set of those who are tuned in is informed, curious, and engaged.

Given this, what should we do to promote conversation?

It turns out that about one-third of Facebook users either "like" or "follow" a news organization or individual journalist (Pew, "The Role of News"). These users are far more likely to have a high news consumption level and much more likely to share news with friends and comment on news stories. This is a recipe for returning our young (and not so young) to a higher level of political involvement. It would be great if Facebook took it upon itself to promote news literacy. Perhaps it could offer a news default system in which users would need to opt out of news consumption rather than the reverse.

The U.S. government used to push its broadcasters to produce news and public affairs shows; the FCC insisted on it as a condition for station contract renewal (Mindich). Since the Reagan era of deregulation, the FCC has watered down these requirements. The FCC doesn't control cable or Facebook in the same way, but it is not impossible to imagine the government finding ways to incentivize greater news and public affairs programming, the kind that promotes young people to be more informed and muscular voters. The government has no place in choosing parties or even news outlets, but it could bring back pre-deregulation requirements that broadcasters operate as good citizens with a heavier dose of serious programming. And if we wanted to, we could incentivize cable networks and social networks to do the same.

★ ★ ★

This is our challenge: To insist that more Americans, particularly young Americans, tune back into news. If we commit to this challenge, we should go all in. Journalists need take their audiences seriously. Teachers and parents need to talk to their kids about news and politics. Politicians need to create a society in which civic engagement and politics are discussed and valued. We need to create the conditions to compel more young people to embrace a tuned-in mind-set of curiosity, intelligence, and political muscularity.

Clay Shirky tells us that we are sitting on a vast national (even international) treasure, a cognitive surplus waiting to be tapped; Shirky says that even a *1 percent* shift would be staggering. We don't need Americans to spend all their time consuming news. But learning that the Affordable Care Act and Obamacare are the same thing would be a good place to start.

References

Beaujon, Andrew. "Pew: Half of Americans Get News Digitally, Topping Newspapers, Radio." Poynter, September 27, 2012, http://www.poynter.org/latest-news/mediawire/189819/pew-tv-viewing-habit-grays-as-digital-news-consumption-tops-print-radio/.

Biskrupic, Joan. "Has the Court Lost Its Appeal? In Poll, 59% Can Name 3 'Stooges,' 17% Can Name 3 Justices." *Washington Post*, October 12, 1995.

Carey, James W. "AEJ Presidential Address: A Plea for the University Tradition." *Journalism Quarterly* 55 (1978): 846–55.

Carter, Bill. "Fox Viewers May Be Graying, but Their Passion Still Pays." *New York Times*, July 23, 2013.

Dropp, Kyle, et al. "The Less Americans Know about Ukraine's Location, the More They Want U.S. to Intervene." *Washington Post*, April 7, 2014.

Friedman, Thomas L. *The Lexus and the Olive Tree.* New York: Anchor Books, 2000.

Greenwald, Robert, dir. *Outfoxed: Rupert Murdoch's War on Journalism*. Carolina Productions and MoveOn.Org, 2004.

Manjoo, Farhad. "The End of the Echo Chamber: A Study of 250 Million Facebook Users Reveals the Web Isn't as Polarized as We Thought." Slate.com, January 17, 2012, http://www.slate.com/articles/technology/technology/2012/01/online_echo_chambers_a_study_of_250_million_facebook_users_reveals_the_web_isn_t_as_polarized_as_we_thought_.html.

Mercer, Rick. "Talking to Americans," posted December 20, 2006, http://www.youtube.com/watch?v=BhTZ_tgMUdo.

Milbank, Dana, and Claudia Deane. "Hussein Link to 9/11 Lingers in Many Minds." *Washington Post*, September 6, 2003.

Mindich, David T. Z. *Tuned Out: Why Americans under 40 Don't Follow the News.* New York: Oxford University Press, 2005.

Parton, James. *The Life of Horace Greeley, Editor of "The New York Tribune," from His Birth to the Present Time.* Boston: Houghton, Mifflin and Co., 1889.

Patterson, Thomas E. *Informing the News: The Need for Knowledge-Based Journalism.* New York: Vintage Books, 2013.

Pew Research Center. "In Changing News Landscape, Even Television Is Vulnerable," 2012, http://www.people-press.org/2012/09/27/in-changing-news-landscape-even-television-is-vulnerable/.

———. "The Role of News on Facebook: Common Yet Incidental," 2013, http://www.journalism.org/2013/10/24/the-role-of-news-on-facebook/.

———. "The State of the News Media, 2013," http://stateofthemedia.org/2013/overview-5/.

———. "Well Known: Clinton and Gadhafi. Little Known: Who Controls Congress," 2011, http://www.people-press.org/2011/03/31/well-known-clinton-and-gadhafi-little-known-who-controls-congress/.

Poindexter, Paula Maurie. *Millennials, News, and Social Media: Is News Engagement a Thing of the Past?* New York: Peter Lang, 2012.

Rosenstiel, Tom, Carl Gottlieb, and Lee Ann Brady. "Time for Peril for TV News: Quality Sells, But Commitment and Viewership Continue to Erode." *Columbia Journalism Review* (November/December 2000): 84–92.

Sapolsky, Robert M. "Investigations: Open Season." *New Yorker*, March 30, 1998, 57.

Shirky, Clay. *Cognitive Surplus: Creativity and Generosity in a Connected Age.* New York: Penguin Press, 2010.

Thornton, Paul. "Jimmy Kimmel's Obamacare Stunt: How Infallible Is Public Opinion?" *Los Angeles Times*, October 2, 2013.

Times Mirror. "The Age of Indifference," 1990, http://www.people-press.org/files/legacy-pdf/19900628.pdf.

Watercutter, Angela. "Yes, We've Been Talking a Lot More about Twerking Than Syria on Twitter." Wired.com, September 18, 2013, http://www.wired.com/2013/09/twitter-data-twerking-vs-syria/.

7

Catching Our Eye

THE ALLURING FALLACY OF KNOWING AT A GLANCE

Maggie Jackson

HEADING HOME after a morning walk in Central Park, I saw a man on his hands and knees, peering at a patch of plants sprouting between the cobblestones at the park's perimeter. Tall and gaunt, he had a Lincoln-like beard and aura of calm. Lost key or contact lens? I stopped to ask. No, just looking, said the man, running his fingers across a tuft of grass and a mossy cushion of green. Two plants that normally flower in April and August were blooming simultaneously in May, he explained. Standing up beside his bicycle, he gazed down at the ragtag greenery at his feet. I asked if he was a botanist. No, he answered, just interested.

I am not a naturalist, and I wouldn't have caught this tiny glitch in the rhythm of the seasons no matter how hard I had looked. A certain expertise had primed this man's eye. But something beyond this feat of knowledge intrigued me. Willing to pause and look, he had seen a bit of wilderness pushing up through city stones. Lingering and considering, he had begun to comprehend an innocuous detail that had the potential to speak volumes about our warming earth. Could this brief encounter illuminate a larger paradox of our lives? I had stopped that day out of curiosity—and surprise. As I had rushed by, the man's moment of contemplation had seemed strikingly out of step with the tenor of our hurried and fragmented days. Screens in hand and bodies on the fly, we rarely let our roving eyes settle down to observe the tableau of life unfolding before us. Workers switch tasks on average every three minutes and typically open 70 percent of email within six seconds (Gonzalez and Mark; see also Jackson et al.). Nearly a third of teens trade one hundred or more texts a day (Lenhart). Film trailers average nearly forty cuts per minute, triple the rate in the 1950s (Palmer). Reading, like truffle hunting, has become a search-and-grab operation, with deep analysis growing passé (Baron). We see what's before us, virtual or physical, only momentarily. Casting looks here and there like fishhooks into a stream, our sight is caught and tossed by torrents of shifting wonders. Yet how much can one fathom in a heartbeat or know deeply at a glance? How are speed and brevity, the twin markers of our day, redefining what it means to see and understand? Vision is our master sense, the main gateway to awareness, knowledge, and understanding. Operating on quick-cut glimpses, are we increasingly, as T. S. Eliot asked in "The Dry Salvages," having the experience but missing the meaning? Could the art of observation be worth a second thought in an age when looking grows cheap?

★ ★ ★

Seeing is believing, or so the saying goes. It's easy to assume that vision is fabulous camera-work, a series of clear, continuous readings of our ever-changing surroundings. After all, 70 percent of the body's sense receptors cluster in the eyes, the light-gatherers of perception (Ackerman). Sight literally expands our horizons, allowing us to imbibe detail and distant prospects alike. Nevertheless, we were not built to take in all before us. By necessity, survival is a constant process of simplification, at all levels of cognition. Even the most rudimentary mechanisms of perception engage in a ceaseless work of cognitive culling. The lowly neuron, foot soldier of the brain, doesn't, as was once assumed, simply funnel raw sensory data to the higher-order regions that "think." Instead, these front line cells shift their synaptic tunes as much to our higher goals, expectations, and focus as to the pulsing environment. The ceaseless sifting and interpreting of information up and down the food chain of cognition—one of science's greatest recent discoveries—keeps us from being snowed by our surroundings, as schizophrenic and autistic minds sadly are.

Still, our efficiency comes with a cost: perception is the art of the assumption, a first glance most of all. Moment to moment, we construct experience largely based on wish, expectation, and slices of reality, while presuming that we are seeing and comprehending all.

Consider the "gorillas in our midst" experiment, one of the most famous psychology studies of recent times. Shown a sixty-second video of students tossing a basketball back and forth and instructed to count the passes, half of the viewers fail to spot a woman in a gorilla suit amble for a full nine seconds through the game (Simons and Chabris). Our "change blindness" is vivid proof of the triumph of selective perception. We did the job in counting the passes. What more could one ask? Yet in concentrating as instructed on the ball, we miss to our surprise a dramatic shift in the environment. In the running narrative of experience, "things that do not fit the script," observes neuroscientist Vilayanur Ramachandran, "are wiped wholesale from consciousness" (Ramachandran and Ramachandran). When one thousand vision scientists familiar with the gorilla experiment were shown an updated version of the video, most completely missed striking changes—a departing player, a curtain that changed color—in the scene. (Else). To err is human, to select is to prioritize. We cannot see all. But what if the setting were a crime scene and the gorilla an overlooked clue? What happens in the boardroom when we miss the peripheral yet crucial point? The opposite of understanding is not ignorance, notes Jerome Bruner: "To understand something is first to give up some other way of conceiving it" (122–23). Expecting to know everything at a glance is our most mistaken inference of all.

Such hubris inspired a Yale doctor more than a decade ago to turn to art as a balm for the hurried eye. Irwin Braverman, a dermatologist, grew concerned as high-tech, high-paced medicine dethroned the careful physical exam, the thorough patient history, and the role of sensory perception in care, undermining skills once thought indispensable. Taught simply to recognize patterns—if symptom A, then illness B; if test result C, then treatment D—young doctors, in particular, lack practice in close observation, a physician's fundamental tool. The sharp diagnostic eye of the Scottish doctor Joseph Bell, after all, inspired the invention of the brilliant Sherlock Holmes. Frustrated one day by his residents' struggles to identify subtleties of skin lesions, Braverman brought them to a university museum to expose them to a puzzle they could not assume to solve instantly: a painting. Afterward, their ability to describe patients improved dramatically. In a now-mandatory program that he and a museum curator created, Yale medical students each examine a painting for fifteen minutes, then discuss their observations with a guide and their peers. "Look at the normal," not just the eye-catching, the students are told. Approach the work with an open mind, moving past first assumptions. Revisit the subject, again and again.

Observing a painting of a pale young man lying prone in a darkened room, students often quickly assume that he's drunk or sleeping. Gradually noticing the blue-gray of his lips and an empty vial nearby, they uncover the truth: Henry Wallis' 1856 *Chatterton* depicts the suicide of a young eighteenth-century poet after his literary forgeries were unmasked. "We are trying to slow down the students," said Yale Center for British Art curator Linda Friedlander, the program's cofounder. "The artwork is a means to an end" (quoted in Finn; also, personal interview with author, March 2014). In effect, the painting, with its hidden stories and ambiguous subtleties, *becomes* a substitute patient. Adopted by dozens of other medical schools, the brief intervention was shown in a three-year study to boost diagnostic observational skill by nearly 10 percent (Dolev et al.; see also Braverman). At Harvard Medical School, students given eight hours of similar training produce nearly 40 percent more observations and offer more sophisticated, accurate notations on a visual skills exam than those not enrolled in the course (Naghshineh et al.).

What happens when we look closely? How does vision deepen into knowledge? A breakthrough understanding of the mechanisms of slow observation began to emerge a generation ago when psychologists seeking to deconstruct perception looked to the work of World War II code breakers led by the brilliant mathematician Alan Turing (Fleming). Rather than study just one sample of enemy code, Britain's

Bletchley Park spies cracked Germany's infamous Enigma cipher by accruing samples over time in order to sift better signal from noise. Intriguingly, our brains seem to work similarly, weaving various slices of sketchy information together before making perceptual or even high-order judgments, from discerning a shadowy object to choosing between two rewards. Our minds must do so because their own activity, expressed in the flickering firing of neurons, is irregular and unpredictable, a noisy business at best. "When the accumulated evidence reaches a critical threshold, a judgment—a decision—is made," explains Columbia University neurologist Michael Shadlen, a leader in the study of decision-making's neural basis (quoted in Perry; see also Shadlen and Roskies). This core building block of cognition underlies the famous speed-accuracy trade-off, the finding that slower judgments in novel situations tend to be less prone to error. In difficult, complex environments, we must be code breakers, endeavoring to decipher an ambiguous world through painstaking refinement of our assumptions. A first glance is just a beginning, the bare makings of understanding. Could close looking be a missing link to the depth in thinking that we increasingly sense we lack?

Forty percent of technology experts worry that hyperconnectivity is turning tech-immersed generations into impatient thinkers with a "thirst for instant gratification" (Anderson and Rainie, 2). More than one-third of workers report that they are so busy or constantly interrupted that they do not have time to process or reflect on the work they do (Galinsky et al.). American adults and children have become over two decades far less able to see things from multiple angles, synthesize information, and work out a creative endeavor in detail, longitudinal studies show (Kim). The upshot is clear: We are not thinking before leaping. Our eyes and minds alike are too often scattershot. The dynamism of speed promises endless downloadable progress. Instantaneity is the new frontier of Industrial Age efficiency. But increasingly, the costs of lives built on one tempo, march-step with the machine, have grown too dear to ignore. "Great understanding is broad and unhurried; small understanding is cramped and busy," wrote the Taoist Zhuangzi (32). Could skilled observation be a training ground and gateway to the construction of knowledge? A few months after meeting the man in the park, I took my hurried eyes to New York's Metropolitan Museum of Art to try an improbable challenge: gazing at a painting for three solid hours.

A young art historian's epiphany inspired my experiment. Around 2010, Harvard's Jennifer Roberts sensed that she not only had to engineer more explicitly the practice of close looking for her students, but defend its value as well. Opportunities to unlock the poetry and stories of their surroundings were no longer a given, and skill in doing so was waning. Roberts responded by placing one of her assignments, a three-hour "visual analysis" of an artwork, at the center of her teaching to show her charges that learning is not synonymous with access, that knowledge is not available at a glance. At first, many resist, incredulous that any analog object could contain enough information to occupy them at such length. When they learn of the assignment, there is a "look of terror in their eyes," Roberts, a professor of the humanities, told me in April 2014. To help, students are given clues to looking: see with fresh eyes, keep questioning, explore multiple aspects of the object from its proportion and function to its content and sensuality. To inspire, she tells them how long it can take—twenty-one minutes, forty-five minutes, or hours—even for her, an expert, to notice crucial connections in paintings central to her research. For Roberts, introducing her students to the practice of "naïve observation" as preparatory research has become something more than a simple homework assignment. Time, she seeks to show, is not the enemy but the vehicle of understanding. Slowness is not an obstacle to progress but a key to the practice of knowledge-making. And close looking is preface to the hard-won *making* of thought. At heart, she is coaxing her students to question what's beyond surface appearances—of a painting, a frown, a flower, or an idea. By the end, many of her students tell her that they are astonished at what they have seen and learned. I had always considered myself observant, the quintessential sharp-eyed reporter. But settling down to begin the experiment, I wondered whether I'd really looked at anything before.

Leutze, Emanuel Gottlieb (1816–1868). Washington Crossing the Delaware. *1851. Image copyright © The Metropolitan Museum of Art. Image source: Art Resource, NY. Used by permission.*

I chose Emanuel Leutze's *Washington Crossing the Delaware* for its famous subject, mammoth size, and handy nearby bench. Despite all that I'd learned about close looking, sizing up the work at first seemed easy. In the 1851 painting, the imposing general stands at the prow of a crowded rowboat, eleven soldiers at his side, crossing the ice-strewn river hours before their pivotal Christmas 1776 victory in Trenton. We all know the story, the patriotic motif, and the hero who inspired this iconic yet seemingly dated image. What more could I possibly uncover? Fearing that I would rapidly fail the assignment, I began counting and categorizing: the men in the boat and their hats, their facial expressions and postures, and the splashes of eye-catching red—a blowing scarf, the stripes of a flag, the watery reflection of a soldier's scarlet tunic—sprinkled across a canvas dominated by tones of earth, wood, ice, and sky.

Then slowly, with each revisit of the canvas, inference led to guesswork, and detail built to overarching whole. Moment by moment, I began to see stories hidden in the painting. I quickly had noticed the bursts of red across the work, but in time I began to wonder: Were they harbingers of the blood to be shed in the battle to come? In twenty minutes, subtler signs of tense expectancy emerged: the muted flag held erect but furled, the chill emptiness of the approaching riverbank, guns and bayonets held aloft, mute yet ready to do violence. In eighty minutes, the painting's stillness and silence hit me. With just a tiny splash at bow and oars, the boat hardly seems to move. No one, not even Washington, speaks. Nearly all vigilantly look ahead, one collective breath held in anticipation. In the time that I often spent racing past dozens of paintings, I had begun to decipher a familiar artwork's long-unseen artistry. The painting was telling me, when I took the opportunity to look, a tale of expectation—of the moment before a perilous landing, a daunting battle, and a fateful turn in a war to create an untested country. Was I right or wrong in my observations? What mattered most was the process of deciphering the artists' intentions, the texture of a long-past day, and an iconic story newly told. I had passed by the image many times, blind to its secrets. In just a few hours, I had begun unlocking a code that I'd never even realized existed.

The process was hardly pure, a series of easy epiphanies. I took breaks and checked the clock. My focus at times bounced around the canvas and the room. I hit multiple seeming dead ends: focusing on Washington's steely posture, I overlooked until the end the humanizing curves of his flowing cape and middle-aged girth. Looking often gave me scattered particulars and snippets of information that demanded repeated consideration. Nothing worthwhile in those hours came automatically, without an effort of tenacity and synthesis. But if we are willing, the work of close looking combines a visual with an intellectual journey of meaning-making. We begin to see and consider detail, weigh and bypass the irrelevant, and reconsider first assumptions, emerging in time with a more textured understanding of what's before us. Looking closely *is* thinking, as we are beginning to understand. Even brief guided encounters with artworks, for instance, can boost children's critical thinking skills. In one yearlong study, Arkansas students, many of whom hadn't visited a museum before, showed modest but significant gains in thinking ability, mostly due to improved observation skills, after seeing five paintings on an hour-long museum tour. Minority, low-income, and rural children made double to triple the improvements of their peers (Bowen, Greene, and Kisida). Given time and effort, eye and mind work toward mutual discovery.

There is much we still do not know about how the world shapes and moves us, and how we do so in return. But in an age of quick-cut speed and machine-driven attention, times and spaces for training the human eye deeply matter. Immersive virtuality is explicitly designed to grab and splice our focus. It preys upon our minds. Physical objects—an artwork, an element of nature, or a printed page—in all their stillness and solidity, better allow us to navigate and manage the pace of our learning. In the museum I was on my own in seeing and understanding, as long as I resisted the click that would rescue me from the conundrum before my eyes. Of course, there is no magic in the analog. It's unusual today to spend even as long as a minute in front of a great work of art (Smith), and I would guess we similarly rush past the evocative people or telling blossoms that surround us. Skill and time in looking are a necessity to decode any aspect of our environment. Yet in an age of increasing expectation of immediate clarity, we urgently need to cultivate counterpoints to quick, machine-fed knowledge: the mysteries that we ourselves slowly and imperfectly decode. Think of a painting or a face or flower as canvases for the art of looking, as old media for practicing crucial skills that our screens may be too busy and predatory to allow. When I bothered to look closely, a painting that I carelessly had chosen to observe conveyed to me a slow-told story of endurance and forbearance. But the experience of contemplation itself taught me all the more.

★ ★ ★

Just twenty minutes before I turned to go, a young tour guide shepherded a group up to the painting. One of the most iconic of American images, the work is a symbol of hope and liberation, he said. It is a painting of rebellion against tyranny. Yet the artist deliberately chose to depict not the triumph and glory of a wartime victory, said the guide, but the suspense of an unknown outcome. I listened, reassured. My efforts had not unlocked all truths about this painting. Yet my time before the canvas had put me on the path to knowledge. In looking, I had begun to see.

References

Ackerman, Diane. *A Natural History of the Senses.* New York: Random House, 1990.

Anderson, Janna, and Lee Rainie. "Millennials Will Benefit and Suffer Due to Their Hyper-Connected Lives." Pew Research Center's Internet and American Life Project, February 29, 2012, http://www.pewinternet.org/2012/02/29/millennials-will-benefit-and-suffer-due-to-their-hyperconnected-lives/.

Baron, Naomi. "Redefining Reading: The Impact of Digital Communication Media." *PMLA* 128 (2013): 193–200.

Bowen, Daniel, Jay Greene, and Brian Kisida. "Learning to Think Critically: A Visual Art Experiment." *Educational Researcher* 43 (2014): 37–44.

Braverman, Irwin. "To See or Not to See: How Visual Training Can Improve Observational Skills." *Clinics in Dermatology* 29 (2011): 343–46.

Bruner, Jerome. *On Knowing: Essays for the Left Hand.* Cambridge, MA: Belknap Press of Harvard University Press, 1962.

Dolev, J. C., et al. "Use of Fine Art to Enhance Visual Diagnostic Skills." *Journal of the American Medical Association* 286 (2001): 10920–21.

Else, Liz. "Would You Spot the Gorilla?" *New Scientist*, June 2010, Vol. 206 (2010): 32–33.

Finn, Holly. "How to End the Age of Inattention." *Wall Street Journal*, June 1, 2012.

Fleming, Steve. "Hesitate!" *Aeon Magazine*, January 8, 2014.

Galinsky, Ellen, et al. *Overwork in America: When the Way We Work Becomes Too Much.* New York: Families and Work Institute, 2005.

Gonzalez, Victor, and Gloria Mark. "'Constant, Constant Multi-Tasking Craziness': Managing Multiple Working Spheres." *Proceedings of the ACM* CHI'04 Vol. 6 (2004): 113–20.

Jackson, Thomas W., et al. "Understanding Email Interaction Increases Organizational Productivity." *Communications of the ACM* 46 (August 2003): 80–84.

Kim, Kyung Hee. "The Creativity Crisis: The Decrease in Creative Thinking Scores on the Torrance Tests of Creative Thinking." *Creativity Research Journal* 23 (2011): 285–95.

Lenhart, Amanda. "Teens, Smartphones and Texting." Pew Research Center's Internet and American Life Project, March 2012, http://www.pewinternet.org/2012/03/19/teens-smartphones-texting/.

Naghshineh, Sheila, et al. "Formal Art Observation Training Improves Medical Students' Visual Diagnostic Skills." *Journal of General Internal Medicine* 23 (2008): 991–97.

Palmer, Katie. "Movie Trailers Are Getting Insanely Fast." Wired.com, June 18, 2013.

Perry, Susan. "Decision-Making," Brainfacts.org, October 1, 2009.

Ramachandran, Vilayanur, and Diane Rogers-Ramachandran. "How Blind Are We?" *Scientific American* (Special Edition) S18.2 (2008): 16–17.

Roberts, Jennifer L. "The Power of Patience: Teaching Students the Value of Deceleration and Immersive Attention." *Harvard Magazine*, November–December 2013.

Shadlen, Michael, and Adina Roskies. "The Neurobiology of Decision-Making and Responsibility: Reconciling Mechanism and Mindedness." *Frontiers in Neuroscience* 6 (April 2012): 1–12.

Simons, Daniel, and Christopher Chabris. "Gorillas in Our Midst: Sustained Inattentional Blindness for Dynamic Events." *Perception* 28 (1999): 1059–74.

Smith, Jeffrey K. "Art as Mirror: Creativity and Communication in Aesthetics." *Psychology of Aesthetics, Creativity and the Arts* 8 (2014): 110–18.

Zhuangzi. *Zhuangzi: Basic Writings*. Trans. Burton Watson. New York: Columbia University Press, 2003.

8

The Rise of the Self and the Decline of Intellectual and Civic Interest

Jean M. Twenge

"MR. SCHUE TAUGHT me the second half of the alphabet," says high school student Brittany on the television show *Glee*. "I stopped after M and N. I felt they sounded too similar and got frustrated." In another episode, Brittany refers to two universities in Northern California as "Stanford and Son or the University of California at Charles Barkley's house" and mentions she has a 0.0 grade point average. Yet when she exits the show in a 2013 episode, it's because MIT has suddenly discovered she's a math genius. "It wasn't until . . . I joined this club that I really started believing in myself," Brittany explains. "And as soon as I did that, as soon as I started believing that maybe I was smart after all, I think the whole world did, too."

The message: The key to academic success is not studying, reading, problem sets, parental involvement, inborn ability, or dedicated teachers, but believing in yourself. Brittany's story arc is played for humor, but her farewell speech about self-belief—complete with tears—is clearly intended to be inspirational, not funny. Throughout *Glee* (and many other shows aimed at today's young people), self-belief is presented as the solution to virtually every problem.

The pervasive—and recent—focus on self-belief appears throughout mainstream American culture, not just in television shows aimed at teens (Uhls and Greenfield). The phrase "believe in yourself" appeared six times more often in American books in the 2000s than it did in the 1960s. "You are special" appeared more than thirty times more often (these analyses use the Google Books Ngram

Viewer, which allows the examination of the full text of 5 million books; see Michel et al.). The use of other individualistic words and phrases ("unique," "personalize") and individual pronouns (I, me, you) also increased significantly in American books (Twenge et al., "Increases in"; "Changes in Pronoun Use") and popular song lyrics (DeWall et al.). In contrast, words focusing on moral character and caring (e.g., "virtue," "honesty," "politeness"—Kesebir and Kesebir) and giving (Greenfield) declined over time (for example, the use of "give" declined while "get" increased).

In this chapter I document the effect of the cultural shift toward self-focus and individualism and its consequences for the state of the American Mind as embodied in youths. Individualism per se is not necessarily related to cognitive performance, intelligent dialogue, or the existence of an informed citizenry, but the specific way in which TV shows, movies, fashions, music, advertising, and goods have emphasized self-belief has resulted in a reluctance, especially among today's young generation, to focus on anything else. This research suggests a particularly disabling tendency to favor self-belief in academic ability over actual academic ability.

Because today's young generation (variously referred to as Generation Me [GenMe], GenY, and Millennials) has grown up with this culture, they are its most prominent proponents. This does not mean that we should blame them for the cultural emphasis on self-focus. They did not create the culture into which they were born and which they have absorbed. As I note in *Generation Me,* this group (born after 1980) has never known a world that emphasizes anything over the self—for instance, putting duty before gain. This generation thus reflects, even though it did not originate, the cultural shift toward self-focus. (So, I'm often asked, whose fault is it? The baby boomers? In my view, assigning fault or blame is not necessary. Cultures change, and generations reflect those changes.)

Nor is the shift toward individualism entirely negative. For example, individualism promotes tolerance and equality, arguably the most pervasive and positive cultural change of the last fifty years. For example, recent generations are more supportive of women's rights (Donnelly et al.) and more tolerant of marginalized out-groups (Twenge et al.). As with any cultural system, individualism presents a cost-benefit trade-off. Without ignoring the many benefits, however, I argue that the current flavor of American individualism has the cost of encouraging unjustified self-belief and forsaking interest in issues outside the self.

Self-Belief versus Actual Performance

Like Brittany on *Glee*, American culture now promotes the idea that self-belief is more important than actual performance. Believing that you are great is sufficient; actually learning or accomplishing something is not necessary.

Evidence for this generational shift appears in data from the American Freshman (AF) study, which has surveyed a nationally representative sample of entering college students every year since 1966 ($N = 9$ million). Students are asked to rate themselves "compared to the average person your age" on a list of attributes including "self-confidence (intellectual)," "academic ability," "writing ability," "mathematical ability," "drive to achieve," and "leadership ability." Compared to students entering college in the 1960s, recent students are much more likely to rate themselves as above average in every one of these attributes (Twenge et al.).

For example, 39 percent rated themselves as above average in intellectual self-confidence in 1966, compared to 59 percent in 2014. The percentage who believed themselves above average in writing ability rose from 30 percent to 46 percent, in academic ability from 64 percent to 71 percent, and in mathematical ability from 39 percent to 48 percent. Sixty percent believed they were above average in their drive to achieve in 1966, compared to 78 percent in 2014.

These shifts, we should note, were not due to gender or ethnicity; in fact, the demographic groups formerly underrepresented in college populations (women, Latinos, Asian Americans) rate themselves *lower* on such measures on average, a disposition that would have pushed self-ratings down, not up, with their increasing college enrollment. Changes in college selectivity cannot explain the results; more high school students go on to college now than did in 1966, so the survey respondents are a *less* select population and thus have less reason to see themselves as above average. Most crucially, objective performance has not increased. Scores on standardized tests such as the SAT and the National Assessment of Educational Progress (NAEP) exams for seventeen-year-olds and twelfth-graders are either unchanged (math) or down (verbal, writing, and reading). Meanwhile, the number of entering college students who need remedial coursework is astronomical. In the Cal State University system, for instance, fully 68 percent of the incoming freshmen test into remedial courses in English, math, or both (National Center for Public Policy and Higher Education). Thus, self-belief has increased, while actual performance has not.

Similar results for increasingly positive self-views appear among a nationally representative sample of high school students in the *Monitoring the Future* (MtF) study (Johnston et al.). In the 1976–78 period, 56 percent of twelfth-graders believed they were above average in intellectual ability; by 2010–12, that figure had jumped to 64 percent. Fifty-seven percent believed they were above average in school ability in 1976–78, compared to 61 percent in 2010–12 (Twenge and Campbell).

The percentage who believed that they were below average was about the same in the two eras, but the percentage who believed they were merely average declined (from 37 percent in 1976–78 to 29 percent in 2010–12 for intellectual ability, and from 37 percent to 32 percent for school ability).

Why are members of Generation Me more likely to think more highly of themselves despite the objective evidence? As noted above, this shift is cultural rather than simply generational. Members of GenMe did not just wake up one day and decide they were awesome. Given their rates of consumption of television, the Internet, movies, and so on, the emphasis on self-belief in popular media certainly has played a role. Another factor may have had an even more direct effect on self-beliefs in ability in academic subjects: grades, or the more subjective feedback students receive from teachers. Sure enough, 37 percent of high school seniors had an A average in 2012, nearly twice as many as in 1976 (19 percent). More than half (53 percent) of entering college students in 2014 had an A average in high school, up from 19 percent in 1966 (Twenge and Campbell). The grade inflation continues into college classes. While in the 1960s the most common grade was a C, by 2000 the most common grade was an A. Only 15 percent of college grades were As in the 1960s, compared to 42 percent in 2009 (Rojstaczer and Healy). Thus, more students are told, and probably believe, that they are in fact "A students."

Perhaps students are studying for more hours, thus justifying the higher grades. But they are not. In the AF survey, 43 percent of 2014 students said they studied for six hours a week or more during their last year in high school, compared to 47 percent in 1987 (Twenge et al., statistics updated). College students now study fewer hours, and the decline is not due to shifting majors, paid work, or computers (Babcock and Marks). Nevertheless, more students now believe they are above average in their "drive to achieve."

This decline in study time may be partially due to college students being a less select portion of their generation than in decades past. Among high school students in MtF, however, where the decline in college selectivity is not an issue, 23 percent of students said they studied ten or more hours a week in 1976, compared to 21 percent in 2012 (Twenge and Campbell). Thus, students are not receiving higher grades because they are studying more, nor because they are performing better. More than likely, students are receiving higher grades because academic culture is part of American culture, which increasingly promotes the idea that praise for mediocre performance is just as good as objectively superior performance. Another folk theory suggests praise will lead to better performance, but evidence is lacking. Most teachers go with the flow, and those few who resist the trend and stick with lower grades look like curmudgeons and suffer lower enrollments and lower student evaluations.

Narcissism, defined as an inflated sense of self, is also more prominent among more recent generations. Across three different samples, recent college students score higher on the Narcissistic Personality Inventory compared to their predecessors (Twenge and Foster). The lifetime prevalence of Narcissistic Personality Disorder is three times higher (!) among those in their twenties than those in their sixties (Stinson et al.). Interestingly, those who score high in narcissism believe they are smarter than others but actually earn lower grades in college (Robins and Beer). This mismatch may occur because they have an unrealistic view of their abilities, and their narcissism helps them overlook their inferior performance or explain it away with external causes. Grade inflation helps them do so; indeed, the lowering of standards is so widespread that it affects even those with low narcissism ratings, so that today's students may not even need to be narcissistic to develop an inflated view of their abilities. Needless to say, their overestimation prevents them from recognizing weaknesses and gaps in their formation and hinders further learning and intellectual engagement.

The disconnection arises outside the classroom as well, where self-belief and work ethic diverge and affect young people's attitudes toward jobs. Although GenMe is more likely than boomers to value money and status in a job, they are less willing to put in the work necessary to earn it. In the 2010–12 period, 39 percent of high school students in MtF said they might not get the job they wanted due to "not wanting to work hard," up from 25 percent in 1976–78. GenMe also seems more disconnected from work: 34 percent of 2010–12 students agreed that "work is just making a living," compared to 23 percent in 1976–78 (Twenge et al.). Another study found that the percentage of adult Americans who said they would work if they were independently wealthy declined significantly since the 1980s from 77 percent to 68 percent (Highhouse et al.). In sum, self-beliefs are high, and work ethic is low.

Interest in Intellectual Life

What do students value, and are those values any different from those of previous generations? Both MtF and AF ask students about their life goals and reveal further characteristics that distinguish Generation Me from prior cohorts. A consistent trend in these data is the decline in interest in abstract and intellectual concerns and the increase in practical and materialistic ones. Among the goals in AF, the largest decline over the years appears in the query "developing a meaningful philosophy of life," with 86 percent of students saying this was important in 1966, compared to 45 percent in 2014. The largest decrease in MtF life goals emerges in the prompt "finding purpose and meaning in my life" (Twenge et al.).

As for the opposite trend, the largest increase in AF is in the importance of "becoming very well-off financially" (42 percent in 1966 vs. 82 percent in 2014), while the largest increase in MtF is "being a leader in my community"—notably the item most highly correlated with narcissism in a validation sample (Twenge et al.).

The AF survey also asks about reasons students decide to go to college. The largest decrease appears in "to gain a general education and appreciation of ideas," the largest increase in "to be able to make more money."

Data from the California Psychological Inventory confirm this decline in interest in intellectual pursuits. Compared to 1980s undergraduates, undergraduates in the mid-2000s scored markedly lower on scales measuring intellectual engagement, including conceptual fluency ("deal easily with abstract and complex concepts") and achievement ("strong drive to do well"; Stewart and Kilmartin).

Civic Engagement

Perhaps intellectual interests have been replaced not by self-interest but by civic engagement. For example, many authors argue that Millennials are more interested than previous generations in helping others, becoming involved in the community, and participating in politics. The opinions and behaviors of Millennials themselves, however, do not support these views.

In both the MtF survey of high school students and the AF survey of entering college students, every item measuring civic engagement was lower among Millennials than it was among boomers in the late 1970s, including interest in social problems, interest in government, actions to help the environment, and political participation. Moreover, all but two items were lower among Millennials than they were for Generation X students in the 1980s–1990s. Concern for others showed a similar, though smaller and less consistent, downward trend (Twenge et al.). Although the trends for some of these items reversed during the recent economic recession, they did not return to the levels seen in the late 1970s (Park et al.). Another study found that Millennials were lower in empathy than boomers and GenXers (Konrath et al.), an unsurprising finding in light of Millennials' higher narcissism.

One reason Millennials have been lauded as a new civic generation is the increase in the number who perform volunteer community service during high school. But we may attribute that volunteerism not to empathy or citizenship, but to ambition, given that community service has been increasingly required for high school graduation and for admission to selective colleges over the same time period. That may explain why it is the only "concern for others" item to increase while all others decreased (Twenge et al.). Other scholars point to increased voter participation rates since 2000 and affirm in Millennials a new political consciousness. Youth voter participation in 2012, however, was 45 percent, lower than the boomers' rate in 1972 (52 percent) and GenXers' in 1992 (49 percent). Even at its highest mark, in the 2008 election, Millennial voter participation was 49 percent—hardly a sign of breakthrough civic engagement. If participation rates are averaged for each generation across all presidential election years, the numbers come out to 51 percent (boomers), 46 percent (GenX), and 48 percent (Millennials/GenMe)—in other words, not that different.

In his in-depth study of today's emerging adults, *Lost in Transition*, Christian Smith and his colleagues found that only about 4 percent were civically engaged and interested in politics. They conclude, "The idea that today's emerging adults are as a generation leading a new wave of renewed civic-mindedness and political involvement is sheer fiction. The fact that anyone ever believed that idea simply tells us how flimsy the empirical evidence that so many journalistic media stories are based upon is and how unaccountable to empirical reality high-profile journalism can be" (Smith et al.). And why are today's young people so uninterested? Smith's explanation is similar to mine: "They are so focused on their own personal lives, especially on trying to stand on their own two feet, that they seem incapable of thinking more broadly about community involvement, good citizenship, or even very modest levels of charitable giving" (Smith et al.).

In other words, we have an inverse relationship between self-focus and community/political/charitable focus. Studies from abroad show similar trends. In the 1980s, Finnish teens worried the most about global issues such as war and terrorism but when the same survey was administered to teens in 2007, most of them instead highlighted personal worries such as loneliness and finding a job (Lindfors et al.). These results mirror those from the United States perfectly, with interests becoming ever more centered on the narrow world of the self.

This is not to say that Millennials/GenMe are completely focused on their individual selves. They do care about their personal relationships with friends and family, deeply so. For most of them, however, interest in others does not extend beyond their personal circle (Smith et al.).

Conclusion

American culture has become more individualistic, imparting messages of self-esteem and personal fulfillment that overlook genuine accomplishment and disregard interests beyond immediate experience. Youths have come to maturity in this environment of self-belief and internalized its premises, setting the acquisition of self-confidence above actual learning, civic awareness, and charitable conduct. While this uncritical individualism has produced praiseworthy benefits, especially progress in equality and tolerance, it has yielded a generation of youths absorbed by personal concerns and lacking the objectivity to judge their actions and talents constructively. In this chapter I have presented abundant empirical evidence for these trends on the negative side. Given the results of standardized tests, population surveys, and time-lag studies, we cannot doubt the tendency to value self-belief over actual performance and the focus on the self to the exclusion of intellectual interests and civic engagement. And we can no longer ignore their costs, either.

Millennials/GenMe are not to "blame" for these trends, but they do embody them. Those concerned about the state of American young people are often tempted to deny these trends, claiming that acknowledging them resorts to "stereotyping." I have, indeed, been accused of much worse due to my forthright presentation of the evidence for narcissism. But there is no gainsaying the evidence here based on the opinions and behaviors of young people themselves. As a first step toward improvement, we should listen to what today's young people have to say.

Next, we need not passively accept the current state of the culture. First, we must communicate to young people that self-belief, although pleasant, does not actually lead to superior performance. On the other hand, self-control—the ability to persevere at difficult tasks—does (see, e.g., Baumeister et al.). One prime example: In the United States, the ethnic group with the lowest self-esteem is Asian Americans. Asian American children also demonstrate the best academic performance, possibly because their culture emphasizes hard work rather than self-belief. We might also propose that self-belief may actually discourage hard work, for why work hard to accomplish something if you already believe in your own superiority? Or why work hard, only to risk discovering that you cannot complete the task well, and thus face direct evidence against self-belief?

Third, we must communicate to our children and our students that intrinsic values (such as intellectual life and community feeling) are more fulfilling to human existence than extrinsic values (such as money). Research consistently finds that those who emphasize intrinsic values are happier and more mentally healthy than those who favor extrinsic values (Kasser and Ryan). In recent years, however, American culture has promoted the opposite message, and recent generations have absorbed it. Teachers, parents, journalists, foundations, and other groups and organizations that can influence youth must reiterate the value of hard work and self-criticism, functioning in a sense to dispel the false messages that youth culture purveys. Generation Me did not create this world, but they must live in it. Let us teach them how to learn and work, and with luck we may find that they will aim to change the culture and restore better values and expectations at the center of our national life.

References

Babcock, P., and M. Marks. "The Falling Time Cost of College: Evidence from Half a Century of Time Use Data." *Review of Economics and Statistics* 93 (2011): 468–78.

Baumeister, R. F., J. D. Campbell, J. I. Krueger, and K. D. Vohs. "Does High Self-Esteem Cause Better Performance, Interpersonal Success, Happiness, or Healthier Lifestyles?" *Psychological Science in the Public Interest* 4 (2003): 1–44.

DeWall, C. N., R. S. Pond, W. K. Campbell, and J. M. Twenge. "Tuning In to Psychological Change: Linguistic Markers of Psychological Traits and Emotions over Time in Popular U.S. Song Lyrics." *Psychology of Aesthetics, Creativity, and the Arts* 5 (2011): 200–207.

Donnelly, K., J. M. Twenge, and N. T. Carter. "Change over Time in Americans' Attitudes toward Women's Work and Family Roles, 1976–2013." *Psychology of Women Quarterly* (Forthcoming).

Greenfield, P. M. "The Changing Psychology of Culture from 1800 through 2000." *Psychological Science* 25 (2014): 1722–31.

Highhouse, S., M. J. Ziclar, and M. Yankelevich. "Would You Work If You Won the Lottery? Tracking Changes in the American Work Ethic." *Journal of Applied Psychology* 95 (2010): 349–57.

Johnston, L. D., J. G. Bachman, P. M. O'Malley, and J. E. Schulenberg. "Monitoring the Future: A Continuing Study of American Youth (12th-Grade Survey), 1976–2012." ICPRS25382-v2, 2013 (computer files and codebook). Ann Arbor, MI: Inter-University Consortium for Political and Social Research.

Kasser, T., and R. M. Ryan. "Further Examining the American Dream: Differential Correlates of Intrinsic and Extrinsic Goals." *Personality and Social Psychology Bulletin* 22 (1996): 280–87.

Kesebir, P., and S. Kesebir. "The Cultural Salience of Moral Character and Virtue Declined in Twentieth-Century America." *Journal of Positive Psychology* 7 (2012): 471–80.

Konrath, S. H., E. H. O'Brien, and C. Hsing. "Changes in Dispositional Empathy in American College Students over Time: A Meta-Analysis." *Personality and Social Psychology Review* 15 (2011): 180–98.

Lindfors, P., T. Solantaus, and A. Rimpela. "Fears for the Future among Finnish Adolescents in 1983–2007: From Global Concerns to Ill Health and Loneliness." *Journal of Adolescence* 35 (2012): 991–99.

Michel, J. B., S. Y. Kui, A. A. Presser, et al. "Quantitative Analysis of Millions of Digitized Books." *Science* 331 (2010): 176–82.

National Center for Public Policy and Higher Education and the Southern Regional Education Board. "Beyond the Rhetorical: Improving College Readiness through Coherent State Policy," 2010, http://www.highereducation.org/reports/college_readiness/CollegeReadiness.pdf.

Park, H., J. M. Twenge, and P. Greenfield. "The Great Recession: Implications for Adolescent Values and Behavior." *Social Psychological and Personality Science* 5 (2014): 310–18.

Robins, R. W., and J. S. Beer. "Positive Illusions about the Self: Short-Term Benefits and Long-Term Costs." *Journal of Personality and Social Psychology* 80 (2001): 340–52.

Rojstaczer, S., and C. Healy. "Where A Is Ordinary: The Evolution of American College and University Grading, 1940–2009." *Teachers College Record* 114, no. 7 (2012): 1–23.

Smith, C., K. Christoffersen, H. Davidson, and P. S. Herzog. *Lost in Transition: The Dark Side of Emerging Adulthood.* New York: Oxford University Press, 2011.

Stewart, K., and C. Kilmartin. "Connecting the Dots: The Decline in Meaningful Learning." *Journal of Faculty Development* 28, no. 2 (2014): 53–61.

Stinson, F. S., D. A. Dawson, R. B. Goldstein, S. P. Chou, et al. "Prevalence, Correlates, Disability, and Comorbidity of DSM-IV Narcissistic Personality Disorder: Results from the Wave 2 National Epidemiologic Survey on Alcohol and Related Conditions." *Journal of Clinical Psychiatry* 69 (2008): 1033–45.

Twenge, J. M. *Generation Me: Why Today's Young Americans Are More Confident, Assertive, Entitled—and More Miserable Than Ever Before.* New York: Atria Books, 2014.

Twenge, J. M., N. T. Carter and W. K. Campbell. "Time Period, Generational, and Age Differences in Tolerance for Controversial Beliefs and Lifestyles in the U. S." *Social Forces.* (Forthcoming): 1972–2012.

Twenge, J. M., S. M. Campbell, B. R. Hoffman, and C. E. Lance. "Generational Differences in Work Values: Leisure and Extrinsic Values Increasing, Social and Intrinsic Values Decreasing." *Journal of Management* 36 (2010): 1117–42.

Twenge, J. M., and W. K. Campbell. *The Narcissism Epidemic: Living in the Age of Entitlement.* New York: Atria Books, 2009.

Twenge, J. M., W. K. Campbell, and E. C. Freeman. "Generational Differences in Young Adults' Life Goals, Concern for Others, and Civic Orientation, 1966–2009." *Journal of Personality and Social Psychology* 102 (2012): 1045–62.

Twenge, J. M., W. K. Campbell, and B. Gentile. "Changes in Pronoun Use in American Books and the Rise of Individualism, 1960–2008." *Journal of Cross-Cultural Psychology* 44 (2013): 406–15.

———. "Generational Increases in Agentic Self-Evaluations among American College Students, 1966–2009." *Self and Identity* 11 (2012): 409–27.

———. "Increases in Individualistic Words and Phrases in American Books, 1960–2008." *PLoS ONE* 7 (2012): e40181.

Uhls, Y. T., and P. M. Greenfield. "The Rise of Fame: An Historical Content Analysis." *Cyberpsychology: Journal of Psychosocial Research on Cyberspace* 5 (2011), http://www.cyberpsychology.eu/view.php?cisloclanku=2011061601.

9

Has Internet-Fueled Conspiracy-Mongering Crested?

Jonathan Kay

SINCE THE PUBLICATION of my 2011 book, *Among the Truthers: A Journey through America's Growing Conspiracist Underground*, I have received many angry responses from conspiracy theorists who believe (with some justification) that I am seeking to discredit their views about the events of September 11, 2001, Barack Obama's place of birth, the medical effects of vaccines, and the true identity of Lee Harvey Oswald. In one case, a 9/11 conspiracist I described in the book, Canadian university professor Anthony J. Hall, published a seventeen-thousand-word rebuttal to my assertions, which he claims are just one small "part of a larger campaign to prevent the consolidation of conditions that might elevate the prospects for peace over the imperatives of war." Another blogger, displeased with my dismissal of *The Protocols of the Learned Elders of Zion* as a notorious fraud denounced my "vain effort" to fool "the unsuspecting gentile goyim at this state of the Zionist conspiracy." The heated moral universe in which these voices circulate makes genuine engagement impossible, the debate soon sinking into charges such as this addition by the blogger: "Kay's cunning is as blatant, transparent and distastefully disgusting as the images of the charred remains of the Palestinian corpses" (RadicalPress.com).

But I also have received sad emails—from (invariably female) spouses of (invariably male) conspiracy theorists. These correspondents have watched their mates slide down Internet rabbit holes to such depths that their relationships have broken down entirely. I have much sympathy for these people. A marriage often can survive between mates who embrace different religious faiths or political views. But it is hard to feel any sense of companionship with someone who sees dark plots everywhere he looks, and so comes to inhabit a dark and entirely separate *reality*.

In one sad story related to me, a man told me about a brother of his who recently had come out as gay. Their father was an intelligent and well-respected man, but he simply could not accept the truth of his son's sexuality. When the son declared himself a homosexual, the father obstinately denied it, instead concocting theories about how this or that group of people had conspired to lure his son into a sinful lifestyle. By the time his family members gave up on the father, he had become convinced that homosexuality and AIDS were both the result of a fiendish Jewish conspiracy to depopulate Western nations. Like almost all conspiracy theorists, this man was drawn to such plots as a tool to explain evil (as he saw it), serving him as rationalizations that made a difficult experience psychologically manageable. This pathological formula underlies the conspiracy mind-set—that is to say, that anger and paranoia often cause less psychic disruption and pain than sadness and disappointment. But having pursued a conspiratorial solution to his son's sincere and arduous declaration, he created a reality so twisted and absurd that none of the people around him could communicate constructively with him.

Such examples help explain why conspiracism becomes popular in any society that has suffered an epic, collectively felt trauma. In the aftermath, millions of people find themselves casting about for an answer to the ancient question of why bad things happen to good people. The French Revolution, World War I, the Russian Revolution, the Holocaust, and the 2008 financial crisis all provide illustrations. The assassination of JFK, in particular, recently memorialized on its fiftieth anniversary, was a huge landmark in the development of conspiracism in the United States, as surveys of the population about the event consistently show. To this day, a half century after it took place and with no further evidence of conspiracy having emerged, less than one-third of Americans nonetheless believe the Warren Commission's conclusion that the assassination was the work of a lone gunman (Gallup).

In this climate of distrust, an uncountable number of conspiracy theories have proliferated. A 2013 poll in the United States, for instance, found that 28 percent of respondents agreed with the statement that a "secretive power elite with a globalist agenda is conspiring to eventually rule the world." Fifteen percent of respondents believe media or government adds secret "mind-controlling" technology to television broadcast signals (another 15 percent said they weren't sure). And in a separate poll, 47 percent of respondents said they thought it either "very likely" or "somewhat likely" that Princess Diana was killed by some sort of conspiracy (newsPolls .org). At these rates, we can't speak of conspiracy thinking as a fringe phenomenon, nor one that has only a negligible impact on the civic sphere and cultural values.

The resultant conspiracy theories are many, and they are not confined to people's personal lives. They produce a fracturing of political discourse, a breakup in civic relations, precisely because the various camps that emerge invariably become paranoid and cultish, deeply suspicious of mainstream politics and news sources, all the while dignifying their suspicion as a higher discernment. Indeed, hostility toward mass-market media outlets and their unaware audiences often forms a central theme at many of these sites. For instance, GlobalResearch (http://www.globalresearch.ca/), a hub for left-wing conspiracy theory, solicits web surfers and financial contributions with the claim that it is "fighting the battle against mainstream media disinformation." Such ventures claim to form a digital vanguard that uses new communication technologies to bypass and expose traditional media and liberate the ignorant masses ("sheeple," as they are sometimes labeled in conspiracist parlance) from lies peddled by the old, corrupt establishment.

The theorists behind these projects tend to congregate within their own echo chambers, a process that has become much easier since the creation of the World Wide Web and the subsequent popularization of the Internet in the mid-1990s. Indeed, this echo-chamber effect extends well beyond the problem of conspiracism, as people of all strong forms of ideological commitment generally seek news media that reinforce existing opinions, a natural disposition in anyone who prefers ease over discomfort. A 2011 University of Chicago study, for instance, found that 91 percent of the visitors to the right-leaning news site humanevents.com were conservative, while at townhall.com it was 89 percent and at drudgereport.com it was 78 percent. On the other end of the spectrum, thinkprogress.org attracted visitors who are 83 percent liberal, whereas the proportion of liberals watching Fox News on cable reaches just 13 percent (Gentzkow and Shapiro).

The popularity of these outlets means that polarized attitudes, which include suspicion of the other side, are no indication of oddball status in our society. Rather, they are altogether commonplace, with the numbers to reinforce themselves and ignore pleas of moderation and civility. In some contexts, polarization and congregations of the like-minded have drawn the culture of conspiracism into the mainstream, with serious and damaging implications in regard to the advancement of knowledge and the conduct of public debate. It is impossible to discuss the problem of terrorism in any serious way, for instance, with someone who truly believes that the 9/11 attacks were an "inside job" perpetrated by George W. Bush and Dick Cheney. It is impossible to discuss macroeconomics with someone who believes that Barack Obama is scheming to bankrupt the United States and destroy capitalism (as Glenn Beck and other conservative figures have argued). It is impossible to discuss public health issues with alternative-medicine advocates who believe that the products manufactured by Big Pharma are knowingly designed to spread cancer or autism. And it is impossible to discuss the proper response to global warming with someone who believes that the whole notion of anthropogenic climate change is an invention of left-wing scientists and United Nations officials who seek to deindustrialize the planet. Once people adopt the conspiracist mind-set, they cannot accept the pluralist condition of an open society whereby beliefs and values swirl and compete in a marketplace of opinion and decisions run through a process of persuasion and policy making. Not only do they think that decision making operates underground, the panorama of public debate nothing more than a screen tactic, but they regard people who don't possess their conspiracist point of view as part of the conspiracy, whether they are aware of it or not!

The result is a balkanization of the marketplace of ideas that threatens normal political dialogue, which relies on a certain baseline quantum of consensually accepted truths. On scientific issues, for instance, politicians and policymakers typically have settled their disagreements by reference to the opinions of experts as expressed in the form of research published in peer-reviewed scientific journals. Yet the power of ideology often trumps scientific method as soon as experimental findings leave the circles of practicing scientists and enter the public domain. Many conservatives, for instance, reject peer-reviewed evidence of man-made global warming as an artifact of a corrupt and left-leaning scientific establishment. Many liberals who campaign against genetically modified foods likewise insist that scientists hide information about GMOs at the behest of big food companies. For instance, when a Harvard scientist recently challenged the Green Party of Canada's anti-GMO agenda by sending its leadership a batch of seventy peer-reviewed studies, he was dismissed with the claim that all such literature is contaminated by "ties to corporate profit" (Hopper).

These disputes exceed the ordinary disagreements of an open society. They are marked by accusations of dishonesty and attributions of malign motive. Democracy acknowledges the inevitability of clashing interests and outlooks, and it frames a process by which they may be worked through without violence and vitriol. But it presumes some starting point at which minds on all sides meet, concurring on at least a few basic values and facts. Conspiracy thinking finds no common ground with the conspirators; it can't. Any contention by those on the other side it casts as mendacious and manipulative, and so it trusts nothing others say, takes no statement or action at face value. Civil society relies on a forum of ideas and fair-minded methods to winnow truth from falsity, but conspiracism interprets everything from its adversaries as falsehood. Democracy cannot work this way.

The situation seems dark and the intensity of the conspiracists hasn't lessened, but I believe that there are signs of hope. The shrill tone of American politics during the last few years seems to have caused many Americans to become more intellectually self-aware and moderate, and one now can observe a certain backlash against conspiracist thinking. Perhaps they have noticed the civic costs of partisanship in the apparent inability of political leaders to discuss pressing issues without turning to accusation and blame games, or maybe they have grown weary of political bickering that seems to produce no improvements in the American economy, or maybe they are just bored with the theatrics of conspiracist talk. Whatever the reason, conspiracism has lost some of the appeal it possessed but a few years ago. The University of Chicago study cited above, for instance, suggests that "ideological segregation" on the Web may have peaked some time during the last decade and is now in decline, in large part thanks "to a moderation in the audience of very conservative sites" (Gentzkow and Shapiro, 1819).

Indeed, I would argue that the start date of this backlash can be identified with some precision. On April 27, 2011, Barack Obama released his Hawaii long-form birth certificate, a document indicating quite clearly that his place of birth was the Kapiolani Maternity & Gynecological Hospital in Honolulu. The release of the birth certificate received wide coverage in the American media—as did the disturbing side question of why so many Americans apparently suspected that their president was an illegal Kenyan immigrant.

From the time of Barack Obama's election in 2008, the usual self-appointed guardians of the marketplace of ideas at NPR, PBS, CNN, and the *New York Times* had been sounding the alarm about crackpot populism—as they saw it—within GOP ranks. Sarah Palin, in particular, served as a lightning rod for such criticism. By mid-2011, as the "birther" tag—like "truther," in the 9/11 conspiracism context—had entered the mainstream lexicon as a term of abuse and mockery, even establishment Republicans had become concerned with the trend, especially when they envisioned its uses in the coming presidential election. As the primaries began, in fact, not all of the leading 2012 Republican presidential candidates completely firewalled themselves from conspiracy thinking. Mitt Romney was accused of dropping hints of birtherism in his speeches, and Ron Paul gave interviews to Alex Jones, an advocate of all sorts of lurid conspiracy theories (including 9/11 trutherism). Perceiving the media as biased toward Democrats, and knowing how poorly conspiracists could look in interviews and on camera, Republican strategists came to realize that prudent political brand management meant they had to keep a safe distance from the conspiracy theorists whom many of the party's grassroots voters embraced.

This development was and remains important. Many political commentators on the left allege that the Republican Party has cheapened political discourse with its members' caustic attacks on Barack Obama—with some justification. In the reddest states, Republican candidates faced with primary challenges have felt pressured to embrace radical positions. But fearful of alienating centrist voters and having lost the 2012 contest for the White House, Republican Party leaders tend to use rhetoric that is less shrill and less conspiratorial than the views embraced by many ordinary Republican voters and Fox News commentators. Their calculations show how the discipline imposed by the need to win elections can indirectly serve to rein in conspiracism and other forms of political extremism. A somewhat similar pattern played out on the left during the term of George W. Bush, too, when Democratic activists attributed all sorts of evil machinations and Christian theocratic motives to Bush's decision to invade Iraq. Worried about letting them tar the Democratic Party with labels such as "the loony left," not to mention noting their loss in the 2004 election, party strategists likewise tried to contain their influence and promote centrist figures such as James Webb in Virginia as figureheads.

Here in Canada, the hyperenvironmentalist Green Party recently has been pressured to scrub its party platform free of fringe pseudoscience claims—including the false assertion that wi-fi signals might be dangerous to human health. In June 2013, when the Green Party posted a policy document that expressed support for homeopathy, a discredited form of "alternative medicine" that can best be described as placebo therapy, an uproar ensued and references to homeopathy disappeared from the document within days. By my observation as a journalist, the idea that computer signals harm the human body or that highly diluted homeopathic potions can treat diseases beyond the reach of conventional medicine is precisely the sort of false scientific claim that many Green Party supporters are inclined to embrace. But as the Green Party has become competitive in several ridings across Canada in recent elections, the inclusion of both forms of material in the party platform is deemed a threat to the party's expanding mainstream appeal.

I also have observed some encouraging signs in the evolution of the culture of information sharing on the Internet. The reasons that the World Wide Web has served to turbocharge conspiracism are (1) it removes the barriers to entry that formerly blocked fringe authors from wide publication, and (2) it acts to segregate ideologues and political partisans into electronic niches, where they receive a steady diet of positive feedback from other individuals who embrace identical viewpoints. But in the five years since I began writing *Among the Truthers*, I have begun to note that the average citizen is becoming more savvy about which Internet sources can be trusted and which cannot. The astonishing rise of Wikipedia, in particular, has had an extraordinarily positive effect. In my profession, journalism, Wikipedia often is the first resource that reporters turn to when researching a story; its tone is balanced, and its content tends to be rigorously fact-based. By way of example, readers might consult the Wikipedia entries on "9/11 conspiracy theories," or "Barack Obama citizenship conspiracy theories," both of which apply an informed and fair perspective to the phenomena. Students, too, use it as a starting point in their school research, and its citations lead them to authoritative sources and promising lines of inquiry. If they are curious about particular conspiracies, they can find copious, nonpartisan summaries that provide links, footnotes, and references whose tenor and rhetoric lack the feverish drama of conspiracy-theory discourse itself. Wikipedia contains errors, to be sure, and unscrupulous individuals can sometimes game the site's editing system in order to inject false material either as a joke or for propaganda purposes. But in my experience, such episodes are rare, and the cases of fraud and vandalism temporary (especially once they are brought to the attention of Wikipedia editors). As a journalist, I often use the site, though I always make a point of validating its material by double-checking the footnoted source on the material I am citing. In a decade of use, I have never once been burned. Overall, I would say that Wikipedia has probably done more to fight conspiracism than every single cultural commentator and journalist put together.

It is particularly helpful if youths encounter conspiracy thinking through Wikipedia because of the fact that conspiracism has spread conspicuously among young adults, perhaps because their respect for authority has been trending down for decades. This continues to be a problem as adolescents and twenty somethings today express a consistent lack of faith in all branches of public life, including politics, religion, and the media. At the same time, survey data show, Millennials exhibit a similar distrust for all forms of marketing messages, in part because they are bombarded by so many of them every time they go online or watch television. In 2013, the average click-through rate for ads on websites fell to about 0.2 percent, meaning only one in five hundred people click on the average ad. With current technology, however, which enables mass distribution at low cost and effort, even such a microscopic success rate might generate enough attention to promote the practice, and we may expect the avalanche of ads, offers, and other enticements only to increase. Young people are the most exposed to them, and they develop a jaded attitude toward them by the time they turn twenty. We may reasonably assume that it spills over toward all other kinds of information online that seems to have a design on their wallets and attention. Although the effect of this phenomenon is difficult to quantify in the domain of ideology and politics, it seems likely that Millennials' distrust of authority extends to alternative messaging as well, including conspiracist propaganda, which appears to them as bogus as the banners that flash on websites.

Moreover, a separate manifestation of this jaded attitude among hipster Millennials—the pervasiveness of irony culture—also likely acts as a shield against conspiracist movements. As Christy Wampole wrote in a widely cited 2012 *New York Times* op-ed,

> Before he makes any choice, [the hipster] has proceeded through several stages of self-scrutiny. The hipster is a scholar of social forms, a student of cool. . . . It stems in part from the belief that this generation has little to offer in terms of culture, that everything has already been done, or that serious commitment to any belief will eventually be subsumed by an opposing belief, rendering the first laughable at best and contemptible at worst. This kind of defensive living works as a pre-emptive surrender and takes the form of reaction rather than action.

The mind-set that Wampole describes helps insulate young adults from investing themselves in conspiracist movements, particularly because these movements have the quality of humorless intellectual cults. Conspiracists take themselves altogether seriously, never joking about their materials, and they lack the reflective distance that goes with wit and that Millennials cultivate as a generational trait. Immersing oneself in the arcana of 9/11 trutherism, for instance, turns an adherent into just the sort of dogma-spouting bore that self-aware hipsters find tedious and unfashionable. Indeed, in the youth hipster frame of mind, the very notion of "conspiracy theorist" has been reduced to a sociological *type*—such as the religious zealot, the frat boy, and the mall rat.

By way of example, consider xkcd, an award-winning artistically minimalist "geek humor" webcomic that has achieved a massive following among university-educated young adults since its creation by Randall Munroe in 2005. (At last count, it was getting 70 million hits per month, according to Munroe, a statistic I find credible given how frequently I see his comics pop up on social media.) Munroe, a computer programmer and ex-NASA robotics expert, has skewered 9/11 truthers several times, as with a classic panel called "Semi-controlled Demolition" in which a public speaker declares to his audience, "Based on my analysis, I believe the government faked the plane crash and demolished the WTC North Tower with explosives. . . . The South Tower, in a simultaneous but unrelated plot, was brought down by actual terrorists." In another cartoon, a character begins by saying, "The official story of 9-11 is full of holes. . . ." His friend replies, "Please stop, because seeing this happen to you breaks my heart." Wisely, the panel aims not at the content of the conspiracy charge, but at the character making it, stepping out of the evidence game conspiracists play so vigorously.

The less humorous realm of medicine is a more fruitful one for conspiracists, one in which the Internet allows people to spread medical conspiracy theories and pseudoscience. Doctors whom I meet regularly complain that many patients arrive in their offices with thick printouts from discredited sources, such as websites that promote the unfounded notion that vaccines cause autism. But even here, the momentum of conspiracism is waning. Many of the most notorious medical conspiracy theories of the 1990s and 2000s circulated quickly because web surfers had not yet learned how to tell truth from fiction on the Internet. But the Web is now two decades old—it has become a mature communications technology—and so almost everyone who uses it now has some awareness of the commercial scams, malware, and identity-theft schemes that have become common risks. By the same token, most users now have become more wary of outrageous-seeming political or medical claims that obscure websites offer.

The evolution of web-search technology has been part of this phenomenon. Google, the Internet's dominant web-search company, does not publicly disclose the algorithms it uses to generate search results. But there is no question that recent refinements have come to emphasize search results containing information from respectable sources, especially peer-reviewed scientific information and archived articles from mainstream media, as opposed to more sensationalist sites (even those that generate high hit counts). To some extent, this is an accidental by-product of technical changes made by Google's Penguin software upgrades, which seek to filter out or down-rank dubious commercial sites that feature questionable link profiles. Under the newest algorithm, Google drills down into a site's internal links to gauge the quantity of relevant information—a process that works to the advantage of well-stocked and well-traveled information hubs such as Wikipedia. Indeed, Google and Wikipedia form a mutually reinforcing dyad in this respect.

"Like an earthquake, 9/11 produced a great fissure through the heart of America's political center," I wrote in *Among the Truthers*, "with two increasingly polarized ideological camps sniping at one another on radio, cable TV, and blogs from either side of the divide" (xiv). That part of my book still rings true to me. Indeed, I am writing these words in late 2013, with the United States teetering on the brink of credit default thanks to the mutually irreconcilable political visions of its two major parties. Yet at least the men and women in Washington are arguing about dollars and cents, programs and policies (Obamacare, in particular). We have not yet degenerated into the dystopia, described in my book, in which political discourse shuts down because both sides are locked in otherworldly conspiracist universes of their own creation.

For the reasons I have described in this essay, most politicians and ordinary citizens have checked themselves before falling into this collective rabbit hole. Whatever one's political affiliation, that counts as good news.

References

Gallup. "Majority in U.S. Still Believe JFK Killed in a Conspiracy," November 15, 2013, http://www.gallup.com/poll/165893/majority-believe-jfk-killed-conspiracy.aspx.

Gentzkow, Matthew, and Jesse M. Shapiro. "Ideological Segregation Online and Offline." *Quarterly Journal of Economics* 126 (2011): 1799–839.

Hall, Anthony J. "The Sacred Myth of 9/11 as Propaganda for Aggressive War." COTO Report, May 27, 2011, http://coto2.wordpress.com/2011/05/27/the-sacred-myth-of-911-as-propaganda-for-aggressive-war/.

Hopper, Tristin. "Elizabeth May's Party of Science Seems to Support a Lot of Unscientific Public Policies." *National Post*, November 15, 2013.

Kay, Jonathan. *Among the Truthers: A Journey through America's Growing Conspiracist Underground.* New York: HarperCollins, 2011.

newsPolls.org. "Survey: SHOH33," http://newspolls.org/surveys/shoh33/19264.

RadicalPress.com. "Counter Force: Deconstructing Jonathan Kay's Lies Regard ing the Design of the Protocols," May 12, 2011, http://www.radicalpress.com/?p=1309.

Wampole, Christy. "How to Live without Irony." *New York Times*, November 17, 2012.

xkcd. "Semicontrolled Demolition," http://xkcd.com/690/.

Part Three

★ ★ ★ ★ ★ ★ ★ ★ ★ ★ ★ ★ ★ ★ ★ ★ ★

National Consequences

★ ★ ★ ★ ★ ★ ★ ★ ★ ★ ★ ★ ★ ★ ★ ★ ★

10

Dependency in America

AMERICAN EXCEPTIONALISM AND THE ENTITLEMENT STATE

Nicholas Eberstadt

EVERY AFFLUENT Western democracy today maintains an expansive social welfare apparatus, but these constructs did not emerge spontaneously, everywhere and all at once. From a historical perspective, the origins of the modern welfare state are quite specifically European. And since its pedigree is basically European, the architecture for the welfare state naturally was designed with European realities in mind.

Perhaps the most important of these realities was the pervasive belief that ordinary people in Europe in poverty or need were effectively stuck in it—and through no fault of their own, but rather on account of the Old World's class barriers and attendant lack of opportunity. From the earliest days of the American experiment, however, people in the New World exhibited strikingly different views on poverty and social welfare. To the American Mind, poverty could never be regarded as a permanent condition for any stratum of society, given the possibilities for individual self-advancement across that vast continent. Self-reliance and personal initiative were, in this way of thinking, the critical factors in staying out of need. Generosity was a part of that ethos; the impulse to lend a hand to neighbors in need was ingrained in the immigrant and the settler tradition. But a strong underlying streak of Puritanism parsed the needy into two categories: the deserving and the undeserving poor. To assist the former, the American prescription was community-based charity mostly from "voluntary associations." The latter—men and women judged responsible for their own dire circumstances due to laziness, drink, or other signs of flawed character—were seen as needing assistance in "changing their ways." In either case, charitable aid was a temporary intervention to help good people through a bad spell; long-term dependence upon handouts was "pauperism," an odious condition no self-respecting American would accept.

The American mythos, in short, offered less than fertile soil for cultivating a modern welfare state. This is not to say that the American myth of unlimited opportunity for the rugged individualist always conformed to facts on the ground. That myth rang hollow for many Americans, of course, but it was generally received that the nation displayed an enduring aversion to the trappings of the welfare state. Note, for example, that the share of U.S. national output devoted to public welfare spending (pensions, unemployment, health, and all the rest) not only failed to rise, but apparently declined, over the first three decades of the twentieth century—and that the ratio of government social outlays to GDP in America looks actually to have been *lower* in 1930 than it was in 1890 (U.S. Census Bureau, *Historical Statistics of the United States*). Recall as well that some twenty-six European and Latin American countries already had put in place nationwide "social insurance" systems for old-age pensions by 1935, when the United States came to pass the Social Security Act, our first federal legislation providing public benefits for the general population (Social Security Administration).

U.S. hesitance in embracing the welfare state continued well after the Depression. In the early 1960s, the welfare state was not dramatically larger than it had been under FDR. In 1961, total U.S. government entitlement transfers to individual recipients accounted for a little less than 5 percent of GDP—as against 2.5 percent of GDP in 1931, right before the start of the New Deal. In 1963 these transfers accounted for about 6 percent of total personal income in America, as against a bit over 4 percent in 1936 (derived from U.S. Bureau of Economic Research NIPA data—see Fishback)

During the 1960s, however, America's allergy to the welfare state collapsed. Three and a half centuries of the self-reliant mentality gave way to a state-dependent mentality and a government bent on reinforcing it, providing care and resources to all the poor and thereby acknowledging (or, to some critics, creating) the dependency mind-set of a significant portion of the citizenry. The "War on Poverty" (declared by President Lyndon Johnson in 1964) and the "Great Society" pledge (1965) ushered in a new era for America, in which Washington finally commenced in earnest to build a massive welfare state. In the decades that followed, America not only expanded provision for current or past workers who qualified for benefits under existing "social insurance" arrangements (retirement, unemployment, disability) but also inaugurated a separate panoply of programs for "income maintenance" (food stamps, housing subsidies, Supplemental Social Security Insurance) where eligibility turned not on work history but officially designated "poverty" status, as well as health-care guarantees for former workers and the officially poor (Medicare, Medicaid, etc.). In other words, Americans could claim economic benefits from the government simply by dint of being citizens; they were now incontestably *entitled* to some measure of transferred public bounty under law.

The expansion of the American welfare state remains a work in progress. The latest addition to that edifice is "Obamacare" (the Affordable Care Act). Compared to some of its European counterparts, the U.S. welfare state may look modest in scope, but nonetheless the remarkable growth of the entitlement state has transformed the American government and the American way of life itself. It is not too much to call those changes revolutionary.

The impact on the federal government has been astounding. In 1963, less than one federal dollar in four (24%) was accounted for by official transfers of money, goods, and services to individual recipients under social welfare programs. By 2013, roughly three out of every five (59%) federal dollars were allocated to entitlement transfers. This tally, incidentally, excludes the considerable bureaucratic costs of overseeing these various transfer programs. Federal politics are now in the main the politics of entitlement programs: activities neither authorized nor even mentioned in the Constitution and its Amendments.

Scarcely less revolutionary has been the remolding of daily life for ordinary Americans. Over the half century between 1963 and 2013, entitlement transfers were the fastest-growing source of personal income in America—registering almost twice the growth rate of real per-capita personal income from all other sources. In 1963, these transfers accounted for less than one dollar out of fifteen in overall personal income for the United States; by 2013 they accounted for more than one dollar out of every six.

This explosion of entitlement outlays was accompanied by a corresponding surge in the number of Americans who would routinely apply for such government benefits. Despite episodic attempts in Washington to limit the growth of the welfare state, as under the Reagan administration, or occasional assurances from Washington that "the era of big government is over," as under the Clinton administration, the pool of entitlement beneficiaries has apparently grown almost ceaselessly. The qualifier "apparently" is necessary because the U.S. government did not actually begin systematically tracking the demographics of America's "program participation" until a generation ago. Such data as are available, however, depict a sea change over the past thirty years.

By 2011—the most recent year for such figures at this writing—Census Bureau estimates indicated that just over 150 million Americans, or a little more than 49 percent of our population, lived in homes that obtained one or more entitlement benefits. Since underreporting of government transfers is characteristic for survey respondents, this likely means that America has already passed the symbolic threshold where a majority of the population is accepting welfare state transfers (Wheaton).

Between 1983 and 2011, by Census Bureau estimates, the percentage of Americans "participating" in entitlement programs jumped by nearly 20 percentage points. One might at first assume this upsurge in recipience was largely a consequence of the graying

Entitlement Dependence in America, 1983 vs. 2011

Recipiency Status and Program	Third Quarter 1983	Third Quarter 2011	Difference, 2011 vs. 1983
	Number in Millions (Percent)	Number in Millions (Percent)	Number in Millions (Percentage point change)
All people	224.3 (100.0)	306.2 (100.00)	81.9 (—)
Received benefits from one or more programs	66.5 (29.6)	150.6 (49.2)	84.1 (19.6)
Social Security	31.7 (14.1)	49.8 (16.3)	18.1 (2.2)
Medicare	26.7 (11.9)	45.9 (15.0)	19.2 (3.1)
One or more means-tested programs (1)	42.1 (18.8)	108.2 (35.3)	66.1 (16.5)
Federal Supplemental Security Income (SSI)	3.2 (1.4)	20.2 (6.6)	17.0 (5.2)
Food stamps (2)	18.7 (8.3)	49.6 (16.2)	30.9 (7.9)
AFDC (3)	9.3 (4.2)	6.1 (2.0)	−3.2 (−2.2)
Women, Infants, and Children (WIC)	2.4 (1.1)	23.2 (7.6)	20.8 (6.5)
Medicaid	17.5 (7.8)	82.2 (26.8)	64.7 (19.0)

MEMORANDUM ITEM: Annual National Statistics on	1983	2011	Difference 2011 vs. 1983
—Unemployment Rate (%)	9.6	8.9	−0.7
—Poverty Rate (%)	15.2	15.0	−0.2
—Median Household Income (2012 $)	45,760	51,100	5,340

(1) Includes free or reduced-price lunch or breakfast, energy assistance, not shown separately.

(2) Now known as the Supplemental Nutrition Assistance Program or SNAP.

(3) Now known as the Temporary Assistance for Needy Families (TANF)

Note: Details may not sum to totals because of rounding, because not all categories are shown, and because people may receive benefits from more than one program.

Source: U.S. Census Bureau, Current Population Reports, Series P-70, No. 1 Economic Characteristics of Households in the United States: Third Quarter 1983, U.S. Government Printing Office, Washington, D.C., 1984, available at: http://www.census.gov/sipp/p70-1.pdf, Table C; U.S. Census Bureau, Survey of Income and Program Participation, Waves 9, 10, and 11, 2008 Panel, July–September 2011. For information on sampling and non-sampling error see: http://www.census.gov/sipp/sourceac/S&A08_W1toW9(S&A-14).pdf; Poverty and Income data: DeNavas-Walt, Carmen, Bernadette D. Proctor, and Jessica C Smith, U.S. Census Bureau, Current Population Reports, P60-245, Income, Poverty, and Health Insurance Coverage in the United States: 2012, U.S. Government Printing Office, Washington, DC, 2013, available at: http://www.census.gov/prod/2013pubs/p60-245.pdf; Unemployment: Bureau of Labor Statistics, Department of Labor, "Labor Force Statistics from the Current Population Survey: Unemployment Rate (LNU04000000)" Washington, DC, accessed February 5, 2014.

of the population, and consequently of the increase in beneficiaries of Social Security and Medicare, programs for older Americans. Such a surmise, however, would be very wrong. Over the period in question, the percentage of Americans in homes receiving Social Security payments increased by only a little over two percentage points—and by just over three points for those in households availing themselves of Medicare. Less than one-sixth of that twenty-point jump could be attributed to increased reliance on those two "old age" programs.

Overwhelmingly, the growth of the recipience in modern America has stemmed from the extraordinary rise of "means-tested" entitlements—also sometimes known as "antipoverty programs," since the criterion for eligibility is an income below some designated multiple of the officially calculated "poverty" threshold.

By late 2011, over 108 million Americans were in homes that obtained one or more such benefits—over twice as many as for either Social Security or Medicare. The population of what we might call "means-tested America" was more than two-and-a-half times as large in 2011 as it had been in 1983. Over those intervening years, total U.S. population grew by 82 million, but the means-tested American population rose by 66 million—an astonishing trajectory, implying a growth of the means-tested population of 80 persons for each 100-person increase in national population over that interval. Put another way, the total number of Americans *not* accepting means-tested benefits was smaller in 2011 than in 1983.

Over the same period, the rolls of claimants receiving "food stamps" (officially renamed in 2008 because of the stigma that phrase had acquired) jumped by more than 30 million, to one American in six. The ranks of Medicaid, the means-tested national health-care program, soared by almost 65 million, to more than one American in four. Supplemental Security Income (SSI), a program originally intended for the disabled poor, likewise swelled. Between 1983 and 2011, the number of Americans in federal SSI homes more than sextupled; by 2011, over 20 million people were counted as dependents on the program.

All in all, over 35 percent of Americans were taking home at least some benefits from means-tested programs by 2011—nearly twice the share back in 1983, even though the annual poverty rate was almost identical for those years. By 2011, indeed, there was no longer any readily observable correspondence between the officially designated condition of poverty and the recipience of "antipoverty" entitlements. In that year, over twice as many people were taking home means-tested benefits as lived below the poverty line—meaning a decisive majority of recipients of such aid were the nonpoor. By 2011, roughly one in four Americans above the poverty line were receiving one or more means-tested benefits.

★ ★ ★

America today is the richest society in history, and more prosperous and productive now than three decades ago, yet our entitlement state behaves as if Americans have never been more needy. The paradox signals how dependency is a mental condition, one that distorts the facts in order to sustain itself. The paradox is easily explained: means-tested entitlement transfers are no longer an instrument for strictly addressing absolute poverty, but instead a device for a more general redistribution of resources.

I risk belaboring the obvious by observing that today's existing American entitlement state, and the habits—including habits of mind—that it engenders, do not coexist easily with the values and principles subsumed under the shorthand of "American exceptionalism." Especially subversive of that ethos, we might argue, are unconditional and indefinite guarantees of means-tested public largesse.

The corrosive nature of mass dependence on entitlements is evident from the nature of pathologies closely associated with its spread. Two of the most pernicious of them are so tightly intertwined as to be inseparable: the breakdown of the American family structure and the flight from work by working-age men.

Between the launch of the "War on Poverty" in 1964 and 2012, the percentage of U.S. children born outside of marriage has gone from 7 percent to nearly 41 percent (National Center for Health Statistics; Hamilton et al.)—with nearly a quarter of all American children under age eighteen living with a lone mother (U.S. Census Bureau, "Family and Living Arrangements"). As for men of parenting age, between 1964 and early 2014, the fraction of men twenty-five to thirty-four years old who were neither working nor looking for work roughly quadrupled: from less than 3 percent to more than 11 percent. In 1965, fewer than 5 percent of men forty-five to fifty-four years old were totally out of the workforce; by early 2014 the fraction was almost 15 percent (Bureau of Labor Statistics). To judge by mortality statistics, American men have never been healthier than they are today, yet they are less committed to working than at any previous point in our nation's history.

We cannot assert as settled fact that the entitlement state is responsible for these trends, but we can say with certainty that the rise of the entitlement state has coincided with them, that it has abetted them, and that its interventions have served to finance and underwrite these developments. For a great many women and children in America, the entitlement state is now the breadwinner in the family.

Changes in popular mores and norms are less easily and precisely tracked than changes in behavior, but we may nevertheless identify some of the ways the entitlements revolution may be shaping the contemporary American Mind.

To begin: The rise of long-term entitlement dependence undermines general belief in the notion that everyone can succeed in America, no matter one's station at birth. At the same time, the traits of personal ambition and hunger for success that domestic and foreign observers have long taken to be distinctively American are now confronted by an unprecedented challenge: a means-based welfare state whose incentive structure invites citizens to accept grants awarded solely on the criterion of demonstrated personal or familial financial failure. The differentiation between the "deserving" and "undeserving" poor is disappearing.

More broadly, the modern politics of entitlement subvert the use of stigma and opprobrium to condition the behavior of beneficiaries, even when the behavior is plainly irresponsible or destructive. For a growing number of Americans—especially younger Americans—the very notion of "shaming" recipients for their personal conduct is regarded as inappropriate, if not patently offensive. A "judgment-free" attitude toward the official provision of social support, one that takes personal responsibility off the table, marks a fundamental break with the past on this basic American precept about civic life and civic duty.

Finally comes the relation between entitlements and middle-class mentality. By the American national myth, anyone can be included in the country's middle class—regardless of income or background. Yet while low incomes, limited education, and other material constraints have not prevented generations of Americans from entertaining middle-class aspirations or entering the middle class itself, the same cannot be said of constraints emanating from the mind. Can members in good standing of the American middle class really maintain that self-conception, while simultaneously taking needs-based government benefits that symbolically brand them and their family as wards of the state?

The qualities celebrated under the banner of American exceptionalism are in poorer repair than at any time in our nation's history. Our political leadership, for its part, has no stomach for taking the lead in weaning the nation from entitlement dependence: apart from resistance by an honorable few, collusive bipartisan support for an ever larger welfare state is the central fact of politics in our nation's capital today. Until and unless America undergoes some sort of awakening that turns the public against its blandishments, or some sort of forcing financial crisis that suddenly restricts the resources available to it, continued growth of the entitlement state looks very much like a foregone conclusion in the years immediately ahead.

References

Bureau of Labor Statistics. Labor Force Statistics from the Current Population Survey query tool, http://data.bls.gov/pdq/querytool.jsp?survey=ln.

Fishback, Price V. "Social Welfare Expenditures in the United States and the Nordic Countries, 1900–2003." National Bureau of Economic Research, Working Paper no. 15982, May 2010, http://www.nber.org/papers/w15982.pdf?new_window=1.

Hamilton, Brady E., et al. "National Vital Statistics Reports." Center for Disease Control, 2013, http://www.cdc.gov/nchs/data/nvsr/nvsr62/nvsr62_03.pdf.

National Center for Health Statistics. "Trends in Illegitimacy, United States—1940–1965," 1968, http://www.cdc.gov/nchs/data/series/sr_21/sr21_015.pdf.

Social Security Administration. "Social Security History," Table 2, Social Security Programs Abroad by Country, Pre-1935, http://www.ssa.gov/history/pre1935table2.html.

U.S. Bureau of Economic Analysis. National Income and Product Accounts (NIPAs), http://www.bea.gov/national/Index.htm.

U.S. Census Bureau, "Family and Living Arrangements Tables CH-1," https://www.census.gov/hhes/families/data/children.html.

———. "Historical Statistics of the United States," 1975, http://www2.census.gov/prod2/statcomp/documents/CT1970p2-01.pdf.

Wheaton, Laura. "Underreporting of Means-Tested Programs in the CPS and SIPP." Urban Institute, http://www.urban.org/UploadedPDF/411613_transfer_programs.pdf.

11

Political Ignorance in America

Ilya Somin

THE SPECTER OF political ignorance hangs over American democracy, undermining a system of government that is supposed to epitomize the rule of the people. If the people often do not know what government is doing or what its effects are, it is far from clear that the people can rule in any meaningful or effective way.

The problem of political ignorance is not a new one. It was a major concern of the Founding Fathers and the focus of debates over democracy going all the way back to ancient Greece (Roberts). James Madison warned that "a popular government without popular information, or the means of acquiring it, is but a Prologue to a Farce or a Tragedy; or perhaps both" (Madison, 790). Survey data suggest that current levels of political knowledge—while low—are roughly comparable to those of fifty or sixty years ago. In that sense, public ignorance is no worse today than in the past. But the problem has become more severe in at least one important respect. The size and complexity of government have grown significantly in recent decades, making it more difficult for voters with limited knowledge to monitor and evaluate the government's many activities. The result is a polity in which the people often cannot exercise their sovereignty responsibly and effectively.

In this essay I survey the extent, causes, and possible solutions for widespread political ignorance. Unfortunately, there is no easy antidote, and significant increases in political knowledge will not likely happen any time soon. But we can mitigate the problem by limiting and decentralizing government—thereby enabling people to make more of their decisions in the private sector, or by choosing between competing state and local governments. In these settings, as we shall see, people have much stronger incentives to acquire relevant information and use it wisely than when they act as voters.

The Extent of Political Ignorance

The low level of political knowledge in the American electorate is one of the best-established findings in social science. Since the start of modern public opinion polling in the 1930s, survey researchers have consistently found that most of the public has only a very limited knowledge of politics and government (Della Carpini and Keeter; Althaus; Shenkman). A few recent examples illustrate the point. President Barack Obama's 2010 health-care bill has been one of the most controversial issues in recent American politics. Yet an August 2013 poll found that 44 percent of the public did not even realize it is still the law (Kaiser Family Foundation). If people were asked what the bill actually says in its many hundreds of pages, we may be sure, knowledge levels would be far lower. The fiscal crisis looming over the federal government is another serious issue facing the nation—and a constant focus of public debate. But most of the public has very little idea of how federal spending is actually distributed. They greatly underestimate the percentage that goes to entitlement programs such as Medicare and Social Security (one of the largest items in the federal budget), and they vastly overestimate that spent on foreign aid (only about 1 percent of federal spending—see Bialik). Some two-thirds underestimate the percentage of federal spending that goes to Medicare, Medicaid, and Social Security; one 2010 survey found that, on average, Americans overestimate the amount of spending on foreign aid by a factor of twenty-five (Bialik).

Public ignorance also extends to the basic structure of government. A 2006 poll found that only 42 percent can even name the three branches of the federal government: the executive, the legislative, and the judicial. (Somin) There is also much ignorance and confusion about the crucial question of which government officials are responsible for which programs and issues. As a result, voters often reward and punish incumbents for events they did not cause—particularly short-term economic trends—while ignoring some of those for which they bear genuine responsibility. Political philosophers dispute the amount of political knowledge voters need to have in order to participate in politics effectively, a debate that extends all the way back to ancient Greece, where Plato, Aristotle, and others disagreed over this very issue. Modern political theorists have developed several distinct theories of democratic participation, some of which implicitly require far greater political knowledge than others (Somin; Kelley). Voter-knowledge levels clearly fall short of the more demanding versions of democratic theory, such as deliberative democracy, which requires the public to engage in sophisticated and unbiased deliberation about political issues. But current levels also undershoot the requirements of more modest theories, such as the idea that voters need only know enough to reward good performance by incumbent officials and punish them at the polls when things go badly (Somin).

The enormous size and scope of modern government exacerbate the problem of political ignorance. In the United States today, government spending accounts for close to 40 percent of GDP; that figure does not include many other government policies that function through regulation of the private sector. The vast network of agencies, programs, offices, and departments often makes government impenetrable to even the most dedicated voters. Even if voters followed political issues more closely than most do, they still could not effectively monitor more than a small fraction of the activities of the modern state.

Some argue that voters have a right to make decisions in any way they choose, because casting a ballot is simply an exercise of individual freedom or of the majority's inherent right to rule. John Stuart Mill effectively refuted such claims in his 1861 book *Considerations on Representative Government*, where he pointed out that "the suffrage" is not an individual "right" that the voter is entitled to wield "for his particular use and benefit," but rather a "public trust" that involves the exercise of "power over others" (Mill, 154–55; for a modern elaboration on Mill, see Brennan). When we elect government officials based on ignorance, they rule over not only those who voted for them but all of society. When we exercise power over other people, we have a moral obligation to do so in at least a reasonably informed way. Moreover, in a democratic society, majority public opinion often has a major impact on government policy. If the majority is poorly informed or does a poor job of evaluating the information they do know, the consequences often include terribly harmful, unjust, and counterproductive policies.

Rational Ignorance and Rational Irrationality

Widespread ignorance is not the result of stupidity or lack of availability of information. It has persisted despite the fact that the Internet, cable television news, and other modern technology have made basic political information more readily available than ever. It has also been largely unaffected by substantial increases in American IQ scores over the last several decades (Flynn). Measured adult intelligence on the Information subtest of the Weschler Adult Intelligence Scale rose 8.4 points between 1950 and 2004, while Vocabulary gains were even greater (17 points). Both scores are relevant to understanding political information, since sophisticated vocabulary is useful in understanding complex texts discussing policy issues.

For most people, political ignorance is actually rational behavior. If your only incentive to follow politics is to be a better voter, that turns out not to be much of an incentive at all, because there is so little chance that your vote will actually make a difference to the outcome of an election: about 1 in 60 million in a presidential contest, for instance (Gelman et al.). For most people, it is rational to devote little time to learning about politics, and instead to focus on other activities that are more interesting or more useful. As former British prime minister Tony Blair puts it, "Most people, most of the time, don't give politics a first thought all day long. Or if they do, it is with a sigh . . . before going back to worrying about the kids, the parents, the mortgage, the boss, their friends . . . sex and rock 'n' roll" (70–71). Few voters precisely calculate the odds that their ballot will make a difference. But they do have an intuitive sense that the likelihood is small, and act accordingly. Such people are "rationally ignorant" (for the first formulation of rational political ignorance, see Downs).

Obviously, some Americans learn political information for reasons other than becoming better voters. Just as sports fans love to follow their favorite teams even though they can't influence the outcomes of games, "political fans" enjoy following political issues and cheering on their favorite candidates, parties, or ideologies (see Somin for a discussion of parallels between sports fans and political fans). There is nothing necessarily wrong with being a political fan. But when people seek out information for the purpose of enhancing the fan experience, that objective is often at odds with the goal of seeking out the truth. Like sports fans, political fans tend to evaluate new information in a similarly biased way. They overvalue anything that supports the position of their political "team" and undervalue or ignore new data that cut against it. A classic 1954 study of sports fans watching a football game found that people overestimate the number of penalties committed by the opposing team and underestimate those committed by their own (Hastorf and Cantril; for further discussion, see Somin). Moreover, those most interested in political issues are also particularly prone to discuss it only with others who agree with their views and tend to follow politics only through like-minded media (Somin).

Such behavior is highly illogical if the goal is truth seeking. A truth-seeker should make a special effort to consider opposing viewpoints. But it makes perfect sense if the goal is not so much truth as it is enhancing the political fan experience. Economist Bryan Caplan calls this kind of behavior "rational irrationality": when the goal of acquiring information is something other than truth seeking, it is often rational to be highly biased in the way you evaluate what you learn (Caplan).

The combination of rational ignorance and rational irrationality severely undermine the quality of democratic decision making. The vast majority of the electorate is rationally ignorant. Among the relatively knowledgeable minority, many are political fans who do a poor job of evaluating the information they have because of partisan or ideological bias.

Why Political Ignorance Is Difficult to Overcome

Some scholars argue that voters do not need to know much about politics and government because they can rely on "information shortcuts" to make good decisions. Shortcuts are small bits of information that we can use as proxies for larger bodies of knowledge of which we may be ignorant (Somin). Rationally ignorant voters understandably use shortcuts to make political decisions, because they have little time to devote to studying policy issues in detail.

Perhaps the most popular shortcut is "retrospective voting": the idea that voters don't need to follow the details of policy but only need to know whether things are going well or badly. If things are looking up—if the economy is improving, for example—they can reward the incumbents at election time. If not, they can "vote the bums out."

Unfortunately, effective retrospective voting requires greater knowledge than most voters actually have. In order to reward or punish incumbents for their performance, voters need to know what events the incumbents actually caused and which ones were beyond their control. Studies show that voters repeatedly reward and punish political leaders for events over which they have little control. Most national electoral outcomes are primarily determined by short-term economic trends, despite the fact that incumbents have little influence over them. Incumbents also often get the credit or blame for such things as droughts, shark attacks, and victories by local sports teams (Somin).

The other major shortcoming of shortcuts is that voters often choose them for reasons other than their utility for getting at the truth. For example, some scholars argue that "opinion leaders" are useful shortcuts. Instead of learning about government policy themselves, voters can follow the directions of opinion leaders who share similar values but who know more than the voters themselves. Unfortunately, if we look at the most popular opinion leaders, most of them are not people notable for their impressive and objective knowledge of public policy issues. They are people like Rush Limbaugh and Jon Stewart, whose main asset is their skill at entertaining their audience and validating its preexisting biases. Relying on such opinion leaders is another example of rational irrationality at work. Other information shortcuts have similar flaws, including reliance on party identification and voting based on knowledge acquired through everyday life.

If political ignorance is widespread and shortcuts do relatively little to alleviate it, perhaps the solution is to increase political knowledge. The most obvious way to do so is through education. Unfortunately, political knowledge levels have increased very little over the last fifty to sixty years, even as educational attainment has risen enormously (Nie). The failure of public education to increase political knowledge may be connected with its failure to achieve improvements in student achievement in other subjects such as English, science, and mathematics, despite massive increases in per-pupil expenditures over the last forty years (Hanushek).

Perhaps a better curriculum might ensure that high school students don't graduate without learning basic political and historical knowledge, as many currently do. The difficulty here is that governments have little incentive to ensure that public schools really do adopt curricula that increase political knowledge. To the contrary, political leaders who owe their positions to a largely ignorant electorate may be reluctant to endanger those positions by increasing political knowledge. Historically, governments have tended to use public education to indoctrinate students in their preferred ideologies (or those advocated by influential interest groups), rather than increase political knowledge in an evenhanded way. Indeed, indoctrination was one of the main motives for the initial establishment of public education in both the United States, where the goal was to indoctrinate mostly Catholic immigrants in Protestant values, and Europe, where governments used it to inculcate nationalism (for a discussion of the relevant history and political incentives, see Somin).

Political incentives could change if the voters carefully monitored education policy and rewarded elected officials for using public schools to increase political knowledge. But if the voters were that knowledgeable, we would not have a political ignorance problem.

Informational Advantages of Foot Voting

The problem of political ignorance has no easy solution. But we can help alleviate its worst consequences by making more decisions through voting with our feet and fewer decisions through voting at the ballot box. People can vote with their feet in two ways. The first is in the private sector, by choosing which products to buy or which civil society organizations to join, such as churches and clubs. The other is choosing what state or local government to live under in a federal system—a decision often influenced by the quality of those jurisdictions' public policies.

Both types of foot voting have important informational advantages over ballot-box voting. Most people probably spend more time and effort acquiring information to decide which car or TV to buy than which candidates to support for president. That isn't because they believe that a car or a TV is more important than the presidency or more complicated than the issue at stake in a presidential election. The reason is that when they choose a TV, they know that the decision is likely to make a difference.

The key difference between foot voting and ballot-box voting is that foot voters don't have the same incentive to be rationally ignorant as ballot-box voters do. To the contrary, they have strong incentives to seek out useful information. They also have stronger incentives to evaluate objectively what they do learn.

Unlike political fans, foot voters know they will pay a real price in lost money, bad schools for their kids, or weak career prospects if they do a poor job of assessing the information they collect. Consider how many people react to those who point out logical or factual errors in their political views. Usually, they express anger or frustration, treating the other person not as a bearer of useful information but as an irritating or hostile presence. Rarely will they thank the critic for helping them to see the truth. That social norms frown on arguing about politics in politically mixed company is no accident. By contrast, people are usually more open-minded when presented with new information relevant to a foot-voting decision. If you point out to acquaintances that they are passing up a good deal on a car or a TV, or that they might be happier living in a different town, you are likely to get a more positive reaction than if you criticize their choices at the ballot box. For most of us, having our political views attacked is psychological pain with little prospect of gain. But information that improves our foot-voting decisions is much more useful, and therefore we are more willing to put up with criticism of our views on such matters.

Foot voters certainly make their share of mistakes, but on average they do a better job than ballot-box voters do. Historically, foot voters have often acquired and successfully used information even under highly adverse conditions. For example, millions of poorly educated African Americans in the early twentieth-century Jim Crow South managed to figure out that conditions were relatively less oppressive in the North (and also in some parts of the South compared to others), and they migrated accordingly. Foot voting did not solve all the problems of oppressed African Americans in the Jim Crow era, of course. Perhaps nothing could in a society as racist as the early twentieth-century United States. But foot voting did significantly improve their situation compared to what it would have been otherwise, and their actions are an important example of how foot voters can acquire and make use of information even under highly unfavorable conditions (Somin).

Conclusion

The informational advantages of foot voting over ballot-box voting strengthen the case for limiting and decentralizing government. People make better decisions when they have stronger incentives to acquire relevant information and evaluate it in an unbiased way. The more decentralized government is, the more issues can be decided through foot voting. It is much easier to vote with your feet against a local government than a state government (except, perhaps, in a very small state), and much easier to do it against a state than against the federal government.

Foot voting is also usually much easier in the private sector than the public. A given region is likely to have far more private firms and civil society organizations than local governments. We can switch cable providers or enroll our children in a new private school without moving at all.

Political ignorance is far from the only factor that must be considered in deciding the appropriate size, scope, and centralization of government. Some large-scale issues, such as global warming, are simply too big for lower-level governments to address effectively. But the informational advantages of foot voting should lead us to limit and decentralize government more than we might otherwise. At the very least, the problem of political ignorance should play a much larger role in debates over the role of government in society than it has so far.

References

Althaus, Scott L. *Collective Preferences in Democratic Politics*. New York: Cambridge University Press, 2003.

Bialik, Carl. "Americans Stumble on Math of Big Issues." *Wall Street Journal*, January 7, 2012.

Blair, Tony. *A Journey: My Political Life*. New York: Alfred A. Knopf, 2010.

Brennan, Jason. *The Ethics of Voting*. Princeton, NJ: Princeton University Press, 2011.

Caplan, Bryan. *The Myth of the Rational Voter: Why Democracies Choose Bad Policies*. Princeton, NJ: Princeton University Press, 2007.

Delli Carpini, Michael X., and Scott Keeter. *What Americans Know about Politics and Why It Matters*. New Haven, CT: Yale University Press, 1996.

Downs, Anthony. *An Economic Theory of Democracy*. New York: Harper & Row, 1957.

Flynn, James R. *Are We Getting Smarter? Rising IQ in the 21st Century*. Cambridge: Cambridge University Press, 2012.

Gelman, Andrew, Nate Silver, and Aaron Edlin. "What Is the Probability That Your Vote Will Make a Difference?" *Economic Inquiry* 50 (2012): 321–26.

Hanushek, Eric. *Schoolhouses, Courthouses, and Statehouses: The Funding Achievement Puzzle in America's Public Schools*. Princeton, NJ: Princeton University Press, 2009.

Hastorf, Albert H., and Hadley Cantril. "They Saw a Game: A Case Study." *Journal of Abnormal Psychology* 49 (1954): 129–34.

Kaiser Family Foundation. "Kaiser Health Tracking Poll: August 2013," http://kff.org/health-reform/poll-finding/kaiser-health-tracking-poll-august-2013/.

Kelley, Jamie Terence. *Framing Democracy: A Behavioral Approach to Democratic Theory.* Princeton, NJ: Princeton University Press, 2012.

Madison, James. Letter to W. T. Barry, August 4, 1822. In Vol. 9 of *Writings of James Madison*, ed. Gaillard Hunt, 9 vols. New York: G. P. Putnam's Sons, 1900–1910.

Mill, John Stuart. *Considerations on Representative Government*. Indianapolis, IN: Bobbs-Merrill, 1958 (1861).

Nie, Norman, et al. *Education and Democratic Citizenship in America*. Chicago: University of Chicago Press, 1996.

Roberts, Jennifer Tolbert. *Athens on Trial: The Antidemocratic Tradition in Western Thought.* Princeton, NJ: Princeton University Press, 1994.

Shenkman, Richard. *Just How Stupid Are We? Facing the Truth about the American Voter*. New York: Basic Books, 2008.

Somin, Ilya. *Democracy and Political Ignorance: Why Smaller Government Is Smarter.* Stanford, CA: Stanford University Press, 2013.

12

In Defense of Difficulty

HOW THE DECLINE OF THE IDEAL OF SERIOUSNESS HAS DULLED DEMOCRACY IN THE NAME OF A PHONY POPULISM

Steve Wasserman

IT IS COMMONPLACE to bemoan the vanishing of serious criticism in our popular culture. The past, it is said, was a golden age. More than twenty-five years ago, Russell Jacoby put it sharply in his influential book *The Last Intellectuals*, when he decried the disappearance of the "public intellectual" since the heyday of the fevered debates over politics and literature that broke out among Depression-era students in the cafeteria at New York's City College. Much had gone awry: "A public that once snapped up pamphlets by Thomas Paine or stood for hours listening to Abraham Lincoln debate Stephen Douglas hardly exists; its span of attention shrinks as its fondness for television increases" (6). The rising price of real estate was also to blame, for it had led to the gentrification of America's bohemian enclaves, like Greenwich Village in New York and North Beach in San Francisco, spawning grounds for generations of disaffected intellectuals and artists who now could no longer afford independence. Jacoby's verdict was harsh and sweeping: "The eclipse of these urban living areas completes the eclipse of the cultural space" (21). Universities, too, were at fault. They had colonized critics by holding careers hostage to academic specialization, requiring them to master the arcane tongues of ever-narrower disciplines, forcing them to forsake a larger public. Compared to the Arcadian past, the present, in this view, was a wasteland.

It didn't have to be this way. In the postwar era, a vast project of cultural uplift sought to bring to the wider public the best that had been thought and said. Robert M. Hutchins of the University of Chicago and Mortimer J. Adler were among its more prominent avatars. This effort, which tried to deepen literacy under the sign of the "middlebrow," and thus to strengthen the idea that an informed citizenry was indispensable for a healthy democracy, was, for a time, hugely successful. The general level of cultural sophistication rose as a growing middle class shed its provincialism in exchange for a certain worldliness that was one legacy of American triumphalism and ambition after World War II. College enrollment boomed, and the percentage of Americans attending the performing arts rose dramatically. Regional stage and opera companies blossomed, new concert halls were built, and interest in the arts was widespread. TV hosts Steve Allen, Johnny Carson, and Dick Cavett frequently featured serious writers as guests. Paperback publishers made classic works of history, literature, and criticism available to ordinary readers whose appetite for such works seemed insatiable.

Mass-circulation newspapers and magazines, too, expanded their coverage of books, movies, music, dance, and theater. Criticism was no longer confined to such small but influential journals of opinion as *Partisan Review*, *The Nation*, and the *New Republic*. *Esquire* embraced the irascible and caustic Dwight Macdonald as its movie critic, despite his well-known contempt for "middlebrow" culture. The *New Yorker* threw a lifeline to Pauline Kael, rescuing her from the ghetto of film quarterlies and Berkeley art houses. Strong critics like David Riesman, Daniel Bell, and Leslie Fiedler, among others, would write with insight and pugilistic zeal books that often found enough readers to propel their works onto best seller lists. Intellectuals such as Susan Sontag were featured in the glossy pages of magazines like *Vogue*. Her controversial "Notes on Camp," first published in 1964 in *Partisan Review*, exploded into public view when *Time* magazine championed her work. Eggheads were suddenly sexy, almost on a par with star athletes and Hollywood celebrities. Gore Vidal was a regular on Johnny Carson. William F. Buckley Jr.'s *Firing*

Line hosted vigorous debates that often were models of how to think and argue, and, at their best, told us that ideas mattered.

As Scott Timberg, a former arts reporter for the *Los Angeles Times*, puts it in his useful book, *Culture Crash: The Killing of the Creative Class*, the idea, embraced by increasing numbers of Americans, was that

> drama, poetry, music, and art were not just a way to pass the time, or advertise one's might, but a path to truth and enlightenment. At its best, this was what the middlebrow consensus promised. Middlebrow said that culture was accessible to a wide strata of society, that people needed some but not much training to appreciate it, that there was a canon worth knowing, that art was not the same as entertainment, that the study of the liberal arts deepens you, and that those who make, assess, and disseminate the arts were somehow valuable for our society regardless of their impact on GDP. (260–61)

So what if culture was increasingly just another product to be bought and sold, used and discarded, like so many tubes of toothpaste? Even Los Angeles, long derided as a cultural desert, would by the turn of the century boast a flourishing and internationally respected opera company, a thriving archipelago of museums with world-class collections, and dozens of bookstores selling in some years more books per capita than were sold in the greater New York area. The middlebrow's triumph was all but assured.

The arrival of the Internet by century's end promised to make that victory complete. As the *Wall Street Journal* reported in a front-page story in 1998, America was "increasingly wealthy, worldly, and wired" (Blackmon). Notions of elitism and snobbery seemed to be collapsing upon the palpable catholicity of a public whose curiosities were ever more diverse and eclectic and whose ability to satisfy them had suddenly and miraculously expanded. We stood, it appeared, on the verge of a munificent new world—a world in which technology was rapidly democratizing the means of cultural production while providing an easy way for millions of ordinary citizens, previously excluded from the precincts of the higher conversation, to join the dialogue. The digital revolution was predicted to empower those authors whose writings had been marginalized, shut out of mainstream publishing, to overthrow the old, monastic self-selecting order of cultural gatekeepers (meaning professional critics). Thus would critical faculties be sharpened and democratized. Digital platforms would crack open the cloistered and solipsistic world of academe, bypass the old presses and performing arts spaces, and unleash a new era of cultural commerce. With smart machines there would be smarter people.

Harvard's Robert Darnton, a sober and learned historian of reading and the book, agreed. He argued that the implications for writing and reading, for publishing and bookselling—indeed, for cultural literacy and criticism itself—were profound. As he gushed in *The Case for Books: Past, Present, and Future*, we now had the ability to make "all book learning available to all people, or at least those privileged enough to have access to the World Wide Web. It promises to be the ultimate stage in the democratization of knowledge set in motion by the invention of writing, the codex, movable type, and the Internet" (33). In this view, echoed by innumerable worshippers of the New Information Age, we were living at one of history's hinge moments, a great evolutionary leap in the human mind. In truth, it was hard not to believe that we had arrived at the apotheosis of our culture. Never before in history had more good literature and cultural works been available at such low cost to so many. The future was radiant.

Others, like Leon Wieseltier, the *New Republic*'s former longtime literary editor, and critics Sven Birkerts, Evgeny Morozov, and Jaron Lanier, were more skeptical. They worried that whatever advantages might accrue to consumers and the culture at large from the emergence of such behemoths as Amazon, not only would proven methods of cultural production and distribution be made obsolete, but we were in danger of being enrolled, whether we liked it or not, in an overwhelmingly fast and visually furious culture that, as numerous studies have shown, renders serious reading and cultural criticism increasingly irrelevant, hollowing out habits of attention indispensable for absorbing long-form narrative and sustained argument. Indeed, they feared that the digital tsunami now engulfing us may even signal an irrevocable trivialization of the word—or, at the least, a sense that the enterprise of making distinctions between bad, good, and best was a mug's game that had no place in a democracy that worships at the altar of mass appeal and counts its receipts at the almighty box office.

★★★

Karl Kraus, the acerbic fin de siècle Viennese critic, once remarked that no nation's literature could properly be judged by examining its geniuses, since genius always eludes explanation. A better metric is the second-rate, which is to say, the popular literature and art that makes up the bulk of what people consume. The truly extraordinary defy taxonomy. More fruitful by far would be to map the ecosystem of the less talented for whom craft and tenacity and ambition are no insult. By that measure, postwar America's middlebrow culture, a culture whose achievements often mistook the second-rate for top-tier work (see, for example, the novels of Herbert Gold, Herman Wouk, James Michener, Edna Ferber, Irving Stone, and John Steinbeck, to name a few), appears almost to have been a golden age. Or, as Timberg says, a silver age, at the least. What is missing today is a cultural ecology that permits the second-rate to fail upward.

That failure is a body blow against the broader culture. The world that had once permitted such efforts to flourish is gone. Today, America's traditional organs of popular criticism—newspapers, magazines, journals of opinion—have been all but overwhelmed by the digital onslaught: their circulations plummeting, their confidence eroded, their survival in doubt. Newspaper review sections in particular have suffered: jobs have been slashed, and cultural coverage vastly diminished. Both the *Los Angeles Times* and the *Washington Post* have abandoned their stand-alone book sections, leaving the *New York Times* as the only major American newspaper still publishing a significant separate section devoted to reviewing books. Such sections, of course, were always few. Only a handful of America's papers ever deemed book coverage important enough to dedicate an entire Sunday section to it. Now even that handful is threatened with extinction and thus is a widespread cultural illiteracy abetted, for at their best the editors of those sections tried to establish the idea that serious criticism was possible in a mass culture. In the nineteenth century, Margaret Fuller, literary editor of the *New York Tribune* and the country's first full-time book reviewer, understood this well. She saw books as "a medium for viewing all humanity, a core around which all knowledge, all experience, all science, all the ideal as well as all the practical in our nature could gather" (cited in Hamilton, 132). She sought, she said, to tell "the whole truth, as well as nothing but the truth." The editors of the *New Republic* echoed her severe and sound standard when they wrote not long ago that "the intelligent discussion of a book has the power to change its reader's ideas about how he votes or who he loves—to furnish nothing less than a 'criticism of life,' in the old but still sterling Arnoldian phrase." Newspapers and magazines are businesses, of course, but the *New Republic* editors insisted, "There are properties that are not just properties, but also pillars of a culture and institutions of a society." The editors argued that book reviewing, done right, is not blogging.

The arrival of the Internet has proved no panacea. Its vast canvas has done little to encourage thoughtful and serious criticism. Mostly it has provided a vast Democracy Wall on which any crackpot can post a manifesto. Bloggers bloviate and insults abound. Discourse coarsens. More is less. Information is abundant, wisdom scarce. It is a striking irony, as Wieseltier noted in an April 2007 interview with Charlie Rose on PBS, that with the arrival of the Internet, "a medium of communication with no limitations of physical space, everything on it has to be in six hundred words." The Internet, he said, is the first means of communication invented by humankind that privileges one's first thoughts as one's best thoughts. And he rightly observed that if "value is a function of scarcity," then "what is most scarce in our culture is long, thoughtful, patient, deliberate analysis of questions that do not have obvious or easy answers." Time is required to think through difficult questions. Patience is a condition of genuine intellection. The thinking mind, the creating mind, said Wieseltier, should not be rushed. "And where the mind is rushed and made frenetic, neither thought nor creativity will ensue. What you will most likely get is conformity and banality. Writing is not typed talking."

Wieseltier is among the few who have chosen to resist "the insane acceleration of everything," preferring instead to embrace the enduring need for thought, for patient analysis, so necessary in an increasingly dizzying culture. He also knows that the fundamental idea at stake in the criticism of culture generally is the self-image of society: how it reasons with itself, describes itself, imagines itself. Nothing in the excitements made possible by the digital revolution banishes the need for the rigor such self-reckoning requires. It is, as he has said, the obligation of cultural criticism to bear down on what matters.

★ ★ ★

Where is such criticism to be found today? We inhabit a remarkably arid cultural landscape, especially when compared with the ambitions of postwar America—ambitions that, to be sure, were often mocked by some of the country's more prominent intellectuals. Yes, Dwight Macdonald famously excoriated the enfeeblements of "mass cult and midcult," and Irving Howe regretted "this age of conformity," but from today's perspective, when we look back at the offerings of the Book-of-the-Month Club and projects such as the Great Books of the Western World, their scorn looks misplaced. The fact that their complaints circulated widely in the very midcult worlds Macdonald condemned was proof that trenchant criticism had found a place within the organs of mass culture. One is almost tempted to say that the middlebrow culture of yesteryear was a high-water mark.

The reality, of course, was never as rosy as much of it looks in retrospect. Cultural criticism in most American newspapers, even at its best, was almost always confined to a ghetto. You were lucky at most papers to get a column or a half page devoted to arts and culture. Editors encouraged reporters, reviewers, and critics to win readers and improve circulation by pandering to the faux populism of the marketplace. Only the review that might immediately be understood by the greatest number of readers would be permitted to see the light of day. Anything else smacked of "elitism"—a sin to be avoided at almost any cost.

This notion was coarse and pernicious, one that lay at the center of the country's long-standing anti-intellectual tradition. From the start of the republic, Americans have had a profoundly ambivalent relationship to class and culture, as Richard Hofstadter famously observed. He was neither the first nor the last to notice this self-inflicted wound. As even the vastly popular science-fiction writer Isaac Asimov understood, "Anti-intellectualism has been a constant thread winding its way through our political and cultural life, nurtured by the false notion that democracy means that 'my ignorance is just as good as your knowledge.'"

The effort to insinuate more serious standards into the instruments of mass culture was always difficult, even when a rising middle class made possible the notion of increasing cultural sophistication. A single story from the near-decade I served as literary editor of the *Los Angeles Times* tells the tale.

In 1997 Penguin announced that it would publish a volume of Sor Juana Ines de la Cruz's selected writings. Years ago, Carlos Fuentes had told me of this remarkable seventeenth-century Mexican nun and poet. I had never heard of her. Nor was I alone. Much of her work had yet to be translated into English, even some three hundred years after her death. It was, Fuentes said, a scandal, as if Shakespeare had still to be translated into Spanish. The whole of Spanish literature owed a debt to her genius. Thus I decided that an anthology of her writings, newly translated by the excellent Margaret Sayers Peden and published under the imprimatur of Penguin Classics, ought to be treated as news. After all, about a quarter of the readers of the *Los Angeles Times* had Latino roots.

I asked Octavio Paz, Mexico's greatest living poet and critic, to contribute a lengthy essay on Sor Juana. When he agreed, I felt I had gotten something worth playing big on the front page of the Book Review. But when I showed my superiors the color proof of the cover, I was met with incomprehension. Sor Juana who? A nun who'd been dead for almost half a millennium? Had I taken complete leave of my senses? Couldn't I find something by someone living who might be better known to our many subscribers, say, the latest thriller from James Patterson?

Dispirited, I trundled up to the paper's executive dining room to brood upon the wisdom of my decision. When Alberto Gonzalez, the paper's longtime Mexican American waiter, appeared to take my order, seeing the proof before me, he exhaled audibly and exclaimed, "Sor Juana!"

"You've heard of her?" I asked.

"Of course," he said. "Every schoolchild in Mexico knows her poems. I still remember my parents taking me as a boy to visit her convent, now a museum. I know many of her poems by heart." At which point, in a mellifluous Spanish, he began to recite several verses. *So much for my minders,* I thought; *I'm going to trust Alberto on this one.*

After Paz's paean appeared in the Sunday edition, many people wrote to praise the Book Review for at last recognizing the cultural heritage of a substantial segment of the paper's readers. Their response suggested, at least to me, that the best way to connect with readers was to give them the news that stays news. In the end, it hardly mattered. In the summer of 2009, four years after I left, the Tribune Company, which had bought the *Times* for more than $8 billion, shuttered the Book Review. The staff was mostly sacked.

Today such an ambition seems absurdly quixotic. Perhaps it always was. After all, the very idea of cultural and intellectual discrimination is regularly attacked for the sin of "snark," and notions of authority and expertise are everywhere under siege. Richard Schickel, the longtime film critic for *Time* magazine, writing in a 2007 op-ed in the *Los Angeles Times*, objected to the "hairy-chested populism" that increasingly dominates and enfeebles what passes for cultural commentary. "Criticism—and its humble cousin, reviewing—is not a democratic activity," he insisted. "It is, or should be, an elite enterprise, ideally undertaken by individuals who bring something to the party beyond their hasty, instinctive opinion of a book (or any other cultural object). It is work that requires disciplined taste, historical and theoretical knowledge and a fairly deep sense of the author's (or filmmaker's or painter's) entire body of work, among other qualities." Sure, he seemed to be saying, let 100 million opinions bloom; but let's also acknowledge the truth that not all opinions are equal. In these matters, I, like Schickel, am a Leninist: Better fewer, but better.

The necessity of literary hygiene as a way of keeping a culture honest and astute is in danger of being forgotten. Too few remember William Hazlitt's intemperate and imperishable essay on "the pleasure of hating." Hazlitt complained that "the reputation of some books is raw and *unaired*" (186), and he rightly saw that "the popularity of the most successful writers operates to wean us from them, by the cant and fuss that is made about them, by hearing their names everlastingly repeated, and by the number of ignorant and indiscriminate admirers they draw after them" (185). Today what is needed, more than ever, is what Wieseltier has called "the higher spleen." A good recent example is Francine Prose's lacerating takedown of Donna Tartt's best-selling and widely admired novel *The Goldfinch*, or the late Christopher Hitchens' mighty evisceration of Henry Kissinger—or, in an earlier period, Susan Sontag's salutary critique of Leni Riefenstahl's fascist aesthetics at a time when her Nazi past had been largely forgotten. None of these critics banished difficulty or avoided complexity of thought; on the contrary, they tried hard to think seriously and deeply, to express themselves with vigor and clarity, without shirking the moral obligation to treat readers as adults. They understood the necessity of making distinctions between the good, the bad, and the ugly. Doing so, they knew, was a critic's highest calling.

★ ★ ★

When did "difficulty" become suspect in American culture, widely derided as antidemocratic and contemptuously dismissed as evidence of so-called elitism? If a work of art isn't somehow immediately "understood" or "accessible" by and to large numbers of people, it is often dismissed as "esoteric," "obtuse," or even somehow un-American. We should mark such an argument's cognitive consequences. A culture filled with smooth and familiar consumptions produces in people rigid mental habits and stultified conceptions. They know what they know, and they expect to find it reinforced when they turn a page or click on a screen. Difficulty annoys them, and, having become accustomed to so much pabulum served up by a pandering and invertebrate media, they experience difficulty not just as "difficult," but as insult. Struggling to understand, say, Faulkner's stream-of-consciousness masterpiece *The Sound and the Fury* or Alain Resnais's Rubik's Cube of a movie, *Last Year at Marienbad*, needn't be done. The mind may skip trying to solve such cognitive puzzles, even though the truth is that they strengthen it as a workout tones the muscles.

Sometimes it feels as if the world is divided into two classes: one very large class spurns difficulty, while the other very much smaller one delights in it. I was taken aback, for example, when I met a woman at the annual *Los Angeles Times* Festival of Books some years ago who confessed that she was afraid to enter her local bookstore. She found herself bewildered by the vast number of books, intimidated by the embarrassment of riches on offer, nearly paralyzed with indecision. Crushed by the weight of her ignorance, she fled. (Not too many years later, she would be spared the trouble as the store would close, like so many other book and record stores.) Similarly, there are readers who, when encountering an unfamiliar word, instead of reaching for a dictionary, choose to regard it as a sign of the author's contempt or pretention, a deliberate refusal to speak in a language ordinary people can understand. Others, encountering the same word, happily seize on it as a chance to learn something new, to broaden their horizons. They eagerly seek a literature that upends assumptions, challenges prejudices, turns them inside out, and forces them to see the world through new eyes.

The second group is an endangered species. One reason is that the ambitions of mainstream media that, however fitfully, once sought to expose them to the life of the mind and to the contest of ideas have themselves shrunk. We have gone from the heyday of television intellection, which boasted shows hosted by, among others, David Susskind and David Frost, men who, whatever their self-absorptions, were nonetheless possessed of an admirable high-mindedness, to the pygmy sound-bite rants of Sean Hannity and the inanities of clowns like Stephen Colbert. Remnants such as Charlie Rose and *National Review*'s web show "Uncommon Knowledge" are hardly models of Socratic dialogue, but at least they have pretensions—pretensions that, alas, garner a minuscule viewership. They haven't the numbers to secure a space for serious civic reflection as an indispensable feature of popular culture in America. Once upon a time, the ideal of seriousness may not have been a common one, but it was acknowledged as one worth striving for. It didn't have to do what it has to today—that is, fight for respect, legitimate itself before asserting itself. The class that is allergic to difficulty now feels justified in condemning the other as "elitist" and antidemocratic. The exercise of cultural authority and artistic or literary or aesthetic discrimination is seen as evidence of snobbery, entitlement, and privilege, lording it over ordinary folks. A perverse populism increasingly deforms our culture, consigning some works of art to a realm somehow more rarified and less accessible to a broad public. Thus is choice constrained and the tyranny of mass appeal deepened in the name of democracy.

Consider, by contrast, Theodor Adorno's exemplary response to his good friend Gershom Scholem upon receiving Scholem's translation of the *Zohar*, the masterpiece of Kabbalah, as mysterious as it is magnificent. In 1939, Adorno, living in exile in New York after fleeing Nazi Germany, wrote Scholem who had long since settled in Jerusalem,

> I'm not just being rhetorical when I say that the *Zohar* translation you sent me gave me more joy than any gift I have received in a long time. Don't read into this remark anything pretentious, because I am far from claiming to have fully grasped the text. But it's the kind of thing whose indecipherability is itself an element of the joy I felt in reading it. I think I can say that your introduction has at least given me a topological notion of the *Zohar*. A bit like someone who goes high into the mountains to spot chamois bucks but fails to see them, because he's a near-sighted city dweller. After an experienced guide points out the precise spot where the bucks congregate he becomes so thoroughly acquainted with their territory that he thinks he must be able to discover these rare creatures immediately. The summer tourist cannot expect to glean anything more than this from the landscape, which is truly revealed only at the price of a lifetime's commitment—nothing less. (Scholem, 298)

The ideal of serious enjoyment of what isn't instantly understood is rare in American cultural life. It is under constant siege. It is the object of scorn from both the left and the right. The pleasures of critical thinking ought not to be seen as belonging to the province of an elite. They are the birthright of every citizen. Such pleasures are at the very heart of literacy, without which democracy itself is dulled. More than ever, we need a defense of the Eros of difficulty.

References

Blackmon, Douglas. "Forget the Stereotype: America Is Becoming a Nation of Culture." *Wall Street Journal*, September 17, 1998.

Darnton, Robert. *The Case for Books: Past, Present, and Future.* Philadelphia: Perseus Books, 2009.

Hamilton, John Maxwell. *Casanova Was a Book Lover: And Other Naked Truths and Provocative Curiosities about the Writing, Selling and Reading of Books.* Baton Rouge: Louisiana State University Press, 2000.

Hazlitt, William. "On the Pleasure of Hating." In *The Plain Speaker: Opinions on Books, Men, and Things.* London: George Bell and Sons, 1870.

Jacoby, Russell. *The Last Intellectuals.* New York: Basic Books, 1987.

Juana Ines de la Cruz, Sister. *Poems, Protest, and a Dream: Selected Writings.* Trans. Margaret Sayers Peden. New York: Penguin Books, 1997.

Schickel, Richard. "Not Everybody's a Critic." *Los Angeles Times*, May 20, 2007.

Scholem, Gershom Gerhard. *A Life in Letters, 1914–1982.* Ed. and trans. Anthony David Skinner. Cambridge, MA: Harvard University Press, 2002.

Timberg, Scott. *Culture Crash: The Killing of the Creative Class.* New Haven, CT: Yale University Press, 2015.

13

We Live in the Age of Feelings

Dennis Prager

Western history has been marked by eras with monumental names such as "the Renaissance," "the Reformation," and "the Enlightenment," to cite three prominent examples. We are living in another such era, and I suggest it be named "the Age of Feelings." Not feelings as they were ennobled by figures during the Romantic period such as Jean-Jacques Rousseau and William Wordsworth, who respected not just any average person's average feelings but the feelings of heightened souls undergoing sublime experiences. Today's version spreads that privilege to everyone and everywhere—although, of course, some people and some experiences are more equal than others.

The Age of Feelings as we now know it really began in the 1960s and 1970s, when for the first time in Western history, feelings were exalted above everything, from reason to law to facts, and most importantly, to standards—especially in morality and the arts. Those years marked a genuine cultural revolution, and the triumph of sensitivities, preferences, dispositions, experiences, and personal choices over objective norms and traditional authorities fueled the more overt political and cultural changes that the revolution wrought. We witnessed the rising power of feelings whenever someone stood up in a public forum to declare, "You don't know how it feels to be . . . ," and the audience responded with deference, not debate. It happened in cases of special pleading and double standards, when bad behaviors were rationalized by appealing to the feelings motivating them, asking others not to judge, but "to understand."

We see it today in the case of rap music, whose misogynistic and violence-glorifying lyrics are papered over by assertions about their authenticity and expressive force.

I say "for the first time in Western history" not because people in the West (or anywhere else) have always exalted rationality above emotion. They haven't. I believe racism and sexism are irrational, for instance, and that some religious beliefs are, too. But holding irrational religious beliefs is not the same as elevating personal feelings to decisive status. Irrational theological beliefs can easily exist alongside objective moral standards, as faith in God may originate elsewhere than in reason but nonetheless adhere to the Ten Commandments. When feelings are supreme, however, individuals consult their own responses before they heed objective customs, rules, and traditions. The moral order comes second to the fluctuating emotional state of each person.

Religions recognize the challenge, knowing well the dangers that underlie the ostensibly benevolent decree that we appreciate how people feel. Hence, Judaism and Christianity have always warned people against trusting their hearts:

- Numbers 15.39. "Do not follow your hearts and your eyes after which you prostitute yourself" (literal translation).
- Jeremiah 17.9. "The heart is deceitful above all things, and desperately wicked."
- Proverbs 28.26. "He who trusts in his heart is a fool."
- Matthew 15.19. "For out of the heart come evil thoughts—murder, adultery, sexual immorality, theft, false testimony, slander."

In our society, those admonitions have largely disappeared, replaced by the contrary belief that to constrain the heart is itself a harmful and wicked ruling. Imagine what would happen if a public speaker were to respond to an audience member who stated in the question-and-answer session, "I am offended by your remarks," with a blunt dismissal: "Your feelings of offense are your business—let's stick to the issue. Do you have a question? Would you like to cite any evidence I haven't covered?" A politician who did so would kill any chance of reelection. A teacher who did so might be fired.

Morality Rooted in Feelings

The ascent of feelings has penetrated so far into our culture that it is expressed in the most basic and decisive terms. Instead of asking, "Is it right?" a generation of Americans has been raised to ask, "How do I feel about it?" Indeed, while the advent of the Age of Feelings fifty years ago may have started as an injunction to respect others' feelings—allowing people to make judgments, yes, but keeping them quiet, or at least positioning them within a context of sensitivity—young Americans sometimes seem to lack the very equipment to decide a moral question in their heads. Recently, *New York Times* columnist David Brooks wrote vehemently about this incapacity, summarizing the disturbing findings of a research team led by "the eminent Notre Dame sociologist Christian Smith" that studied the moral reasoning of young people:

> The default position, which most of them came back to again and again, is that moral choices are just a matter of individual taste. "It's personal," the respondents typically said. . . . "I would do what I thought made me happy or *how I felt*. I have no other way of knowing what to do but *how I internally feel*." . . . As one put it, "I mean, I guess what makes something right is *how I feel about it*. But different people feel different ways, so I couldn't speak on behalf of anyone else as to what's right and wrong." . . . All judgments are based on *how we feel* at the moment. . . . Morality was once revealed, inherited, and shared, but now it's thought of as something that emerges *in the privacy of your own heart*. (all emphasis added)

Call it emotional relativism, the idea that the best foundation for judgment is emotive response and the best one for choice is emotive preference. And because every individual has a distinct emotional makeup, as many moral yardsticks and cultural tastes exist as there are individuals. To apply any broader criterion that is based upon nonemotive, impersonal reality or truth is not only mistaken, it's oppressive—which is why the young lean so far in the direction of liberalism: not because of its political content (they know little about progressive tax policy, regulations, and specific government programs), but because conservatism sounds too much like someone telling them what to think and do. Political correctness is as coercive as any right-wing dogma, of course, but it escapes the tyranny charge because it locates its demands precisely upon feelings.

Culture is the first casualty. A healthy culture stocked with superb examples of human creativity relies on standards to filter the good from the bad, the beautiful from the vulgar, the profound from the superficial. Museums collect masterpieces that have stood the test of time, teachers stock their syllabi with the best that has been thought and said, and "the moral obligation to be intelligent" (a phrase from twentieth-century critic Lionel Trilling) prevails over the lure of cheap entertainment. But art is such a matter of taste already that as soon as feelings come to dominate standards, the effect on literature, TV, movies, songs, and visual art is nearly instantaneous. Indeed, the cultural revolution that celebrated feelings had its avant garde in the Beat Generation writers of the 1950s who cultivated bohemian lifestyles and extreme experiences as a precondition of their art. Once their adversarial critique of bourgeois society vanquished mainstream norms and became, in turn, another species of popular culture, concepts such as excellence and greatness looked downright reactionary and stuffy. To judge a critically acclaimed film such as *American Beauty* (which makes a mockery of family values) a warped and meretricious version of great family dramas of the past such as *Death of a Salesman* would be disdained as the act of a backward curmudgeon.

When judged by the standards of artistic and musical excellence developed through the ages, much art and classical music of the twentieth century appears vacuous and ephemeral. But what else could happen when artists and critics ground their creation and reception in something as transient and inconsistent as their own feelings? When standards decline in a wash of feeling, accelerated by the treatment of tradition as the biased product of white European males, then we may expect art to degenerate as well, so that blotches of paint, fecal matter, graffiti ("urban art"), and other gimmicks are deemed worthy of presentation in the greatest museums and galleries, while tonality-free, harmony-free, and melody-free music is deemed worthy of performance by the greatest orchestras.

Love über Alles

I first realized how much things had changed when in the 1970s, just out of college, I began asking high school students if they would save their dog or a stranger if both were drowning. Back then and to this day, aside from some (not all, unfortunately) religious Jewish and Christian schools, I have always received the same results: around one-third say they would save the dog, one-third say the stranger, and one-third find the question too difficult to answer. When asked why they would save their dog first, the near-universal answer is, "I love my dog; I don't love the stranger." No moral examination, no contrast between animals and humans, nothing about duty to others, no appeal to religious doctrine over such grave matters, just a simple calculation of personal feelings. Tellingly, the object of their love seems to matter less than the amount of love they have for it, even if it means elevating an animal's life above that of another human being. In the Age of Feelings, it's love über alles, including religious belief. Judeo-Christian values have always taught that human life, not animal life, is sacred—the first, not the second, created in the image of God. But when feelings determine judgment (or nonjudgment) and action (or inaction), natural and moral hierarchies such as those indicated in the story of Genesis collapse. Indeed, the youths' response to my question demonstrates a pernicious end point of the Age of Feeling: not toward empathy for others, but empathy for oneself, my feelings counting more than anybody else's.

As this version of love displaces Judeo-Christian standards, it undermines all the institutions based upon those standards. Note, for instance, the astonishing redefinition of marriage that has transpired in the last ten years, progressing from an unthinkable advent in mainstream culture to a *bien-pensant* attitude sweeping our society and framing defenders of the traditional custom of one-man-one-woman as shameful. The argument for same-sex marriage rests on a pointedly guileless appeal to love, not to anything fundamental about marriage, family, sexuality, children, monogamy, or the state. We have two people who happen to be both male or both female, but who care deeply about one another and wish to solemnize their devotion in a ceremony that enjoys the same status as a male-female ceremony. How can we deny their request, or, more deeply, how can we deny their love? That recognizing their wedding entails redefining marriage by gender for the first time in Western history makes no difference once we pose its meaning in terms of love alone.

The same conclusions apply to child-rearing, which in the Age of Feelings alleges that having a mother and father is not necessary to the healthy development of children. Instead, the argument goes, children only need love, a transfer of emotion, not two parents who can stand as representatives of the two sides of humanity. It sounds like a positive position until we see what happens when someone asserts the opposite, that a male and female parent each provide emotional and social benefits that the other cannot. As University of Texas sociologist Mark Regnerus found out after he published research indicating the possible harm ensuing in children of parents who'd had same-sex relationships, an "academic auto-da-fe" followed (as an article in the *Chronicle of Higher Education* termed it—see Smith), with Regnerus vilified by social science colleagues and the editor who published his findings targeted with Freedom of Information Act requests.

The abortion debate follows the same feeling-based logic. According to recent survey data, for about half of the American people the worth of a human fetus is determined by the feelings of the mother. On their premise, the living being growing inside her has no independent existence, his or her living status deriving wholly from the way the mother views her own pregnancy. Whereas the pro-life position determines the condition of the fetus itself as firm and unchanging, a life to be cherished, the pro-choice position makes the fetus a wavering entity, sometimes wanted and sometimes unwanted.

All this explains why feelings-based advocates regard Judeo-Christian values as their primary enemy. Too many doctrines expressly outlaw certain actions no matter how much one wants to do them. Recall, too, how common abortion, infanticide, and prostitution were in the ancient world in which these religions originated and against which they defined themselves. More generally, Judaism and Christianity insist on natural law and God-given morality constituting a baleful resistance to the personal-impulse mandate, and hence the Age of Feelings must renounce them. The essence of both religions is that a commanding God tells us what is right and what is wrong, the opposite of "How do I feel about it?" They acknowledge the power of feelings, but know that giving in to them without restraint is a false liberation, not a progressive freedom, even proclaiming them a sin unless the voice of God and reason moderate them. The Ten Commandments direct people how to behave, but implicit in each one is a selfish feeling that needs to be curtailed (greed behind "Thou shalt not steal," lust for thy neighbor's wife, envy of thy neighbor's property, . . .). Moses brings from the mountaintop the command, "Honor your father and mother," a decree that implicitly admits children quite naturally may hate or resent their parents, but in the Age of Feelings, this obligation is meaningless. What if a father has done hateful things? What if the parents' declining health proves an infringement upon the son's slacker lifestyle? When feelings reign supreme, one properly honors one's parents only if one feels like doing so.

More and more people operate on this attitude, not only young children, but even more so adult children. Based on what callers to my radio show have told me for decades and what I have confirmed at speeches around America (asking members of the audience to raise their hands if they know any parents whose adult child refuses to speak to them), I have noted a veritable epidemic of adult children who have chosen to have no contact with one or both of their parents. They live near or far away, but have broken the generational tie, their anger or hurt or just plain indifference eclipsing the duty to take care of or simply keep in touch with the father and mother. The notion that each one owes a parent honor (not love, significantly—the Bible commands that one love God and neighbors, but not one's parents) is foreign to those who are guided by feelings. Sadly, many psychotherapists reinforce the attitude, telling patients that their feelings about parents trump any moral obligation to them.

The Age of Feelings doesn't stop with personal lives and cultural tastes, either. Feelings also guide half the nation's political policies, regardless of how costly and ineffective they are. We see it happen when current debates over food stamps and other welfare programs settle into an emotive polarity: conservatives who don't care about the poor versus liberals who do. President Obama articulated it bluntly in a March 2012 speech on Republican attitudes:

> Their philosophy is simple: You're on your own. You're on your own if you're out of work, can't find a job. Tough luck, you're on your own. You don't have health care: That's your problem. You're on your own. If you're born into poverty, lift yourself up with your own bootstraps, even if you don't have boots. You're on your own.

This isn't a statement of policy or a discussion of best practices. It's an accusation against the other side of greed, selfishness, insensitivity, callousness, and arrogance. Here, the president converts what should be a programmatic question—how best to bring the most people out of poverty?—into a division of personalities, those with compassion and those without. Once the issue gets framed in this way, the question, "Does a policy work—does it justify the expense?" is irrelevant, especially when the policy in its ideal version sounds so warm and humane. At the same time that we hear the denunciation of one side, we implicitly discern the self-congratulation of the other side, "We are the ones who care, the good souls." The people who espouse the policy feel good as they do so, for they think the policy is good, and whether a policy does sufficient good to warrant the resources devoted to it is an impertinent query.

Does affirmative action—lowering admissions and test standards for selected racial groups—help those groups? In the recent Supreme Court case challenging the practice (*Fisher v. University of Texas*), the plaintiff submitted fresh social science research showing the hazards of admitting one set of students to a selective college in which they have to compete with other students who earned higher grades and test scores in high school. The evidence researchers compiled showed how the "mismatch" (admitting students with credentials significantly inferior to the rest of the entering class) leads to higher dropout rates and, for those students who manage to stay in school, shifts toward less competitive majors (that is, where there is more grade inflation) that have weaker career prospects. If those students had been admitted to a Tier II institution instead of a Tier I, researchers concluded, they would have remained in school and in more promising majors at higher rates. Affirmative action, then, more often hurt the recipients of it than helped them. This was an empirical conclusion, not an ideological one, and the social scientists presented their findings openly for others to examine and dispute. In fact, one set of researchers at Duke University who identified the drift of affirmative action beneficiaries out of STEM fields and into "softer" humanities and "studies" programs were themselves firm liberals with no hostility to race-based admissions criteria (Arcidiacono et al.). But they were rigorous and honest enough to follow the evidence where it led, and they were shocked when, after the Black Student Alliance and black alumni protested the study, Duke president Richard Brodhead expressed his dismay. After citing the importance of free and open debate, he stated at a university-wide faculty meeting,

> I can see why students took offense at what was reported of a professor's work. Generalizations about academic choices

> by racial category can renew the primal insult of the world we are trying to leave behind—the implication that persons can be known through a group identity that associates them with inferior powers. A further insult was that the paper had been included in an amicus brief submitted by opponents of affirmative action urging the Supreme Court to hear [*Fisher v. University of Texas*]. (Brodhead)

This conversion of standard social science practice into a "primal insult" is extraordinary—but only from a perspective outside the Age of Feelings. And the indulgence of thin-skinned reactions over a scientific study ("I can see why students took offense. . . .") only serves to legitimate such childish complaints. Brodhead seeks to vindicate the students' objection to factual evidence by devoting the preceding paragraphs to what black Americans have endured in the past, but what that has to do with whether affirmative action does work or doesn't work for its intended beneficiaries remains unstated. The important thing is that one racial group was offended.

Apart from turning youths into children who can't manage their discomforts except by broadcasting their hurt feelings, the bigger problem here is that when facts and evidence are subordinated to emotions, you can't develop effective policies. Indignation and guilt are no basis for political decision making, which involves even-handed trade-offs and practical choices, and when they become too mixed up with policy making, we can be sure that corruption and distortion will soon set in. Policies first have to be just, and justice is guided by standards, not by feelings. If a poor man and a rich man are in a legal dispute, justice demands ruling in favor of whichever party is in the right. Feelings, on the other hand, often dictate a ruling in favor of the poor man, even if he is in the wrong. That is social justice, one of the most fervent movements in the Age of Feelings. Here, too, we find another example of the conflict between biblically-based and feelings-based positions. The biblical demand was that judges rule on the basis of justice: "Do not favor the poor in judgment" (Exodus 23:3; Leviticus 19:15).

We shouldn't be surprised that to foster social justice in a feeling-full era, reformers target education as well. Exhibit A comes from California, home of the 1967 Summer of Love and today the nation's largest purchaser of textbooks. Recently, the state legislature approved a mandate that requires history textbooks to devote a certain amount of space to women, to various ethnic groups, and to gays, lesbians, bisexuals, and the transgendered. The result is a skewed historical record in favor of these groups, leading inevitably to other, more important historical material getting shortchanged. But an accurate picture of the past is a lesser concern, an aim secondary to an Age of Feelings goal: to have students who are members of those groups feel good about themselves. As with scientific results (when the data cross the feelings of certain groups), historical truth succumbs to the sanctioned reactions of the moment.

Leftism: Rooted in Feelings

By now, readers will have realized that feelings-based positions complement left-wing positions as they have evolved in the twenty-first century. Prior left-wing positions sympathized with the misery of the poor and working classes, but emphasized union activity, progressivist legislation, and welfare programs on financial grounds, not on individual feelings. But today's leftism is feelings-based. Though the left often obscures this fact with intellectual-sounding rhetoric, and though intellectuals disproportionately hold left-wing positions, leftism highlights the experience of victims, especially the way in which racism, sexism, homophobia, patriotism, and American exceptionalism victimize different identity groups. For all his dry economic analyses and scientific pretensions, even the originator of left-wing thought, Karl Marx, gave in to feelings at key moments in his writings. He described his views as "scientific," to be sure, for example, declaring it a scientific law that societies evolve from feudalism to capitalism to socialism. But he hated capitalism with a passion. He hated rich capitalists, too, and material inequality, and religion as well.

This is one reason that fighting leftism in the current climate is so frustrating. Nothing is more difficult than fighting feelings, especially when society's elite lead people to believe that their feelings are perfect guides to determine how to live one's life and how to decide what policies society should pursue. Are we supposed to respond to Barack Obama's accusations with, "I do, too, care for others!"? It sounds so defensive and feeble, but if we let the accusation slide, it sinks in as common knowledge (and more people do, indeed, agree with the statement "Republicans are heartless" than disagree with it).

When people on the left, then, announce that they are "offended" by conservative positions, they wield a powerful rhetorical weapon. Pro-choice women, for example, frequently say that they are "offended" by pro-lifers, yet one rarely encounters pro-life women who declare that they are offended by pro-choice people. The "I'm offended" response doesn't tally a conservatism that maintains objective moral standards. Another example: Pro-choice women frequently assert that men have no right morally to object to any abortion since only women carry babies. This, too, is an entirely feelings-based argument, for men cannot feel what pregnancy is like.

All people, even the most evil among us, want to feel good about themselves—in fact, in surveys of different groups' self-esteem, no people feel better about themselves than violent criminals. In addition, most people don't relish being told that they have to answer to a higher moral authority, which is the basis of Judaism and Christianity, especially if the authority proscribes what they like to do and urges what they don't like to do. Leftism, on the other hand, combines those two powerful drives—you are your own moral authority, and your feelings are your morals—making it almost irresistible to most people, especially the young.

What could be nicer than doing what feels good, whether in one's own life or in the social positions that one takes—and feeling wonderful about oneself while doing so?

That is leftism in a nutshell. In my personal life, I do what feels good—sometimes drugs, sex, and cheating on tests, but also working in a shelter or walking through the park—and in choosing social and political positions, all I have to do is consult what feels good and what I think makes others feel good.

I feel for the poor, and so I favor ever-expanding government programs to help the poor. I feel for the poor, and so I resent the rich and want to see them disproportionately taxed. I feel for black Americans because of America's history of slavery and racial discrimination, so I will support lowering college admissions standards on their behalf and I will not judge the 70 percent out-of-wedlock black birthrate. Instead, I will blame white racism, not black criminality or the disproportionate number of black males in prison for violent crime. I feel for gays, so I will support redefining marriage for the first time in history from the union of a man and a woman to the union of any two (and eventually three or more) people.

I feel good about myself and my motives. Therefore those who oppose my positions must be bad people. They only care about white privilege and about protecting the rich.

It is no wonder, then, that leftism, being so in tune with the heart, has been the most dynamic religion of the past century—considerably more so than Christianity, not to mention Judaism. Indeed, it has influenced Judaism and Christianity far more than those religions have influenced anybody, let alone leftists. Given the power of feelings, only two things can reverse this trend. One is the collapse of left-wing economic and political systems, which are currently straining under the financial burdens of social programs and public employee salaries and benefits. As Europe demonstrates to anyone willing to face reality, the welfare state is failing. The welfare state, even when well-intentioned, is a Ponzi scheme that inevitably will fall upon the shoulders of the young, who will one day recognize how they have been suckered. I worry, however, that their realization will not guarantee a rejection of leftism, but may render voters more receptive to populist demagogues.

The other trend is for those of us who understand how morally weak the human heart is, and therefore how much we need religion, to fight back with a war of ideas and values. We need to convince broad audiences that the appeal to feelings that sounds so compelling and thoughtful and generous has, in fact, dark implications, and we can point them out in objective detail. We need to revive the old truism, "The road to hell is paved with good intentions," and teach ordinary Americans to mistrust the politician and pundit who promise to "feel your pain" and act in your interest. The available evidence is so copious that I can't imagine that an informed, forceful presentation of the disaster of feelings-based policy can fail. Here, too, though, I worry that a vigorous assault on ideas and values of the Age of Feelings will produce a fevered counterattack using all the cheap tools of feelings-based rhetoric ("They don't care about poor people. . . . They hate gays. . . .")—a tactic that has worked well up to this point, as we see with the ineffective Republican response to the "War on Women." From what I've seen, not enough people can articulate the moral decline that feelings-based, religion-free policies produce, and many articulate opponents of leftism—such as libertarians—only oppose large government, not secular, feelings-based morality.

Nevertheless, there is hope.

Across our northern border, though many Canadians have been seduced by leftism, at this moment its prime minister, Stephen Harper, has emerged into a great moral leader in the world. As a religious man and a conservative, he is not only opposed to ever larger government, but he is also guided by a clear understanding of good and evil—hence his uniquely robust support for Israel and opposition to Iran acquiring nuclear weapons.

But we cannot await the coming of an American Stephen Harper, an American Margaret Thatcher, or another Ronald Reagan. We need, first and foremost, to understand, and to teach every generation, that the heart—even a good heart—is a very poor guide to making a good world.

References

Arcidiacono, Peter, et al. "What Happens after Enrollment? An Analysis of the Time Path of Racial Differences in GPA and Major Choice." *IZA Journal of Labor Economics* 1 (2012): 1–24, http://public.econ.duke.edu/~psarcidi/grades_4.0.pdf.
Brodhead, Richard. "Duke and the Legacy of Race." Speech at the Annual Meeting of the University Faculty, March 22, 2012, http://m.today.duke.edu/2012/03/rhbfacultytalk.
Brooks, David. "If It Feels Right." *New York Times*, September 12, 2011.
Obama, Barack. "You're on Your Own," speech delivered at University of Vermont, Burlington, March 30, 2012.
Smith, Christian. "An Academic Auto-da-Fe." *Chronicle of Higher Education*, July 23, 2012.

14

How Colleges Create the "Expectation of Confirmation"

Greg Lukianoff

"THEY DECIDED NOT to cancel the lecture, so we decided to cancel it for them," said Brown University student Jenny Li (Shallwani). Li and a group of Brown students made headlines when they successfully shut down a campus speech by former New York City Police Commissioner Ray Kelly on October 29, 2013.

Kelly is a controversial figure. His stop-and-frisk program is credited by some with reducing violent crime in New York City and condemned by others for its treatment of black and Hispanic New Yorkers. Having failed to convince Brown to call off Kelly's speech, the protestors decided that rather than ask Kelly hard questions during the time he had agreed to take questions from them, they would stop the speech altogether.

Roughly one minute into the lecture, the protestors stood and began chanting so loudly that they drowned out Kelly's words. After nearly half an hour of disruption, Kelly was forced to leave. When administrator Marisa Quinn lamented that she had "never seen in [her] 15 years at Brown the inability to have a dialogue," the protestors cheered (Morgan).

The Brown/Kelly incident is only one of the more notorious stories in an increasing trend of students organizing to prevent figures they disagree with from speaking on campus. In 2013, students at Johns Hopkins University teamed up to get black conservative Ben Carson disinvited as a commencement speaker, as did students at Swarthmore College when a former top George W. Bush administration aide and former World Bank president, Robert Zoellick, was tapped to address the school (see, respectively, Blake; Budryk). While those two speakers withdrew in the face of the intense protest, at the University of Michigan, Morehouse College, and the University of Pennsylvania's Wharton School that same year, speakers didn't have the chance to do so before they were disinvited by administrators heeding student objections to their purported views (see, respectively, Jaschik; Gammage; Bhowmick). While there are certainly examples going back decades of students chasing speakers they disliked off campus, in my work at the Foundation for Individual Rights in Education I have noticed a decided uptick in the frequency and intensity of such suppressions, with the push for disinvitation now a favored tactic.

The modern disinvitation movement represents a dramatic (if gradual) shift away from the ethic of robust debate to which both higher education and American society itself nominally subscribe. Protesting students may regard themselves as descendants of the landmark campus upheavals of the 1960s and early 1970s, but their strategies directly contradict the values of the Free Speech Movement, which, at least in principle, would demand not that speakers be prevented from speaking, but that opponents would get the chance to challenge and debate. Antiwar activists circa 1969 had thick skins and went to jail, accepting the rough-and-tumble of heated controversy. Disinvitation operates, however, on a different premise. It is the logical outgrowth of a campus environment that privileges emotional states over hard-nosed discussion and encourages a belief among students that there is a "right not to be offended."

We have passed from a campus climate in which robust, meaty, and sometimes harsh debate and discussion was regarded as a precondition of genuine learning and maturation, to one in which it is too often seen as a violation properly suppressed before it even happens. Decades after the supposed heyday of political correctness, I fear, campus culture has only moved farther away from a free speech ethic: the mythical "right not to be offended" is morphing into a stricter "right to have your views confirmed and not challenged."

Indeed, students are coming to believe that speakers with whom they disagree should not even be allowed on campus.

This move toward what I call an "expectation of confirmation" has troubling implications for American society as a whole. In this chapter I explore how the expectation of confirmation not only worsens the intellectual atmosphere on campus but also America's broader problem of political polarization.

Polarization and the Thickening Walls of Our Echo Chambers

In his 2008 book, *The Big Sort: Why the Clustering of Like-Minded America Is Tearing Us Apart*, journalist Bill Bishop compellingly argues that the United States is growing more politically polarized partially because Americans are increasingly moving to cities, neighborhoods, and counties that reflect their values and political beliefs. The reality of this clustering was laid out in even greater detail in Charles Murray's 2012 book, *Coming Apart*, which cited extensive data about the increasing isolation of neighborhoods according to both political viewpoints and economic class.

At the same time, the physical isolation that Bishop and Murray discuss is accompanied by increased opportunities to interact in online environments that reflect our existing biases. This trend was already fostered by twenty-four-hour news networks appealing respectively to conservatives and liberals, but has only accelerated as the amount of media produced by partisan websites has grown enough to occupy devoted readers every minute of every day. Left to their own devices, humans have a tendency to prefer to hear their existing views reflected back to them—and technological advancement has only increased our ability to achieve twenty-four-hour confirmation.

We should be concerned about creating echo chambers. Well-documented social science research demonstrates that people are prone to becoming more radical, and less understanding of opposing viewpoints, the more they cluster together with the like-minded. This affinity can lead to polarization and an intensified sense of tribalism in society, as we see our opponents increasingly as something more akin to alien enemies than fellow citizens with whom we disagree (Sunstein).

It's important, however, to step back for a moment and think about how this polarization may very well be the natural result of what we might otherwise consider progress. The aggregation of people into mutually sympathetic niches not only accords with the basic American right to assembly, but it also follows from the general advance of prosperity and leisure. Ronald Inglehart has outlined the clustering of communities around shared values in his theory of modernization progressing toward the "post-materialist society." Starting with work he published in the 1970s up through and including his work today, Inglehart theorizes that as societies become more affluent and move up Maslow's hierarchy of needs, they increasingly seek greater opportunities not only to express themselves and their values but also to have a sense of belonging in like-minded communities.

Seen in this light, the clustering of like-minded Americans seems only natural and is indeed part of the vision of a society we might all find seductive. In my everyday life I call these "problems of comfort," in that increasingly affluent societies generate problems that are the result of relative historic abundance and security. (The modern obesity epidemic, for example, is a "problem of comfort.") In this case, polarization is the natural result of people seeking out comfortable, self-affirming, morally coherent, and sympathetic communities. We therefore can probably expect political clustering and a propensity for groupthink to be tendencies that increase over time—as well as the illiberal mores and communication breakdowns that accompany them. It is all the more pressing, then, that we model and reform cultural institutions to combat these downsides.

The Role of Higher Education in Battling Self-Affirming Cliques

There is, in fact, an existing institution that can help America minimize the negative consequences of a society whose citizens increasingly are able to cocoon themselves in self-affirming communities: higher education.

Whereas once only a small percentage of Americans enrolled in college, as of 2012, as many as two-thirds of high school graduates attend college for at least some amount of time (National Center for Education Statistics). That percentage gets even higher when we factor in the number of citizens who take college classes at some point in their lives. Both the Bush and Obama administrations have pressed for more access and admissions to college, and employers increasingly demand workers with skills typically acquired in postsecondary coursework. The result is an everybody-should-go-to-college mode of thought that makes higher education a central feature of American culture and society.

Given its power and reach, higher education would seem to provide a ready-made solution to the problem of a society that naturally fragments into tighter echo chambers. After all, in theory at least, higher education valorizes the Socratic style of skeptical questioning and the systematization of doubt as represented by great scientific heroes such as Newton and Einstein. Also, in the 1960s and 1970s, the academy largely embraced the free-speech, "question authority" culture, and its impact reached beyond the campus walls to become a standard feature of popular culture and political discussion. American higher education should, therefore, be at the vanguard of teaching students to examine their assumptions, to engage in debate and discussion, to seek out opposing viewpoints, and to cultivate the crucial intellectual habit of applying skepticism to one's most dearly held beliefs.

Unfortunately, as I illustrated in my 2012 book, *Unlearning Liberty: Campus Censorship and the End of American Debate*, higher education is failing to instill in students these intellectual habits, and is, to a surprising degree, teaching students not to question much at all.

In *Unlearning Liberty*, I discuss my twelve years fighting for free speech, academic freedom, and the right to dissent on college campuses at the Foundation for Individual Rights in Education (FIRE).

My experience and that of my colleagues leaves me consistently appalled by how transgressions can land a student or professor in trouble. I cannot do justice to the thousands of cases I've seen of censorship on campus (see FIRE's blog, The Torch— http://thefire.org/torch—for an ongoing record of issues and incidents), but some standout examples over the years include

- A professor at Brandeis University was found guilty of racial harassment for explaining the historical origins of a racial epithet (Guess).
- Numerous cases where campuses refused to recognize Christian student groups because of their stance on sexuality and traditional marriage (Shibley).
- A student at Modesto Junior College who was refused the right to hand out copies of the Constitution in the public areas of campus on Constitution Day because he did not request advance state permission and did not limit his activities to the campus's tiny free speech zone (Kopan).

For the better part of two decades, researchers have studied the reservations college students seem to have about sharing their opinions and engaging in debate in class. While sociologists scratch their heads as to why this might be, a 2010 study by the Association of American Colleges and Universities might provide insight (Dey). The study simply asked students, professors, and staff if they believed it was "safe to hold unpopular positions on college campuses." Note how this question is worded: it does not ask if it is safe to express unpopular points of view, play devil's advocate, or engage in challenging thought experimentation, but *merely if it is "safe" simply to "hold" a point of view.* Despite this weak wording, only 40 percent of college freshmen strongly agreed. That percentage gets worse when put to sophomores, and then worse still when put to juniors. Notably, only 30 percent of seniors strongly agree. Apparently, as students learn more about the academic environment on their campuses, they become more pessimistic about their ability to dissent, disagree, and debate. Tellingly, the most pessimistic group on campus was college professors, of whom only 16.7 percent strongly agreed that it is "safe to hold" unpopular points of view on campus.

The Chronicle of Higher Education, perhaps the most influential niche publication for higher education professionals, placed an interesting spin on this study (Chapman). Despite the fact that the authors themselves were troubled by the low level of "strongly agree" responses to such a weakly worded question, the *Chronicle* reported the findings as positive because 45 percent of students answered they "somewhat agree" that it is "safe to hold unpopular positions" on campus. If nearly half of students only somewhat agree that it is safe to merely *hold* an unpopular view on campus, this does not indicate a positive environment for dissent or debate on campus. And again, optimism about the openness of the academic environment declined as students, employees, and professors spent more time on campus.

As my experience at FIRE can attest, this pessimism is warranted. But students generally avoid getting in trouble by following four simple rules:

- Talk to the students you already agree with.
- Join ideological groups that reflect your existing beliefs.
- Do not disagree with professors whose egos cannot take it.
- In general, shy away from discussing controversial topics.

These four guidelines can keep most students out of the dean's office and free of their peers' displeasure during their time in college.

Unfortunately, these rules only reinforce a problem of clustering and polarization that Mark Bauerlein and many others have observed accelerating on campus over the years—a problem that we know already exists in broader society. The rules also neutralize the unique opportunity that higher education makes possible: having intelligent discussions across lines of ideological difference.

The harm of these bad intellectual habits was perhaps best illustrated in a 2011 book titled *Academically Adrift: Limited Learning on College Campuses* (Arum and Roksa), which demonstrated that students are not showing improvements in their critical thinking skills from matriculation to graduation. Part of this evaluation tested students' ability to articulate more than one side of an argument. To a disturbing degree, students across institutions could not effectively accomplish this basic intellectual task. If campuses lived up to the promise of encouraging robust debate rather than squelching it, we could expect far better results.

What's more, there can be little doubt that university students are taking the bad habits they learn on campus into the larger society once they graduate. In Diana Mutz's 2006 book, *Hearing the Other Side*, the author cites striking evidence of an inverse relationship between how much education one has acquired and how many political disagreements one undergoes in an average month. In other words, people with a high school education or less are the *most likely* to engage in discussions along lines of political and philosophical disagreement, while those with higher levels of education are less likely. This is precisely the opposite effect that one would expect from an educational environment that properly teaches students that educated people seek out for discussion those with whom they disagree.

Confirmation bias refers to the human tendency to prefer data that confirm preexisting hypotheses and discount contrary evidence. It is, to put it mildly, generally considered to be a problem to be overcome, not only in scientific contexts, but in cultural and political settings as well. Unfortunately, given Mutz's evidence and the caseload at FIRE, we can conclude that higher education seems actually to work toward the opposite goal, promoting in some students a provisional openness to contrary opinions, but an expectation of confirmation: that is, an expectation that their biases should be, at best, validated, but at the very least, not challenged. In a distorted reflection of how fighting confirmation bias helps bring science and other disciplines to better and sturdier ideas, the establishment on campus of this expectation of confirmation threatens to allow thinner, less coherent, and less useful (but more comforting) ideas to flourish.

So, American academia, an institution that should help us fight the tendency of Americans to cluster ourselves in self-affirming cliques, instead encourages citizens to reinforce the walls of their echo chambers. Indeed, colleges today instill in students an unrealistic expectation that their environment should conform to their existing biases and beliefs. As they do so, young people earning college degrees fail to recognize that they inhabit a pluralistic society made up of individuals and groups with discrete and sometimes conflicting interests and outlooks, and when they encounter opposing forces, they judge them as wrongheaded or worse and act toward their suppression.

Can College Help Break Down the Expectation of Confirmation?

Is it possible to set things right? To produce a kind of higher education experience that teaches a generation the creativity, insight, and wisdom that is unleashed by stepping outside our comfortable self-affirming cliques to engage those with whom we disagree and figure out why we disagree?

I'm not always optimistic, but I can chart promising steps toward reform. Perhaps the most important thing that universities can do is simply to require students to engage in formal debates on meaningful and controversial topics as part of general education requirements. Part of students' orientation, too, should involve instruction in productive academic engagement, including the axiom that we fight offensive speech not with censorship but with contrary words. The practice of making oneself take the other side of an argument would help critical thinking skills, and it would also reduce the likelihood of people viewing those on the "other side" as representatives of societal evil. Being able fully to comprehend the opposing side of an argument is a vital skill that will only become more important given that the trend toward self-affirming physical and online environments is unlikely to stop.

Even these modest proposals face serious challenges, the magnitude of which was brought home to me by a student with whom I spoke at Harvard in the spring of 2013. He approached me after a speech, saying that he completely believed in everything I had to say about free speech and debate on campus, but that his attempts to get Oxford-style debates on serious issues to happen was met with constant pushback. On the truly controversial issues, whether they were immigration, affirmative action, or the "War on Terror," he added, the student population would not accept anyone representing the "other side" of the issue.

Obviously, it is hard to have real discussions without a willingness to put an onus on the listener to deal with hearing an opinion he or she might dislike or believe to be wrong. After all, a key measure of being an intellectual used to be how well the thinker in question knew the details of opponents' best arguments. We should instruct students that educated people see it as a duty to seek out intelligent people with whom they disagree for debate and discussion. This would require a major cultural shift away from the way campuses currently operate and is nearly impossible to achieve as long as the "right not to be offended" and the "expectation of confirmation" remain a reality on campus.

If we should be so lucky as to have a global environment in which relative material comfort continues to spread, such progress is going to produce new and emergent problems. Economic advancement, we must realize, may entail certain social and cultural costs that educational institutions must address. In much the same way that regular exercise and a disciplined diet help in the fight against obesity, teaching the intellectual habit of fighting confirmation bias, rather than expecting to have views affirmed, is crucial to the intellectual development and civic health of our society.

Higher education could and should play a crucial role in this process—but it needs to take a long, hard look at itself and ask if it actually creates an environment that is conducive to the bold questioning and uncomfortable discussions that intellectual and societal innovation demands.

References

Arum, Richard, and Josipa Roksa. *Academically Adrift: Limited Learning on College Campuses.* Chicago: University of Chicago Press, 2011.

Bauerlein, Mark. *The Dumbest Generation: How the Digital Age Stupefies Young Americans and Jeopardizes Our Future (Or, Don't Trust Anyone under 30).* New York: Tarcher/Penguin, 2008.

Bhowmick, Nilanjana. "Why Wharton Canceled Narendra Modi's Speech." *Time,* March 5, 2013, http://world.time.com/2013/03/05/why-wharton-canceled-narendra-modis-speech.

Bishop, Bill. *The Big Sort: Why the Clustering of Like-Minded America Is Tearing Us Apart.* New York: Houghton Mifflin, 2008.

Blake, Aaron. "Ben Carson Withdraws as Johns Hopkins Graduation Speaker." *The Washington Post,* April 10, 2013.

Budryk, Zack. "A Speaker Withdraws at Swarthmore." Insidehighered.com, April 8, 2013, http://www.insidehighered.com/news/2013/04/08/swarthmore-commencement-speaker-withdraws-over-controversy.

Chapman, Paige. "Most Students Say It's Safe to Hold Unpopular Views on Their Campuses." *The Chronicle of Higher Education,* September 16, 2010, https://chronicle.com/article/Most-Students-Say-Its-Safe-to/124507/.

Dey, Eric L., et al. *Engaging Diverse Viewpoints: What Is the Campus Climate for Perspective-Taking?* Washington, DC: Association of American Colleges and Universities, 2010, http://www.aacu.org/core_commitments/documents/Engaging_Diverse_Viewpoints.pdf.

Gammage, Jeff. "Controversy Surrounds Philadelphia Pastor's Canceled Speech." *The Philadelphia Inquirer,* April 28, 2013.

Guess, Andy. "Sending in the Class Monitor." Insidehighered.com, November 9, 2007, http://www.insidehighered.com/news/2007/11/09/brandeis.

Inglehart, Ronald F. "Changing Values among Western Publics from 1970 to 2006." *West European Politics* 31 (2008): 130–46.

Jaschik, Scott. "Alice Walker Disinvited." Insidehighered.com, August 16, 2013, http://www.insidehighered.com/news/2013/08/16/university-michigan-rescinds-invitation-alice-walker.

Kopan, Tal. "Student Stopped from Handing Out Constitutions on Constitution Day Sues." *Politico,* October 10, 2013, http://www.politico.com/blogs/under-the-radar/2013/10/student-stopped-from-handing-out-constitutions-on-174792.html.

Lukianoff, Greg. *Unlearning Liberty: Campus Censorship and the End of American Debate.* New York: Encounter Books, 2012.

Morgan, Thomas J. "Protesters Boo NYC Police Commissioner Kelly from Stage at Brown University." *Providence Journal,* October 29, 2013.

Murray, Charles. *Coming Apart: The State of White America, 1960–2010.* New York: Crown, 2012.

Mutz, Diana. *Hearing the Other Side: Deliberative vs. Participatory Democracy.* Cambridge: Cambridge University Press, 2006.

National Center for Education Statistics. *Digest of Education Statistics, 2012,* http://nces.ed.gov/programs/digest/index.asp.

Shallwani, Pervaiz. "Kelly Booed Off Stage during Talk." *The Wall Street Journal*, October 29, 2013.

Shibley, Robert. "Vanderbilt to Religious Students: Are Your Beliefs Really That Important?" *Daily Caller*, January 31, 2012, http://dailycaller.com/2012/01/31/vanderbilt-to-religious-students-are-your-beliefs-really-that-important.

Sunstein, Cass. *Going to Extremes: How Like Minds Unite and Divide*. New York: Oxford University Press, 2009.

15

The New Antinomian Attitude

R. R. Reno

The American Mind has a moral dimension, one transformed in recent decades in a fundamental way. We've all heard about, or lived through, the turmoil of the 1960s. "Make love, not war" was more than a political gesture, more than an antiwar protest. On a deeper level the juxtaposition of violence and lovemaking expressed a new attitude toward desire, one captured succinctly in another slogan of the era: "It is forbidden to forbid." Let's put an end to the repressive attack of the moral "No!" and live in accord with desire's perennial "Yes!" urged leading voices of the time in books, movies, TV shows, speeches, and newspapers. It lay at the root of the sexual revolution, and the fact that it is an injunction that no society can adopt and proceed to thrive didn't slow its progress. Some desires need to be contained, not just criminal ones, but the triumph of desire's "Yes!" spread from the counterculture to social movements to mainstream culture with a momentum that appears at this stage nearly miraculous. The American Mind has reorganized itself to be as solicitous as possible of desire's longings, giving itself a whole different path of obedience. Today, we do our moral reasoning in an Empire of Desire.

These days a man can wake up and say, "Enough! I'm tired of fighting against my innermost feelings. I've always felt myself to be a woman, and I'll be damned if I'll let myself go on like this." Medical professionals stand ready at hand; psychologists are prepared to help. If he has generous and expansive insurance coverage, then the way is clear. Hormones are administered, surgeries performed, wardrobes changed. Eventually, family, friends, and coworkers are informed that Charlie is now Charlene.

In itself this does not shock me. *The Golden Ass*, written by Apuleius in the second century, tells a ribald tale of human depravity and excess, a useful reminder that Michael Jackson was not a uniquely modern phenomenon. The human psyche is unstable and diverse, and, like water finding its way downhill, our intense wants and urgent desires seek paths toward satisfaction.

What's surprising is the moral revolution in our culture, the remarkably swift and forceful change in the way we think about those desires. Charlie can become Charlene—and he can also feel entirely justified in demanding that everyone around him accept and even affirm his decision. We may snicker inwardly and roll our eyes in unguarded moments, but for the most part we fall in line and do our best to make Charlie's transformation seem like any other personal decision—a lifestyle choice, as we often say.

Richard Weaver once wrote, "Every man participating in a culture has three levels of conscious reflection: his specific ideas about things, his general beliefs or convictions, and his metaphysical dream of the world" (18). At the level of specific ideas and general convictions, our age has settled into a number of pragmatic prohibitions and exhortations. No smoking! Count your calories! Build your resume! Save for retirement! Safe sex! Locally sourced food! All this and more testifies to the ongoing and powerful role of behavior-shaping norms.

Yet, underneath all this we find an antinomian sensibility, which means a tacit conviction that human beings flourish to the degree that they're free to satisfy their personal desires, even if those desires run against long-standing moral traditions and (certain) mainstream norms. What makes for happiness and fulfillment—and here we enter into the metaphysical dream that defines our era—is an Empire of Desire. Ministered to by a therapeutic vocabulary of empowerment, the pedagogy of multiculturalism, and our dominant, paradoxical moral code of nonjudgmentalism, this empire has come to dominate the American Mind. We affirm countless little disciplines to ensure health, productivity, success, and social harmony. But we push these social mores, disciplines, and restraints to the margins of our souls, creating space for a bespoke life tailored to our desires. In the Empire of Desire, Charlie can become Charlene without guilt, shame, or social stigma.

It is a profound transformation—not Charlie's transsexual desire, but the social approval of it or of any other desire that doesn't forbid anyone else's. The Empire of Desire compliments us for having adopted a more open and virtuous attitude, and it reassures us that we can shrug off the alarm it causes in people who haven't accepted the new regime of nonjudgmentalism. But our widespread, casual assent to the new regime can't dispel the fact that it overturns religious beliefs and ethical norms that have prevailed in Western civilization from the beginning, nor can it ignore how fundamentally it revises the makeup of the human mind and soul. Much more than a shift in social attitudes has happened. The new status of desire as a primal force to be obeyed rather than one to be contained affects us all, reshaping our sense of what constitutes a good life. We have, in fact, embarked on a radical and hazardous human experiment. Never before have people organized personal and public life around the dictates of desire.

A largely forgotten figure today, Norman O. Brown was for a brief moment an intellectual celebrity. Born in 1913 he came to maturity during two great crises of the twentieth century: the Great Depression and World War II. Like many others, his youthful response was to ally himself with progressive causes. However, in the aftermath of World War II, as the Cold War deepened and American society turned away from revolutionary politics, Brown became demoralized by what he took to be a spirit of complacency. This led him to a broader analysis that drew on psychological and metaphysical theories, not just political ideals. He came to fix on what he identified as the life-destroying impact of culture: its fundamental goal of disciplining desire.

In 1959 he published the results of his reflections, *Life Against Death: The Psychoanalytical Meaning of History*, an ambitious, speculative book that along with *Love's Body* (1966) gave theoretical expression to the counterculture of the 1960s. His muse was Sigmund Freud, a figure to whom many mid-twentieth-century Americans were turning in order to understand the inner workings of the soul and its relation to society.

By Freud's way of thinking, the human person is caught in a painful bind. The psychic energy for life comes from instinctual desires, the so-called id. Against the anarchy of primitive desires, Freud's psychoanalytic theory posits the existence of the ego, the structured reality of our conscious lives that emerges from the way in which the instincts are shaped and redirected by culturally mediated repressions that we internalize.

Freud held out no hope that our instinctual desires can be brought into a deep, satisfying harmony within these repressive disciplines. As Philip Rieff observes in his unsurpassed account of the larger significance of psychoanalytic theory, *Freud: The Mind of the Moralist*, the therapeutic goal, as Freud understood it, is not to achieve a resolution of conflict between id and ego, but rather to seek its humane, scientific management. As someone who acknowledged the irrational roots of culture, yet maintained the necessity of repressive restraint, Freud was an ambiguous thinker. "He was more a statesman of the inner life," writes Rieff. His psychoanalytic approach aimed "at shrewd compromises with the human condition, not its basic transformation" (xx). Freud believed that the repressive limitation of instinctual desires is the fundamental condition for civilized life, and he would have regarded the cultural radicalism of the 1960s with alarm.

Like so many optimistic American readers of Freud, Brown deemed this acquiescence to the inevitable necessity of self-aimed repression intolerably pessimistic, a type of self-destruction. We should not be satisfied with the grim prospect of an unending Cold War between the vigilant ego and the all-desiring id, he insisted. Instead, we should read Freud metaphysically rather than therapeutically. The id—pure desire—must be seen as the deepest, truest source of life, a vital energy to be cherished and worshipped, not repressed and disciplined.

Brown's decision to make desire his redemptive principle was a stroke of genius. Freud (and the rest of modern social science) faced a puzzling fact. What would seem to be the most natural and urgent dimension of the soul—our instinctual desires—must always and everywhere be controlled and dominated by moral ideals and cultural norms. But where do these norms gain their power? In traditional cultures, this power has come from on high. For Plato all reality is tensed with a yearning to return to the transcendent source of being. Biblical religion envisions the more straightforward mechanism of law given by God. Because he was a scientist, Freud was committed to a naturalistic explanation, but it led him to a paradox. Our natural self—that is to say, our instinctual desires—must somehow provide the explanation for its own repression. But how can the self-limiting imperatives of the ego be energized by the very instincts they repress?

Freud brilliantly devised a mechanism to explain how this is possible. A process of sublimation refines and redirects instinctual desires to refresh and renew the psychic potency of the repressive norms. Erotic desire circulates back upon itself, now in the form of the stamping power of social norms that tell us "do this" and "don't do that." From this theory of the instinctual source of culture, Brown draws the obvious metaphysical conclusion: "The essence of man consists, not, as Descartes maintained, in thinking, but in desiring" (*Life Against Death*, 6). From this metaphysical truth, a moral obligation followed: Our goal should be to live in accord with this essence, which he refers to as "the body."

The revolutionary and distinctively postmodern character of *Life Against Death* flows directly from this exaltation of desire. Traditional views see "the body" as subordinate, our desires properly ordered toward something higher. For example, as Plato observes in one of his dialogues, we are erotically attracted to the beautiful body of another person, but we intuitively sense that our desire will not be fully satisfied, for human bodies age, decay, and lose their alluring qualities. So we climb the ladder of desire, as it were, relishing the beauty of statues of beautiful bodies that are made of enduring marble. Yet even this will not satisfy the soul, thinks Plato, and so we take a farther and final step, transforming our erotic desire for beautiful bodies into an intellectual contemplation of the very idea of beauty.

Aristotle had a less dreamy view. As he recognized, we need to be subjected to the disciplining power of cultural norms that habituate and guide our desires into stable forms, the virtues. In the *Poetics*, for instance, Aristotle praises tragedies that inflame our emotions and engage our interests, but then resolve them through plausible developments in the plot, ending in a resolution that leaves audiences enlightened and sobered. This need for external discipline became even stronger in the Christian tradition. Saint Augustine saw that original sin perverts our desires, making them stubbornly ordered toward self-love. Moreover, he believed that we are destined for something higher than the natural nobility of Aristotle's well-trained soul. Fellowship with God extends beyond our natural possibilities. Therefore, we need a divine repair of our disordered desires, as well as a pedagogy that takes us beyond this world. Faith, hope, and love stretch the soul upward. They are, as Saint Thomas put it centuries later, supernatural virtues.

Modern humanism rejects the Christian vision of disciplines of the soul ordained by God and administered by the church, but it nonetheless retains the basic structure of the traditional view. Kant articulated what he took to be the universal moral law for all rational creatures, and he thought this critical principle able to transform external commandments into an internal law that the person can accept as his own, thus becoming his own tutor and disciplinarian. The later Romantics, such as Chateaubriand, Wordsworth, and the Brothers Grimm, emphasized myth, fantasy, and feeling. They were uneasy with Kant's absorption of individuality into a universal humanity defined by reason. Wordsworth and others placed an accent on inner authenticity, moments of intense feeling that unified consciousness and structured a human life. The deepest moral law, therefore, is to be true to oneself. Nonetheless, the consensus remained intact. A law emerges from within the self—from reason, experience, or a lightning flash of self-possession. It properly governs the soul, giving purpose and direction to "the body."

Not surprisingly, in Brown's view, none of these views of human flourishing are satisfactory. All treat desire as something to be disciplined, thus dooming the human person to perpetual alienation—the conflict of life ("the body") against death ("repression"). Brown does not wish to be a reformer, and he has no interest in replacing today's disciplining cultural norms with another, supposedly purified set. He's not even loyal to the nebulous norm of authenticity, because he recognizes that the ideal of a unified consciousness becomes a repressive ideal that disciplines our ever-changing, often conflicting desires. Instead, by his way of thinking, culture *itself* becomes the great enemy of humanity. The goal of a true humanism, he argues, requires a new metaphysical dream, one in which we affirm the supreme redemptive power of desire in all its primitive, polymorphous perversity.

His exhortations are soaring. We should forsake the repressive, habituating project of culture and embrace "that simple health that animals enjoy" (*Life Against Death,* 311). The destruction of civilization—"the abolition of repression"—becomes the great imperative against imperatives. No longer forming life in accord with the projects of progress, competition, and domination that empower the ego, in a postcultural world we shall live in "the mode of unrepressed bodies," cultivating a "Dionysian or body mysticism" that simply seeks and finds satisfaction as an undifferentiated biological mass, "the body" (307–10). An unmitigated loyalty to our essence as instinct-driven animals will usher in the End of History, trigger "the resurrection of the body," and establish the timeless, unchanging, anarchic, and antinomian Empire of Desire.

It's easy to make fun of Norman O. Brown. His appeals to the "dialectical metaphysics of hope" can sound hopelessly jejune and the Dionysian ecstasies overwrought. Nonetheless, his mobile metaphysical imagination allowed him to recognize the larger implications of modern, naturalistic conceptions of culture, and he drew the obvious conclusions in bold, prophetic strokes. Today, nobody talks about "body mysticism," but postmodern cultural theory teaches that social norms and cultural ideals are nothing more than the extruded, solidified manifestations of the primitive, primeval dimensions of the human psyche: sexual desires, will-to-power, a lust for domination, and so forth. Even our selfish goals—to look thin or dress for success—are analyzed as social constructs energized by manipulative advertising driven by capitalist desire for profit. All norms, including those we impose on ourselves, emerge from a more primary circulation of desire.

Moreover, the theoretical gestures that have predominated over the last forty years fit the antinomianism that Brown championed. They are unified by a metaphysical abhorrence of law and preference for spontaneity. Terms such as "metanarrative," "univocality," "foundationalism," and "presence" suggest determinative principles and authoritative truths. Not surprisingly, these pronomian terms are consistently used to refute, denounce, or discredit. In contrast, terms such as "difference," "heterogeneity," and "absence" cut against enduring principles and stable truths, and they are always deployed to evoke positive alternatives. "Marginality" is bathed in luminous light. "Alterity" serves as a liberating force. I can think of no postmodern theoretical gesture, in fact, that does not reflect the broad shift in the West toward the antinomian ideal. True, we have political correctness. It's not a moral vision, though, but instead a regulatory regime that has grown up around postmodern theory over the last few decades and works to impose the singular anti-law in the Empire of Desires: it is forbidden to forbid. Something like Norman O. Brown's metaphysical dream predominates.

The Italian philosopher Gianni Vattimo provides a particularly clear and forthright example. "Philosophy, today," he writes in *After Christianity*, "conceives of Being as event and as destiny of weakening" (44). The modern collapse of Christianity as the source of law for the self and society seems like a failure, but it is in fact the realization of Christianity's true spiritual genius. We are heading, he prophesies, "toward emancipation by diminishing strong structures (in thought, individual consciousness, political power, social relations, and religion)" (91). Indirectly (and unknowingly) evoking the rich tradition of liberal Protestant theology, Vattimo suggests that this antinomian trajectory is "a transcription of the Christian message of the incarnation of God, which Saint Paul also calls kenosis—that is, the abasement, humiliation, and weakening of God" (91). Here we find a wonderfully pure expression of the metaphysical dream of our era: God himself is an antinomian. Christ does not fulfill the law of Moses; instead, he undercuts Moses and evacuates the law of all normative power. Sinai becomes the anti-Christ.

Few contemporary academics have Vattimo's flair for metaphysical rhetoric or willingness to give theological expression to their vision of human flourishing. However, the practice of cultural study over recent decades has been given over almost entirely to what Vattimo calls "weakening." In fact, Norman O. Brown has a long chapter devoted to showing that "money is excrement." The effect is to disenchant the social norms of bourgeois society. The most influential cultural theorist since the 1960s, Michel Foucault, probably never read Brown, but his intellectual life was devoted to detailed studies of cultural norms oriented toward the very same goal. Every gimcrack cultural theorist today has internalized this mode of analysis: what seems like a noble cultural ideal or elevating vision of the good life is, in fact, the intellectually sublimated form of a desire for domination, or a class interest, or the metaphysics of presence. Thus, the critical platitude of our postmodern age: culture is an artificially solidified, socially sanctified, and rhetorically disguised expression of the desires of the powerful.

This presumption about culture is so widespread that it has become an item of almost unconscious conviction. In *Harper's Magazine*, writer and literary scholar Mark Slouka launches a sally against what he regards as the crushing dominance of economic rationality in contemporary higher education. We are, he writes, "hypnotized by quarterly reports and profit margins." Against this show-me-the-money mentality, Slouka pleads for the importance of culture, hoping to revitalize "the deep civic function of the arts and the humanities" (33). Yet, this would-be humanist is a citizen of the Empire of Desire: "I believe that what rules us is less the world of goods and services than the immaterial ones of whims, assumptions, delusions, and lies" (32). Does Slouka really think that this simplistic reductionism will inspire anyone to a renewed and heightened love of the arts and humanities? He probably hasn't given it any thought. The dark turn is typical of our era. Culture isn't really "immaterial" in any metaphysical sense. Instead, what we take to be cultural ideals and norms for living a humane life are disguised and deluded expressions of. . . . Slouka doesn't fill in the blank, but contemporary literary and cultural theory consistently gives this answer: Cultural artifacts are etherealized expressions of our material, instinctual desires for pleasure and domination.

Slouka's plea for humanistic study cannot succeed, because he cannot conceive of an alternative to the Empire of Desire. Why should we concern ourselves with the arts and humanities? Aren't we told that they have nothing to offer other than the desires of others costumed with metaphysical terms and dolled up with artful brushstrokes and well-written sentences? We default to GDP, because, as his own cynicism shows, our metaphysical dreams are dominated by images of desire: desires expressed, satisfied, sublimated, repressed, redirected, imposed, and reified. Students, educators, politicians—all of us to one degree or another—draw the sensible conclusion. As long as we cannot imagine anything real and lasting and true other than primitive instincts, we might as well concentrate our minds on the economic, medical, psychological factors that promise to maximize our satisfaction. If we are fated to be ruled by desire, then we ought to acquaint ourselves with the logic of its circulation and adopt our postmodern roles as bureaucrats, therapists, managers, and other well-groomed functionaries trained to analyze and maintain the Empire of Desire.

It's important to recognize that the downward push of the Empire of Desire—the essence of life is sexual desire and the will-to-power—is entirely consistent with something that looks like moral zeal. Brown styled himself a new Moses: Choose life! The Empire of Desire is a metaphysical dream, something beyond the reach of culture, if not above, then below our present circumstances. We must seek to realize the dream. Life is better, more humane, and more just to the degree that we succeed in relaxing the grip of traditional morality over our interior lives so that our desires can be more freely satisfied, so that Charlie can become Charlene.

To serve this dream we've empowered the dictatorship of relativism, which is closely allied with the harrying mentality of political correctness. Every empire needs rules and regulations, which we certainly have, ranging from a few minimal but bright-line limits (adults having sex with adolescents is absolutely prohibited) to hopelessly vague ones (date rape is a good example). Smokers are subjected to shaming; recycling has become a latter-day sign of environmental virtue. Speech codes regulate the words we use and the thoughts we're allowed to express. Moreover, older traditions endure in diminished forms. Hardly anybody thinks twice about cohabitation before marriage, but when couples get serious they expect monogamy and resent betrayal. Few admire liars, and while we may fail in our own lives, we still honor the sacrifices parents make for the sake of their children. The Empire of Desire's dominion isn't complete.

Nevertheless, in this regime moral authority is largely exercised for a very specific purpose: to minimize the psychological power of moral authority. Middle school teachers catechize their students: One is to be nonjudgmental—one *must* be nonjudgmental. We're now trained to counter the slightest hint of judgment with deflationary gestures: "Speaking as I do from a white, privileged, first-world perspective," and so on. It is forbidden to forbid, and our moral judgments need to be transformed into their true meaning, that is, expressions of class bias, historical circumstances, or (best of all) personal preferences.

The greatest threat we presently face is not Islamic terrorism, global warming, nuclear proliferation, genocide, or poverty, pressing as these problems may be. The antinomian revolution in the postmodern West poses a deeper, more fundamental, and profound existential threat to the human future, because it erodes the cultural capital necessary for a morally robust response to these challenges and others. The richest and most powerful countries in the world are dominated by an elite that, however individually well-intentioned and personally influenced by inherited moral traditions, think as Brown urges, giving priority to desire. We are being trained to live in the Empire of Desire, which begins with changing our minds about the relationship of desire to the law, any law.

In his apocalyptic reveries, Brown failed to see the practical upshot of his hoped for "resurrection of the body." Instead of life abundant, we are sliding toward a world of barbarized masses overseen by often cynical elites who are reconciled to amoral techniques of governance appropriate to human herds animated by raw lusts and fears. We can see the first-fruits of this antinomian world: an expanding underclass disciplined by the threat of incarceration and domesticated by mass entertainment, adolescent boys managed with prescribed drugs, growing industries of therapeutic intervention, and the beginnings of paternalistic controls, whether of the blatant sort proposed by former New York mayor Michael Bloomberg, or the more hidden "nudges" advocated by Harvard professor and former Obama administration official Cass Sunstein.

Today's social theorists are technicians in our metaphysical dream. They work to sustain the Empire of Desire, recommending carefully designed cattle prods with calibrated dials that range from the soft setting of economic incentives to the censorious stigmas of political correctness, culminating in the harsh options of lethal force. The bureaucratic instruments of social management have become increasingly important, justified by philanthropic benevolence and palliated with a therapeutic empathy. Legal regulation of personal behavior, family life, and social interactions expand in order to take over the ordering, harmonizing function once performed by an unofficial but deeply internalized cultural *nomos*. We're policed and regulated and managed. Even the children of the wealthy are disciplined by the brutal competition for spots at top colleges and universities—and then for the top jobs.

There is no revolt building against this regime. We have accepted the bargain—a public culture of petty regulations and forthright economic discipline in exchange for freedom to live in accord with our private, intimate desires. The best one can hope for, I suppose, is to detail the havoc that desire's metaphysical priority produces—broken families, broken relationships, social pathologies. With this sober truth in front of us, we'll become like most upper middle-class Americans, the praetorian guard of the Empire of Desire: people who are disciplined enough to make sure long-term self-interest prevails over short-term desire fulfillment. This will be a more functional world, but it will remain a soulless one that has lost its capacity to dream of something higher than desire—something *to* desire. A true rebellion requires commitment to a deep and fundamental ideal capable of organizing and disciplining desire, something worth living and dying for, something high and noble that haunts our metaphysical dreams.

References

Brown, Norman O. *Life Against Death: The Psychoanalytical Meaning of History.* Wesleyan, CT: Wesleyan University Press, 1959.

———. *Love's Body.* New York: Random House, 1966.

Rieff, Philip. *Freud: The Mind of the Moralist.* New York: Anchor Books, 1961.

Slouka, Mark. "Dehumanized: When Math and Science Rule the School." *Harper's Magazine* (September 2009): 32–40.

Vattimo, Gianni. *After Christianity.* Trans. Luca D'Isanto. New York: Columbia University Press, 2002.

Weaver, Richard. *Ideas Have Consequences.* Chicago: University of Chicago Press, 1948.

Afterword

Mark Bauerlein and Adam Bellow

In the Foreword, we stated that by the mid-1980s, educators, intellectuals, and other cultural elites had stopped talking about a common, essential American anything. But this was not to say that they had ceased talking about any America at all. On the contrary, they have continued to study, interpret, poll, praise and blame, memorialize and revise our nation's past, present, and future all the time. The need for citizens to reflect upon the state whose laws they must obey, upon the government to which they pay taxes, the economic system on which their fortunes rest, and the culture that pours over them every time they turn on the TV or computer doesn't go away. The individuals portrayed in this book seem to have lost that curiosity, but we persist in believing that it lingers, however much muted by other mental traits (entitlement mentality, youth narcissism, voter ignorance . . .). Several small upsurges of civic consciousness have transpired recently, for instance, Barack Obama's 2008 campaign and the rise of the Tea Party. It may be easier than we think to inspire large populations to imagine and respect what America is all about, beyond local facts and news of the moment. Politicians succeed when they do so, as do intellectuals, critics, teachers, and scholars who, in fact, are just as ready to reflect upon America as they ever were. But the assumptions have changed.

A telling example transpired not long ago in the pages of *Dissent* magazine (Winter and Spring, 2010), a symposium entitled "Intellectuals and Their America." It was a deliberate echo of older conversations about American identity and purpose, the editors conceiving it on the model of the 1952 *Partisan Review* symposium, "Our Country and Our Culture." In that prior discussion, thinkers and critics were asked to "examine the apparent fact that American intellectuals now regard America and its institutions in a new way." It wasn't just that the United States of 1950 was drastically different from the United States of 1937, making the America of *The Grapes of Wrath* and Fireside Chats into a fading universe. The geopolitical situation forced new conceptions, too. The Cold War had descended, an age of ideological combat with high stakes, communism making frightening gains in Eastern Europe and Asia and leading some to wonder if the American capitalism that many intellectuals despised in the Depression era was genuinely doomed. In the light of spreading totalitarianism, America looked less like a home of economic suffering and more like a guarantor of individual freedoms.

At least that was the implied development taken up by the participants in the symposium. The result was sober and farsighted, as *Dissent*'s emulation of it suggests. *Partisan* gathered intellectuals who were themselves undergoing ideological change, and they answered variously in ways that displayed prewar liberalism and socialism struggling to adjust to looming Cold War realities of the 1950s. But there was one element common to nearly all of them. They more or less accepted a distinctive American mind, identity, experience, or tradition. Skim the three numbers of that year in which essays appeared and you encounter one term and phrase after another advancing our country and citizens as a unified being, an exceptional one. The opening Editorial Statement itself mentions the "national mind" and "American civilization," and it raises "a recognition that the kind of democracy which exists in America has an intrinsic and positive value."

James Burnham cites "the Great American Promise" and affirms, "America has, it is true, added something new to the world."

Leslie Fiedler states that the "American *mythos*" was "real and effective," though it was always accompanied by "the guilt and terror involved in the American experience."

Reinhold Niebuhr puts "the American way of life" in sneerquotes, but still speaks of saving "our American culture."

Lionel Trilling hails "the great American tradition of non-conformism," and William Phillips mentions "our national experience," the "survival of American civilization," and a "new sense of country."

Irving Howe maintains that we must honor different groups and cultures in the United States, but admits that "only in America does [capitalism] still claim substantial adherence and display a degree of vigor, largely because of the special position of this country."

Arthur Schlesinger Jr., acknowledges our "various and pluralistic society" but still presses "the affirmation of America."

Newton Arvin identifies "the American writer in general," while William Barrett opens his essay, "Do I like being an American? It is a little bit like asking me whether I like being myself." He proceeds to observe, "No doubt, we are on our way to forming a new civilization in this country."

Joseph Frank notes "the special conditions of American culture" and "reaffirming the American tradition," and Richard Chase hails "a new hospitality to serious writing which speaks confidently and lovingly of America and her future."

There are dozens more examples of fundamental "American-ness" in the symposium, not all of them positive. Indeed, the contributors prove that projections of essential American identity can serve criticism as well as approval. During its first decades of existence, the intellectuals at *Partisan* generally fell to the left in matters of politics and to the right in matters of culture, and here they repeatedly express disgust with McCarthyism and mass culture, which they link to American traditions of populist revolt and utilitarian values. But still, positive or negative, *America* means something coherent and mythic—not altogether uniform, but unified. It has a patrimony available to all.

Needless to say, the *Partisan* view is out of fashion. When you hear those American words, a little voice in your head warns you off. You were schooled out of hegemony and patriotism long ago, perhaps by an English teacher who cast your beloved authors as Dead White Males; or a museum exhibit that framed the Constitution as a pro-slavery document; or a diversity orientation at your workplace that issued subtle threats to anyone who doesn't embrace the message; or the influential sections in Jean-François Lyotard's *The Postmodern Condition*, which exploded the "grand narratives" of history and nation; or the sight of Murphy Brown, righteous and solemn, chiding Dan Quayle for upholding the traditional nuclear family. Attentive minds have learned the cost of voicing an essential, fervent conception of America. Twenty-first-century intellectuals and academics know better than to confirm a unified American civilization and tradition or, worse, to wax "lovingly of America."

The contributors to the *Dissent* forum make no such mistakes. The editors likewise ask intellectuals to ponder first principles and core values and respond to the changing position of the United States in the preceding ten or fifteen years. We are more than a year past the economic crisis of Fall 2008, one year into President Obama's tenure, and more months into the occupations of Afghanistan and Iraq than anyone wants to count. Transformation is in the air. The times encourage intellectuals once more to probe beneath current events and pursue a similar reexamination of American meaning and purpose.

The participants are consummate observers of U.S. politics and culture, informed, astute, and literate. You see them on television and at exclusive forums in Washington, DC, and New York City. Regulars at *Washington Post*, *The New Republic*, *New York Times*, *New York Review of Books*, and *The Nation*, and professors at Columbia, Chicago, Georgetown, and Rutgers, by education and experience they have all the qualifications needed to exhibit the American past and present in universal stories, holistic values, and seminal myths. The editors of *Dissent* call upon them to "reflect on issues that bear profoundly on both their craft and their country," the adverb there asking for more than political opinion, personal expression, and current events. We expect depth as well as currency, ethics and *mythos* over partisanship and the news.

It doesn't happen. Rarely do they promote any essential norm or value that counts as uniquely American, nor do they identify a representative American self or mind. The first sign of de-unification lies in the title: the editors have changed the pronoun from "Our" to "Their"—not "Our Country and Our Culture," but "Intellectuals and Their America."

E. J. Dionne discusses patriotism, but his definition is abstract and procedural: "In a democracy, political engagement is an act of patriotism, a declaration of faith in the judgment of our fellow citizens and thus, ultimately, in one's nation." Patriotism includes love, but Dionne won't connect that love to any specific object in our nation. Instead, Dionne's patriotism is mostly adversarial, "the patriotism inherent in embedded criticism." This is a familiar setup. The critic raises universal ideals, de-Americanized abstractions such as "democratic politics demands an ethic of responsibility," then urges intellectuals to highlight our shortcomings. "They will call power to account even when those in power have some sympathy for their goals," he says. "They will lay out the requirements for a better future than the present even during times of progress." What those goals and requirements are remain unclear. The vision is empty; Dionne's model could apply anywhere. There is nothing in it specific to America.

Jackson Lears goes straight to U. S. politics, regretting the resurgence of the right following the countercultural waves of the 1960s. The "left intelligentsia retreated into the academy," he complains, and "farce" ensued. Their takeover of higher education rightly broke up the "hegemonic standard established by white males," but it also "created a new kind of fragmented interest-group politics unmoored from any larger vision of the good society." As we read that admission, we agree and admire Lears for making it in the pages of a magazine of the left. It sounds as if he's about to reverse that fragmentation with a unifying conception of America, citing a "larger notion of commonweal" in the next paragraph. Alas, it never arrives. At the end, Lears mentions once more "the claims of commonweal," but never states what they are. He notes how "The Right has disgraced itself by its inability to govern," opening a "moment of possibility," a great "opportunity for the Left." But to do what? The intellectuals, Lears says, must "articulate that larger vision." But he doesn't specify what it is.

Martha Nussbaum, too, acknowledges the value of national norms and identities. She praises patriotism as "an essential source of political identity and, ultimately, of global concern," adding, "The idea of the nation, however, can be transmitted in a powerfully motivating symbolic form, calling the heart to the service of noble ends." But Nussbaum will not spell out what the American idea is. In fact, for her, a national conception is but a step toward a larger one, "the service of all humanity." She declares herself a "world citizen" and commends Lincoln and Martin Luther King Jr., because they "used a resonant and moving idea of the nation to attach people's hearts to abstract moral values that ultimately acquire a cosmopolitan significance." The national idea, tradition, and identity should be transcended, not observed.

Katha Pollitt renounces patriotism entirely. She does enumerate some essential American attributes: "constitutional democracy; freedom of speech; Huck Finn and *Leaves of Grass*; fighting Hitler; shared prosperity; a general sense of optimism and openness; and, most important, ideals of social justice extended through struggle to more and more people (blacks, workers, women, gays, the disabled)." But it's just a list, perfunctory and random. Pollitt doesn't elaborate. Instead, she cautions us against attaching them too closely to America and overexerting our loyalty. "Why is patriotism so bad for America?" she asks. Because "It prevents us from seeing ourselves the way others see us." If you believe too firmly in American Exceptionalism, if you locate these ideals too much in our country, your mind narrows, you grow arrogant. Better to open it and cancel national commitments: "What if we took seriously the idea of one world?"

Michael Tomasky claims to be a patriot, but here is the object of his faith: "America is vast, weird, anomalous, and I love it. I admire the principles to which the nation aspires in its better moments."

Which principles and what better moments? He doesn't say. Instead, he denounces the Republican Party and Tea Party ("sounding crazier and crazier") and mocks Glenn Beck and his "followers."

Leon Wieseltier announces the prevailing wisdom that restrains these American ruminations: "At this late date in the discussion about identity, almost everybody recognizes that identity is multiple and plural." He admits the impulse to simplify and unify, to draw the experience of diverse peoples into a national bond. But before allowing it the slightest justification, Wieseltier rebuffs it as a "totalizing" process, a "Hegelian illusion," and worse: "A monistic account of human existence is a lie."

Michael Eric Dyson's entry is so focused on African Americans that a comprehensive American civics is out of the question.

Finally, Alice Kessler-Harris's entry reveals best the restraints twenty-first century intellectuals impose when discussing their country. After noting how much the 2008 Obama campaign inspired her and how far the Obama administration has failed those hopes, she promises to get past the year's politics when she accepts that intellectuals have "responsibilities to raise important questions about what is 'American.'" One might expect a few questions and answers to follow, but the scare quotes around "American" reveal a premise that prevents her from doing so. They mark any essential American meaning or entity as a local invention, a historical construct that people like Kessler-Harris regard only from the outside. They aren't part of it and they don't believe in it. And so, when she proposes "constructing a language of shared goals, rather than one of difference," just as Lears does, we aren't surprised that this language is geared to a partisan body, not the American whole. Her summons doesn't project a set of properly American goals for everyone. No, it is invented as an antidote to conservative slogans such as Reagan's "Morning in America" and Milton Friedman's "Free to Choose." It's a rhetoric for progressives, that's all.

We see a pattern here, empty civic universals on one side, party politics on the other, with a blind spot in the center where lies the meaning of America. No doubt, the *Dissent* writers consider their anti-Americanness a principled stance against hegemony and nationalism. To them, traditional patriotism smacks too much of racism, sexism, and exploitation, and the power of the people, when united under the wrong kind of "motivating symbolic form," runs to dark and frenzied ambitions. The Tea Party was launched by Rick Santelli's famous impromptu lecture delivered on CNBC from the floor of the Chicago Mercantile Exchange. It inspired people because it recalled a foundational American event that expressed a core American value. But intellectuals have generally treated the movement with contempt and accusation, partly because it reasserts a traditional American way of self-reliance.

Whether they are right or wrong about American politics and history, there is a contradiction in the position of the *Dissent* intellectuals. They want to mobilize Americans toward liberal and progressive enterprises, and they know they must craft a unifying vision and idiom. But if unification itself is dangerous, if essential American truths are phony and exclusionary, if there is no representative American mind, then they can't bring themselves to do it. All we get are exhortations that are so tepid and distant ("one world," "a better future") that they have no impact at all. Most people want something to believe in, and as citizens they want to connect it to their country. Make the ideal any larger than that and it loses force and specificity, becomes a vacuous religion. If the great civic axioms such as "All men are created equal" can't be grounded in an American condition, if there are no representative American figures and lives, then we have no common civic faith. Maybe that is the point. Social change requires unity, but these commentators eschew an all-American formation. The habits of diversity and group politics run too deep.

The result is a stultified presentation. Reading Dionne and the rest is a frustrating experience, no matter how intelligent and articulate they are. Their paragraphs sound uptight and halting, as if the writers are uncomfortable with the assignment, "Their America." Nothing they say will rouse the individuals portrayed in this volume from distractions and deficiencies. These intellectuals don't find anything typically American that elevates them and fills them with pride, and so they won't influence anyone else. In the *Partisan* symposium, the discussions are fluent and exciting, even when charges are leveled against the United States. There is no atmosphere of withholding in those pages, no sense that there are some things you should not say. A solemn passion runs through their pages, while a solemn guardedness runs through the *Dissent* version. A positive American idea is meaningful to the older figures, and they feel implicated in that meaning. For the younger ones, the only American idea that is meaningful to them is negative: the conviction that traditional notions of the America self, American way, and American Exceptionalism are political formations that marginalize and exclude certain groups.

They believe in the Diversity Idea, but it's a disabling condition. Diversity has no heroes and role models, nothing like Thoreau in the woods or the Joad family on the road or marchers striding across the Selma bridge (who aimed for integration, not diversity). It doesn't set a plan for your life the way Horatio Alger's characters do. There is no great text of diversity, no capacious and energizing words and images equal to those of the Declaration and Booker T. Washington's Atlanta Compromise speech. Self-reliance and the "city on a hill" are ordering notions, diversity a disordering one. It leaves people incognizant of their American being. Take away the devotion that core traditions and ideas provide and one can see why people no longer think past their social circuit, ignore the workings of government, and obsess over personal circumstances.

This restriction is not a political one. It goes deeper than that. It affects what people are capable of thinking. You may disparage the American Dream and regard the American Mind as a bourgeois invention, and you may point out the political purposes of American Exceptionalism, but you must realize that such essentialist conceptions serve a mental purpose. They supply individuals an orientation for their opinions and aims. They ground moral and political standards that can be applied to events and controversies of the day. They frame civic debate when it rises above the bare competition for resources. They allow citizens who may be otherwise rootless and struggling to declare, "I'm an American!" The ideal has to be singular, it has to unify people, not differentiate them, and it has to be familiar to the whole population, enough to help people imagine themselves as part of the whole. Individuals needn't agree on the merits of these essential Americanisms, or even mean the exact same thing when they discuss them; they just have to have a reasonably clear understanding of them, and out of that shared knowledge an intelligent affirmation can follow, and a constructive critique, too. A common language enables a meeting of minds and allows for meaningful disagreement.

An era of diversity and pluralism-without-unity dispels these commonalities. Notwithstanding its group identities, it operates on divisive assertions that fail to anchor individuals in a national community, as we readily see when we derive a diversity version of "I'm an American": "I am one of the many kinds of individuals who make up the population of the United States," or "I'm a female, heterosexual, Generation X, Asian American from Atlanta." The description is specific to her, to be sure, but it doesn't connect her to anyone outside her sub-subgroup. She has no national identity to go along with her sliced-up demographic one, and she mistrusts conceptions that transcend her categories. Multiculturalists and diversity proponents interpret that resistance as a stand against "melting pot" nationalism, a refusal to be absorbed in a myth that denies her (and her group) particular being and experience. But it restricts her mind as well. Her thoughts fall back upon her self. Why should she acquire historical knowledge about our country when she can't find her own identity in it? When she votes, why should she evaluate the candidates apart from her own immediate interests? Why relate to the government in any other way than in what it does for her group? The foundational myths and ideas attach her sole human existence to a historical epoch, a manifest destiny, a civic religion. Remove the essential Americanisms from her education and entertainments and her horizon shrinks—and she sees no reason to expand it.

This is the ironic result of a multiplication of identities, not a richer culture with more engaged citizens, but more disengaged citizens with a parochial outlook. It's a tragic situation. We have gained wider recognition of individuals, but we have lost *our* country and *our* culture. The Americans represented in this volume—students incited to protest disagreeable speakers, adults eager to take public assistance, citizens who see no good reason to vote . . . they are dis-related to America. They do not share in a national identity or character. No heritage inspires them, no ideas guide them. We have respected different races and cultures and sub-groups, but we no longer affirm the one body of all. We have denounced the American past so much (slavery, Wounded Knee, Jim Crow, Manzanar . . .) that our citizens have no legacy left to call their own.

America lies in bits and pieces, and its citizens are disengaged, tuned-out, self-involved. They set social life above civic life, racial and sexual identity over American identity. Our intellectuals are constrained by diversity from drawing the people together and Americanizing them, and so are most educators and politicians. But diversity isn't a faith, it's an anti-faith passing as one. When people hear its dogmas, they shrug, roll their eyes, or nod in thoughtless compliance, then go back to work and play. This is the predominant state of the American Mind, and it's not enough to sustain a free republic. What can we do?

A little more than a half-century ago, the counterculture blossomed in America and began a steady conquest of mainstream culture. The Beats, rock 'n' roll, Hollywood antiheroes, pop art, the free speech movement, Women's Lib, Gay Liberation, the Black Panthers . . . they changed America forever. It was a cultural revolution, not a political one. The conventional wisdom and behaviors of but a few years earlier seemed obsolete and slightly embarrassing once the revolution reached prime-time television. It was a stunning and unpredicted advent. Nobody who might have been asked in 1959 could have foreseen 1969.

It can happen again, another cultural revolution. That is what it will take to undo the delinquent habits and attitudes of our citizens and shake the diversity ideology of the elites. Readers may have read the essays in this volume with dismay, but we can't help but think they indicate a vacuum of civic and cultural meaning waiting to be filled. Something like an eruption of civic consciousness arose in the election of Barack Obama, which ignited national devotions to a degree we hadn't seen since Ronald Reagan's 1980 campaign. But President Obama quickly proved a divider, not a uniter, leaving his opponents bitter and his supporters disappointed. His initial success, however, shows that the American people are still eager for a philosopher-governor to lead them. The phenomenon of social movements such as Occupy Wall Street hasn't waned, either, though the contents of recent examples haven't managed to energize a population large enough to form a threshold occasion in our history ("the 1%" metaphor isn't a durable rallying cry). The popularity of *Fahrenheit 9/11*, Michael Moore's tendentious documentary, reveals a public appetite for large-scale treatments of American policy and purpose. Another transformative era like the sixties is bound to spring forth. We don't know the direction it will take or the politics it will entail, but it will bear animating foundations and picture an integrated future.

It can't be that there will never come another Lincoln, FDR, or Reagan, no more Emerson, Whitman, or Kerouac to define an age. America cannot thrive on entitlement programs, individual freedoms that people invoke only to pursue their own pleasures, new technologies of communication, and a faltering higher and lower education system. It thrives on ideas and visions strong enough to lift disparate and mobile individuals into one identity, a common ground. We await with eagerness the next Federalist Papers and *Leaves of Grass*, another Trust Buster and New Deal, "A Time for Choosing" speech and an eloquent martyr in a Birmingham jail . . .

Contributors

RICHARD ARUM is professor in the Department of Sociology with a joint appointment in the Steinhardt School of Education at New York University. He is also senior fellow at the Bill and Melinda Gates Foundation and was past director of the Education Research Program of the Social Science Research Council. He is the coauthor, with Josipa Roksa, of *Academically Adrift: Limited Learning on College Campuses* (2011) and *Aspiring Adults Adrift: Tentative Transitions of College Graduates* (2014).

MARK BAUERLEIN earned his PhD in English at UCLA in 1988 and has taught at Emory University since then, apart from serving as director of the Office of Research and Analysis at the National Endowment for the Arts from 2003 to 2005. Additionally, he serves as Senior Editor at *First Things* magazine. He is the author of several books, including *Negrophobia: A Race Riot in Atlanta, 1906* (2001) and *The Dumbest Generation: How the Digital Age Stupefies Young Americans and Jeopardizes Our Future; Or, Don't Trust Anyone under 30* (2008).

ADAM BELLOW is editorial director of Broadside Books (HarperCollins) and president, Liberty Island Media. A longtime editor of books by conservative writers, thinkers, and political figures, he is also the author of *In Praise of Nepotism: A Natural History* (2003) and the editor of *New Threats to Freedom: From Banning Ice Cream Trucks in Brooklyn to Abandoning Democracy Around the World* (2010).

DANIEL L. DREISBACH is a professor in the School of Public Affairs at American University in Washington, DC. He received a PhD from Oxford University and a JD from the University of Virginia. His research interests include the intersection of religion, politics, and law in the American founding era. He has authored or edited eight books, including *Thomas Jefferson and the Wall of Separation between Church and State* (2002).

NICHOLAS EBERSTADT holds the Henry Wendt Chair in Political Economy at the American Enterprise Institute. He is also a senior advisor to the National Bureau of Asian Research, a member of the visiting committee at the Harvard School of Public Health, and a member of the Global Leadership Council at the World Economic Forum. His books include *The Poverty of the Poverty Rate: Measure and Mismeasure of Material Deprivation in Modern America* (2008) and *A Nation of Takers: America's Entitlement Epidemic* (2012).

GERALD GRAFF, a professor of English and Education at the University of Illinois at Chicago, is the author of *Professing Literature: An Institutional History* (1987), *Clueless in Academe: How Schooling Obscures the Life of the Mind* (2004), and (with Cathy Birkenstein) *They Say/I Say: The Moves That Matter in Academic Writing* (2005), as well as numerous other books and articles on education. In 2008 he served as President of the Modern Language Association of America.

E. D. HIRSCH JR. is Emeritus Professor of English at University of Virginia and founder of the Core Knowledge Foundation. His books include *Cultural Literacy* (1987), *The Schools We Need and Why We Don't Have Them* (1996), *The Knowledge Deficit: Closing the Shocking Education Gap for American Children* (2006), and *The Making of Americans: Democracy and Our Schools* (2010).

MAGGIE JACKSON is an award-winning former *Boston Globe* columnist and the author of *Distracted: The Erosion of Attention and the Coming Dark Age* (2008), the book that sounded a wake-up call on the fragmentation of attention in modern life. Her next book explores the fate of reflection in a hurried age and the workmanship of thought.

JONATHAN KAY is comment pages editor for the Toronto-based Canadian daily newspaper *National Post*, a columnist for the *Post* op-ed page, and a blogger for the *Post* website. He is the author of *Among the Truthers: A Journey through America's Growing Conspiracist Underground* (2011).

GREG LUKIANOFF is an attorney and the president of the Foundation for Individual Rights in Education (FIRE). He is the author of *Unlearning Liberty: Campus Censorship and the End of American Debate* (2012) and *Freedom from Speech* (2014). He is a regular columnist for the Huffington Post and has frequently appeared on television shows, including the *CBS Evening News*, *Fox and Friends*, and *Stossel*. He is a graduate of American University and Stanford Law School.

DAVID T. Z. MINDICH is a professor of media studies, journalism, and digital arts at Saint Michael's College in Vermont. He has worked as an assignment editor for CNN and has written articles for the *New York Times*, the *Wall Street Journal*, the *Chronicle of Higher Education*, and *Wilson Quarterly*. He is the author of *Just the Facts: How "Objectivity" Came to Define American Journalism* (1999) and *Tuned Out: Why Americans under 40 Don't Follow the News* (2005). In 2006 CASE and the Carnegie Foundation named Mindich the Vermont Professor of the Year.

DENNIS PRAGER'S nationally syndicated radio talk show is heard daily on 150 radio stations across America. His latest of five books is the *New York Times* best seller *Still the Best Hope: Why the World Needs American Values to Triumph* (2012). He is president of the Internet-based PragerUniversity.com, which presents some of the world's finest thinkers giving five-minute courses.

R. R. RENO is editor of *First Things* magazine and author of *Sanctified Vision: An Introduction to Early Christian Interpretation of the Bible* (with coauthor John J. O'Keefe, 2005) and *Fighting the Noonday Devil and Other Essays Personal and Theological* (2011). He earned his doctorate in Religious Studies at Yale University and was professor of theology and ethics at Creighton University until 2013.

Ilya Somin is professor of law at George Mason University School of Law. He is the author of *Democracy and Political Ignorance: Why Smaller Government Is Smarter* (2013), and *The Grasping Hand:* Kelo v. City of New London *and the Limits of Eminent Domain* (2015). He writes regularly for the popular Volokh Conspiracy blog.

Jean M. Twenge, professor of psychology at San Diego State University, is the author of more than one hundred scientific publications and the books *The Narcissism Epidemic: Living in the Age of Entitlement* (coauthor, W. Keith Campbell, 2009) and *Generation Me: Why Today's Young Americans Are More Confident, Assertive, Entitled—and More Miserable Than Ever Before* (2006).

Steve Wasserman, former literary editor of the *Los Angeles Times*; past editorial director of Times Books; and past publisher of Hill and Wang and the Noonday Press at Farrar, Straus, and Giroux, has also worked as a literary agent, representing the late Christopher Hitchens, Linda Ronstadt, Placido Domingo, Geoffrey Wheatcroft, and James Fenton, among others. He is currently editor at large for Yale University Press.

Robert Whitaker is a journalist and author of four books, two of which tell of the history of psychiatry. His last book, *Anatomy of an Epidemic: Magic Bullets, Psychiatric Drugs, and the Astonishing Rise of Mental Illness in America* (2010), won the Investigative Reporters and Editors book award for best investigative journalism in 2010. Prior to writing books, he worked as a science and medical reporter at the *Albany Times Union* newspaper in New York for a number of years.

Index